Charles W. Chesnutt
and the
Fictions of Race

Charles W. Chesnutt
and the
Fictions of Race

DEAN McWILLIAMS

The University of Georgia Press
Athens & London

© 2002 by the University of Georgia Press
Athens, Georgia 30602
All rights reserved
Designed by Walton Harris
Set in 10/14 Carter & Cone Galliard by Bookcomp, Inc.
Printed and bound by Thomson-Shore

The paper in this book meets the guidelines for
permanence and durability of the Committee on
Production Guidelines for Book Longevity of the
Council on Library Resources.

Printed in the United States of America
02   03   04   05   06   C   5   4   3   2   1

Library of Congress Cataloging-in-Publication Data

McWilliams, Dean.
Charles W. Chesnutt and the fictions of race / Dean McWilliams.
p.   cm.
Includes bibliographical references and index.
ISBN 0-8203-2435-3 (alk. paper)
1. Chesnutt, Charles Waddell, 1858–1932 — Criticism and interpretation.
2. Chesnutt, Charles Waddell, 1858–1932 — Views on race.
3. African Americans — Race awareness.   4. Identity (Psychology) in literature.
5. African Americans in literature.   6. Group identity in literature.
7. Race in literature.   I. Title.
PS1292.C6Z77 2002
813'.4 — dc21   2002002787

British Library Cataloging-in-Publication Data available

CONTENTS

Preface   vii

1. Chesnutt's Language / Language's Chesnutt   1

2. Chesnutt in His Journals: "Nigger" under Erasure   23

3. "The Future American" and "Chas. Chesnutt"   43

4. Black Vernacular in Chesnutt's Short Fiction:
   "A New School of Literature"   57

5. The Julius and John Stories: "The Luscious Scuppernong"   76

6. Race in Chesnutt's Short Fiction: The "Line" and the "Web"   100

7. *Mandy Oxendine:* "Is You a *Rale* Black Man?"   122

8. *The House behind the Cedars:* "Creatures of Our Creation"   133

9. *The Marrow of Tradition:* "The Very Breath of His Nostrils"   147

10. *The Colonel's Dream:* "Sho Would 'a' Be'n a 'Ristocrat"   166

11. *Paul Marchand, F.M.C.:* "F.M.C." and "C.W.C."   183

12. *The Quarry:* "And Not the Hawk"   208

Notes   229

Bibliography   247

Index   255

PREFACE

Beginnings and endings may be the sustaining myths of the middle
years; but in the *fin de siècle,* we find ourselves in the moment of transit
where space and time cross to produce complex figures of difference
and identity, past and present, inside and outside, inclusion and exclusion. —HOMI K. BHABHA, *The Location of Culture*

Charles Chesnutt is a writer whose literary fortunes have prospered in the
years when one century ends and another begins. Chesnutt emerged as the
preeminent African American writer of fiction—the first to be published and
praised by the American literary establishment—at the end of the nineteenth
and the beginning of the twentieth century. His earliest stories came out in
the 1880s, but his *anni mirabilis* were the precise junction of two centuries.
From 1899 to 1901, two novels and two volumes of stories appeared bearing
Chesnutt's name, winning appreciative attention by important reviewers.
The young Negro writer seemed on the verge of a major career. But *The
Colonel's Dream,* the novel Chesnutt published in 1905, proved to be a financial and critical failure, and Chesnutt's stream of book-length publications
ended almost as quickly as it began.

One hundred years after his initial success, Chesnutt again attracted significant attention. Important book-length studies of Chesnutt's work had
appeared in the 1970s and 1980s, but scholarly attention to this author
increased significantly at century's end. During the last decade of the twentieth century and the first years of the twenty-first, Chesnutt's journals, his
correspondence, his essays, and his biography of Frederick Douglass were
edited and published, and three novels for which Chesnutt was unable to
gain publication during his life appeared. These publications were supplemented by new paperback editions of Chesnutt's classic novels and stories.

In addition, there were four new scholarly volumes and an outpouring of articles, conference papers, dissertations, and theses. The climax of this activity occurred in 2002 with the appearance of *Charles W. Chesnutt: Stories, Novels, and Essays*, edited by Werner Sollors, in the Library of America series. A Chesnutt volume in this prestigious series, which includes volumes by Melville, Hawthorne, and Steinbeck, caused the *Chronicle of Higher Education* to conclude that Chesnutt's "canonization is nearly complete."[1]

This acceleration of interest in Chesnutt occurred during a decade in which "our ideas of 'whiteness' were interrogated, our ideas of 'blackness' were complicated, and the terrain we call 'American culture' began to be remapped."[2] In the 1990s, more than one hundred scholarly publications appeared exploring the interaction and interpenetration of European American and African American cultural production. For Shelley Fisher Fishkin these new studies "mark a defining moment in the study of American culture" (251). It is no longer possible for those interested in American civilization to isolate "white" and "black" literature, art, and music in mutually exclusive streams. The new wave of historical, critical, and theoretical research has shown us the important ways writers and artists on both sides of the color line influenced one another's work, creating a civilization shared and shaped by both communities.

The recurrent, perhaps obsessive, themes of Charles Chesnutt's writings are racial and cultural mixing. It is not surprising, then, that Chesnutt's work has assumed a new importance in this context. One of the most important contributions, along with Fishkin's own work, to the rethinking of our common culture is Eric J. Sundquist's *To Wake the Nations: Race in the Making of American Literature*. Sundquist justifies devoting nearly one-third of his important study to Chesnutt with the assertion that Chesnutt was "among the major American fiction writers of the nineteenth century" (12). I would do nothing to challenge Sundquist's claim, but I would like to amend it by resituating it historically. Chesnutt's two volumes of short stories appeared at the very end of the nineteenth century, in 1899, but the three novels published in his lifetime came out in the twentieth century, in 1900, 1901, and 1905. In addition, Chesnutt completed two novels in the 1920s, and they are now in print. The way we read an author is influenced by the way we situate him or her historically. It is important to note that Chesnutt's life and career span two very different centuries.

Chesnutt was a liminal figure who straddled and confounded several important American categories. Indistinguishable in appearance from most European Americans, he proudly asserted his identity as an African American. A forty-year resident of Cleveland, he wrote obsessively of the American South, where he spent his youth. Equally interesting and often overlooked is the way Chesnutt's career spans a series of distinct historical moments. Born when blacks were still held as property, he was educated during the brief glow of Reconstruction, and then he spent the remainder of his life under the shadow of segregation. Chesnutt witnessed the flowering of black creativity in the 1920s, and his last novel, had it been published at the time of its composition, would have appeared in same year, 1928, as Claude McKay's *Home to Harlem* and Nella Larsen's *Quicksand*. Born and shaped in the nineteenth century, Chesnutt spent the majority of his creative life in the twentieth.

Of course, more is involved than calendar dates when we try to place a writer in the appropriate historical context. Young Chesnutt was inspired by the idealism of his teachers at the State Colored Normal School in Fayetteville, North Carolina, where he studied, and at a later moment, by the reformers of the Progressive Movement. But as a student of history and of the law, he was angered by America's refusal to live up to its own founding principles. He worked to claim for Americans of African descent their full human and civil rights. However, Chesnutt recognized, better than most writers of his time, the linguistic and literary obstacles that frustrated these claims. A lawyer and a student of languages, he saw the way America's racial thinking was grounded on fictions so universally accepted as to seem part of nature itself. Chesnutt's understanding of what we now call the social construction of race and the way these constructions are supported by the structures of language make him a strikingly modern writer.

Unfortunately, the critical lenses we have used to read Chesnutt have not always helped us to see the modernity of his work. The critical consensus has been that Chesnutt was a late-nineteenth-century realist who skillfully exploited the conventions of local-color fiction to convey a favorable image of the Negro. A significant dissenting minority has argued that Chesnutt's reformist intentions were restricted to the cause of light-skinned mulattoes. For the most part, this discussion of Chesnutt, both pro and con, has been conducted within the methodological framework of biographical and historical criticism, with an admixture of New Critical formal analysis. This has been important work, and William L. Andrews, Sylvia Lyons Render, and Ernestine Pickens, among others, have made possible Chesnutt's recent accession to the American literary canon.[3] But, as valuable as this work has been, it has not set in relief the full complexity of Chesnutt's work. More recent critical theories bring this complexity into better focus and help us appreciate the contemporary relevance of Chesnutt's achievement.

The primary focus of literary theory for the last quarter century has been a critique of language, an exploration of the way language shapes our understanding of the world. Literary and cultural critics have found powerful applications of this theory for exploring the ways we construct racial identities. The critique of "blackness" and "whiteness" to which Fishkin refers has its roots in the new interest in language and the shaping of social identities. Henry Louis Gates Jr., Houston A. Baker, and others have made a direct application of poststructuralist literary theory to black writers. They have called attention to the plight of artists creating in the language of their white oppressors, and they have found recent theory useful for exploring the distinctive tensions in black writing. Poststructuralist literary theory helps us uncover the tensions in Chesnutt's writings, enabling them to resonate anew at the outset of the twenty-first century.

Charles W. Chesnutt and the Fictions of Race is the first extended exploration of Chesnutt's fiction and nonfiction from the perspective of recent theories of language and the construction of racial identity.[4] Like earlier critics, I refer to the times in which Chesnutt worked, but my focus is less on the historical context *outside* Chesnutt's writings than on the historical context *within* them. History is inside language; it shapes its binaries, molds its dialects, and leaves its impress on the narratives we use to organize our experience. Chesnutt understood the way in which we are formed by language in a way that is strikingly modern, although he was not always able to control the implications of this insight for his own texts. My interest here is primarily in these texts, but not in a New Critical search for autonomous, organic form. A good deal of my attention is directed to the conflicts and gaps in Chesnutt's writing; I see them as indications of gaps and contradictions in our cultural narratives. Joseph McElrath, surveying a century of Chesnutt criticism, remarks that "different 'voices' are heard by different critics *within* one story as well as in discrete works" (*Cricial Essays*, 17). These different voices echo the different communities—white, black, and mulatto—in which Chesnutt moved as well as the different historical moments in which he lived and created. The exigencies of these different communicative situations introduce conflicting intentions in his work. To ignore these conflicts—moments when Chesnutt hesitates or contradicts himself—does him no service, for it overlooks the historical difficulties with which he struggled and, as a consequence, it diminishes the magnitude of what he achieved.

I mean to read Chesnutt within his culture, and for this reason my titular phrase "the fictions of race" has a double sense. It refers, of course, to Chesnutt's stories and novels about African American life, but it also refers to the way these fictions interact with, challenge, and, in turn, are shaped by larger cultural narratives, including the American account of racial difference. The first chapter sets out in greater detail the historical and theoretical context, and it discusses a Chesnutt story that illustrates the way his fiction deliberately deconstructs important cultural binaries. This chapter also lays out the claim that Chesnutt's distinctive contribution to American culture resides in the reflections on language embodied in his fictions. These reflections focus both on the immediate topic of black vernacular speech and on the broader problem of language as a signifying system based on binary oppositions. These linguistic concerns come together in the study's broadest theme: the construction of racial identity. I explore these themes and the connection between them in the succeeding chapters. The second chapter focuses on the journals Chesnutt kept as a young man in North Carolina. These diaries provide a poignant record of Chesnutt's struggle within the language and literary tradition he hoped to exploit for his emancipatory purposes. The third chapter examines an important polemical essay that Chesnutt published at the dawn of the century, in 1900. Previous discussions of Chesnutt's nonfiction have used it as biographical context for the fiction. That is not my principal interest in this study. The diary and the essay are texts, complex verbal enactments, and they are treated as such. More specifically, the second and third chapters explore the way the words Chesnutt confided to his journal and to a newspaper's columns reveal the same contradictory tensions and pressures found in his stories and novels. Chapters 4 and 5 analyze the challenge to notions of racial difference posed by the interaction of rural black speech with standard American English in Chesnutt's stories. The opposition between black dialect and standard "white" speech is only one instance of the larger racial binary that has shaped American history, and the focus moves to this larger opposition in the next chapters. Chapter 6 explores the short fiction; here, however, the focus is Chesnutt's use of the mulatto as a means for deconstructing the black-white binary. The succeeding six chapters continue the discussion of language and the construction of individual and racial identity in each of Chesnutt's novels, including the three recent, posthumous publications.

This project began in 1995 when I was editing Chesnutt's *Paul Marchand, F.M.C.* and *The Quarry* for publication. In the intervening years, I have incurred many debts; there is space here to acknowledge only a few of these. At Ohio University and in Athens, Ohio, I was supported and assisted by Leslie Flemming, Betty Pytlik, Tom Scanlan, Marsha Dutton, Bob Demott, Andy Escobedo, Bob Miklitsch, Sam and Susan Crowl, Michel Perdreau, and Nancy Roe. Elsewhere, I have benefited from the friendship and erudition of Noëlle Batt, Roy Rosenstein, Walter Grünzweig, Tom Cooley, Joseph McElrath, Charles Duncan, and Ernestine Pickens. I also want to thank George Hutchinson, who encouraged my Chesnutt research at a crucial juncture, and Courtney Denney, who provided excellent editorial assistance. My greatest debt, however, is once again the one I owe to my wife, Alvi, to whom this book is dedicated.

Charles W. Chesnutt
and the
Fictions of Race

I

Chesnutt's Language /
Language's Chesnutt

Afro-Americans—from Jamestown's first disembarkation of "twenty
negres" to the era of Run-DMC—have been deconstructionists par
excellence. —HOUSTON A. BAKER, *Afro-American Poetics: Revisions of
Harlem and the Black Aesthetic*

At an earlier stage, this book bore the working title "Chesnutt's Language /
Language's Chesnutt." I subsequently changed the title to the designation
on the cover for reasons I will soon explain. Nonetheless, I feel sufficient
attachment to the phrase by which I first identified this project to place it
here at the head of the first chapter. The attachment is due partly to the shape
of the phrase, the satisfying symmetry of the chiasmus. By reversing noun
and modifier, the possessor becomes the possessed: Chesnutt the artist in
control of his medium becomes its captive. The symmetry of these opposed
formulations was, in fact, too neat. Like all binaries, it was too reductive, too
exhaustive of possibilities, without some qualification, and so, unwilling to
abandon the formulation completely, I have put it in at the head of this
chapter, where I can explain and qualify its meaning.

Charles Chesnutt's paradoxical relationship to language remains at the
heart of this enquiry. Chesnutt gained literary recognition in the 1890s for
his skillful rendering of Black English vernacular in his stories featuring
Julius McAdoo. The tales that this former slave narrates in dialect to a

Northern white couple have become anthology pieces. Through the twentieth century, they have assured Chesnutt a minor place in American literary history. Now as another century begins, stronger claims have been made for Chesnutt. However, the question that must be addressed before any historical reassessment can be sustained is the following: what were the nature and the implications of Chesnutt's intervention into American literature and culture? Chesnutt's reputation from the beginning has been associated with language, and with that I would not disagree. It is simply the case that heretofore language has not been defined broadly enough to account for the singularity of Chesnutt's achievement.

The discussion of language in this study encompasses more than the representation of rural black speech—as skillful and as important as Chesnutt's achievement was in that area. Language here is taken as the system of verbal symbols with which we organize reality. This understanding is deeply influenced by both structuralism and poststructuralism. Language, for the structuralists, is a system based on binary oppositions, which relate to the world in a fashion that is purely arbitrary. Meaning derives from the play of these opposed signifiers rather than from a natural connection between these signifiers and the signified elements of the "real" world. Structuralism, in this way, seriously challenged our confidence in the verbal resources we use to shape our experience. Poststructuralism, in its various forms, pushed farther. Deconstruction showed how these binaries are never neutral, for each juxtaposed pair is really a minihierarchy in which one term is privileged over the other. Poststructural Marxists and new historicists have also shown that these hierarchies are not ideal Platonic categories but that they emerge from history. An obvious instance is the privileging of white over black, which was powerfully strengthened by white Europe's need to justify its control over the "dark" continents of Africa, Asia, and America. The choice of the white-black opposition as an example is not innocent in the present context, for it is the contrast around which almost all of Charles Chesnutt's fictions turn. But it is not the only set of contrasting pairs in these works. Indeed, these fictions are not merely about this one binary, but they challenge binary thinking in general; they call into question the structuring of thought by means of two-term hierarchies. The narrative and thematic thrust of Chesnutt's best stories and novels derives from the tension between a series of juxtaposed terms that are gradually questioned, subverted, and reversed.

This study, then, is about Chesnutt's language, understood in both the limited sense of black dialect and the broader structural sense I have outlined.

However, this study is also about language's Chesnutt. Structuralism and poststructuralism have also shown us that we are never outside of language. We have no other resource for questioning language and challenging its power than language itself. We are in language, and, even more fatally, language is in us. Individuals intervening in the discursive practices of their time cannot do so without drawing on those same practices. Ideally, we would like to be able to hoist ourselves by our own linguistic bootstraps, but that is not possible. Any attempt to think past the conditions of our moment begins in that moment with the resources it provides, and it proceeds by a careful critique and transformation of those resources. Thus we find that Chesnutt was profoundly of his moment at the same time he sought to move beyond it, penetrated by the very structures he struggled to change.

Chesnutt's case is particularly moving for the singularity of what he attempted. He sought to create literary art that would reshape America's discourse on race, and he sought to do this at one of the least propitious moments in American history. Chesnutt pursued the bulk of his literary career during the ideological night that extended from the failure of Reconstruction to the beginning of World War I. Supreme Court decisions in 1883 and 1896 condoning Southern segregation were only the most public and official moments in the gradual emergence of a new, nearly universal white consensus on race. Before the Civil War there had been loud debate among white citizens on the identity and status of blacks; but after 1876 there was complacent silence and acquiescence in the "redeemed" South's economic and political subjugation of Americans of African descent. A *New York Times* editorial from 1900 remarked with satisfaction that "Northern men . . . no longer denounce the suppression of the Negro vote in the South as it used to be denounced in the reconstruction days. The necessity of it under the supreme law of self-preservation is candidly recognized."[1]

During this period, language and all forms of discourse—law, science, popular entertainment—were permeated by the ambient racism. Chesnutt sought to change this discourse, but he had no tool except language and those forms of discourse. Chesnutt struggled to reverse and overcome reductive binary thinking, but he could never fully succeed; nor can we, for it is the fundament of language and thought itself. We can reverse binaries and introduce new ones, but we are never free of the need to distinguish. There is a tragic strain in my analysis, for the story of Chesnutt's career is of a struggle that is continually frustrated. Yet I cannot accept the despairing implications of my original title: either total ownership of language or total ownership by language. The story of Chesnutt's struggle is of the in-between position excluded by my neat chiasmus. It is a story in which no ultimate strategic victory is gained—nor, do I believe, is it genuinely anticipated. Nonetheless, there are tactical triumphs, moments of exhilarating insight, instants when literature proves its power to advance our understanding of ourselves and our society. This study explores the in-between in Chesnutt's fiction, the vacillating moments of insight and blindness. To miss what he missed, to overlook the points of entrapment in his own language, is a disservice to his achievement, for it denies the obstacles against which he struggled.

This study's original title highlighted the paradox that is one of its guiding themes, but at the same time it distorted that paradox, eliminating any mediating position, and so it was abandoned. There were other reasons for its removal from the book's cover. It seemed to promise a more theoretical and linguistic treatment than I wished to pursue. What I really wanted to do was to get as close as possible to Chesnutt's writings and to the culture from which they emerged. I also wished to include all of his writings, for in recent years Chesnutt's fictional corpus has expanded by nearly 50 percent, so I have included discussions of the recently published novels from Chesnutt's early and late periods—*Mandy Oxendine, Paul Marchand, F.M.C.,* and *The Quarry.* These works, which existed only in manuscript form until the late 1990s, were ignored or given brief attention in earlier studies of Chesnutt. I also wanted to discuss Chesnutt's journals and one of his essays, but not just as background for the fictions: I wanted to interrogate them as texts. The recent literary theories to which I have alluded have also challenged the distinctions between literary and nonliterary, fictional and nonfictional works. All are texts—impure mixtures rather than mutually exclusive categories. The inclusion of Chesnutt's journals and an important polemical essay illumines his struggle with the language of his time, his struggle with the fictions of race.

This study's title, *Charles W. Chesnutt and the Fictions of Race,* reminds us that our thinking about race is encoded not simply in language's neat binaries but in narratives, fictions that dramatize these binaries and give them cultural life. Chesnutt was a storyteller, but he was also a story-unteller. Chesnutt creates narratives that seek to undo the foundational narratives of his culture. There is also another paradox here, an elaboration of the paradox introduced in my original title. At the same time that Chesnutt deconstructs the racial discourse of his time, his stories have a way of untelling themselves, revealing gaps and fissures in Chesnutt's thinking and that of his time. I do not intend to paper over these cracks, but rather to call attention to them and to explore the personal and cultural tensions that produced them.

In regard to the study's title, I should explain what I mean by referring to race as a "fiction." The biological, religious, and historical narratives that have been used to "prove" black inferiority are clearly invented fantasies. At the same time, however, it seems impertinent to tell individuals trapped in poor housing and low-paying jobs because of their skin color that race is simply a fiction. On the question of the reality or fictionality of race, there are at least three distinct positions. The first position, which has dominated American history, is racial essentialism or racialism. Charles W. Mills prefers to denominate this position "racial realism," with "realism" understood in its ontological sense—the belief that objects exist in the world independent of our cognition. Here is his summary of the essentialist or racial realist position:

> A "racial realist" in the most minimal sense will be somebody who thinks that it is objectively the case—independent of human belief—that there are natural human races; in other words, that races are natural kinds. In the stronger, more interesting sense, a racial realist will also believe that the differences between races are not confined to the superficial morphological characteristics of skin color, hair type, and facial features, but extend to significant moral, intellectual, characterological, and spiritual characteristics also, that there are "real essences."[2]

At the other extreme from racial realism or essentialism is "racial subjectivism." From this perspective, race has no objective existence; it is an illusion projected on one group by another to protect its economic interests or its psychological insecurities. For the subjectivist, one has only to expose these illusions, to unmask the special interests and hidden fears, for them to lose their power and for "race" to disappear from society. If the realist position is clearly false, the subjectivist position seems too simple. A third position is racial constructivism, a perspective that sees race as a false but powerful construct in society. Classic epistemological explanations of consciousness, such as the Cartesian *cogito,* artificially abstract consciousness from society and history. Consciousness in a raced society—a society where race is central to identity—is inevitably raced, if not racist. In such a society, a black person achieves consciousness not simply as a person but as a black person. This consciousness is achieved in active resistance to those who wish to deny or significantly qualify black claims for full personhood. Whites do not escape these epistemological implications, for knowledge of one's whiteness—whether one chooses deliberately to exploit its prerogatives or not—is one of the deepest and most constitutive parts of a white person's self awareness.

Here is Mills's account of the ontology implicit in a constructivist account of race:

> Race is not "metaphysical" in the deep sense of being eternal, unchanging, necessary, part of the basic furniture of the universe. But race is a *contingently* deep reality that structures our particular social universe, having a social objectivity and causal significance that arise out of *our* particular history. For racial realism, the social metaphysics is simply an outgrowth of a natural metaphysics; for racial constructivism, there is no natural metaphysics, and the social metaphysics arises directly out of the social history. Because people come to think of themselves *as* "raced," as black and white, for example, these categories, which correspond to no natural kinds, attain a social reality. Intersubjectivity creates a certain kind of objectivity. (48)

Although the three general approaches to understanding racial difference have been identified, there are, of course, numerous distinctions and gradations within each. W. E. B. Du Bois's famous metaphor of the veil, deployed in *The Souls of Black Folk,* distinguishes two distinct foci within the constructivist position. Du Bois recounts how, when he was a schoolboy in Massachusetts, his greeting card was coolly refused by a white female classmate: Du Bois realized in that moment that a "veil" separated him, as a black person, from the white children in his class. Initially, in the first chapter's second paragraph, the veil stands outside Du Bois, between him and the girl, between all blacks and the white world. This instance of the veil metaphor figures for us one possibility within the constructivist account. Racial difference is not inherent in either the black boy or the white girl, nor is it simply the subjective projection of one on the other. It exists as a palpable, unyielding presence in the social space that separates the two figures. Nonetheless, young Du Bois holds it in contempt and imagines himself living "above it in a region of blue sky and great wandering shadows."[3]

However, in the next paragraph, Du Bois develops his metaphor differently. "The Negro is a sort of seventh son, born with a veil, and gifted with a second-sight in this American world, — a world which yields him no true self-consciousness, but only lets him see himself through the revelation of the other world. It is a peculiar sensation, this double-consciousness, this sense of always looking at one's self through the eyes of others" (102). The veil is now *within* Du Bois. The white girl's othering gaze has entered him, and the veil now divides his consciousness, separating him from himself, forcing him to view and value himself, not only in his own terms, but in the terms imposed by others. Although Du Bois does not address this point directly in this passage, we must also imagine a veil within the white girl as well: "whiteness" is also a construction, and this construct creates a tension between the natural kinship of classmates and internalized social prejudice. The veil metaphor developed in this way leads to a psychological component in the construction of racial identity. Difference exists within us, not biologically but psychologically, in the ways we think, feel, and structure our experience.

This schematic treatment of these three positions does not adequately suggest the complex historical and theoretical interactions between them. Many educated Americans today would ascribe to a version of the constructivist position, but this consensus is relatively recent in American intellectual history and, indeed, still not universal. Well into the second decade of the twentieth century, the belief that black Americans were essentially different and inferior to white Americans was scientific, social, and legal orthodoxy. "The scientific community did not start to move from the paradigm of scientific racism until 1911 with the publication of *The Mind of Primitive Man* by the German-born, Jewish American anthropologist Franz Boas."[4] After Boas, physical and social scientists turned to environment rather than genetic inheritance to explain the most important differences between eth-

nic groups. Nonetheless, the defeat of racial essentialism was hardly immediate or total. Boas himself was willing to acknowledge that the black race
might not produce as many minds of exceptional quality as the white race,
but this, he insisted, could tell us nothing about the abilities of any black
individual.[5] Black intellectuals were not unaffected by racial essentialism. As
late as the mid-1920s, W. E. B. Du Bois, at the same time that he was emphasizing the social construction of race, still spoke of essential characteristics
derived from black "blood."[6] The point here is not to criticize either Boas or
Du Bois but to suggest the difficulty of living exclusively within any one of
the positions so neatly defined above. A constructivist must admit the existence of phenotypical differences between at least some members of distinct
racial groups; subjectivists will often defend some version of race pride; and
an essentialist will acknowledge the existence of false stereotypes, if only in
the minds of his ideological opponents. These points should serve as a prelude to our consideration of Chesnutt, who begins in his journals as a subjectivist and who changes in his maturity to be a constructivist. Nonetheless,
often in a single Chesnutt text elements of all three positions are at work.

The paradoxical ontological status of racial constructs—not real in nature
but real in society and in us—accounts for our difficulties in overcoming
them. They are part of our mental equipment (not hardwired, perhaps, but
embedded at a deep level in our consciousness), the very equipment we use
to change our understanding of ourselves and our world.[7] These constructs
provide the distinctive valences in many of our language's constitutive binaries, transforming them into the minihierarchies discussed. So, although I
have changed the title of my study, substituting "fiction" for "language," I
have not escaped the linguistic concerns with which I began.

Language has from the beginning been central to modern Europe's racial
constructions. After Europe's encounter with Africa in the age of exploration, the key question was where to place the Africans in the Great Chain
of Being, the hierarchical order of nature. Should Africans stand with Europeans at the human level, or ought they be placed at a lower level, interme-
diate between humans and Africa's other exotic fauna? Literacy—the ability
to read and write—was taken as a crucial test to prove or disprove black
humanity. Henry Louis Gates Jr. explains that "after Descartes, reason was
privileged, or valorized, over all other human characteristics. Writing, especially after the printing press became so widespread, was taken to be the

visible sign of reason. Blacks were reasonable, and hence 'men,' if—and only if—they demonstrated mastery of 'the arts and sciences,' the eighteenth century's formula for writing."[8] African languages, most of which were not written, would not serve for these purposes; only mastery of a European language could confer human status. British and Americans who supported black claims for full humanity brought forward English texts written by Africans.

These publishers had, however, first to overcome white readers' deep skepticism about black abilities. Thus for over a hundred years—from Phillis Wheatley to Frances E. W. Harper—texts written by African Americans were introduced by prominent white citizens verifying that the black person had indeed composed the work bearing his or her name. The black voice could be heard only after being validated by a white voice, and, in this way, black claims for autonomous and equal human identity were undercut by the very form that claim was forced to take. The necessity for white sponsorship carried with it the imputation of dependence and inferiority. There was another, perhaps crueler, paradox, in that the very excellence of a black writer's linguistic mastery could be held against her or him. Blacks who wrote poetry or prose in English knew that their work would attract the closest scrutiny, so they were careful to observe the conventions of their time; to do otherwise was to invite summary rejection. But David Hume, Thomas Jefferson, and Immanuel Kant saw in this scrupulous respect for the received forms a sign of the black's innately "imitative" nature. By this logic, blacks were not "creative," that is, fully human.[9] Hume's chosen metaphor for the English-speaking African was the parrot; others, less generous, spoke of the sedulous ape. Frederick Douglass's formidable rhetorical skills posed a different problem. His abolitionist friends advised him to restrain his eloquence. "Better have a little of the plantation manner of speech than not," they urged; "it is not best that you seem too learned."[10] They explained that too great a fluency might call into doubt Douglass's status as a former slave; they did not mention, but may have felt, that too much learning in a Negro might seem presumptuous to his white Northern auditors.

Douglass forcefully defended his expressive autonomy, eventually founding his own newspaper, *The North Star,* against the advice of William Lloyd Garrison and others. Douglass's situation, nonetheless, focuses a key question that he and other blacks faced: what language was appropriate for

African American writers? African languages were taken from them; they had only English, the language of those who had enslaved them. To enter that language was to enter its mental universe, to traffic with its constructs. Douglass's defiant solution was the creation of a literate, highly rhetorical voice, which flaunted its mastery of white linguistic and literary conventions. This voice unequivocally asserted its right to be heard by whites, but it necessarily implied a gap between the writer and the illiterate black masses it sought to represent.

The recently emancipated blacks of the rural South spoke Black English vernacular. This speech variety was familiar to white Americans through its representations on the minstrel stage and the print genres of the dialect sketch and plantation fiction. Black vernacular, or black dialect, is a rule-based variety of English, equal, in linguistic terms, to any of the dialects spoken by white Americans, including Standard English. Nonetheless, whites perceived Black English as a deformation of their own variety, as a failure to master the rules of the socially privileged dialect. This denigration of Black English was a crucial part of the racist argument against fully human status for blacks. The invidious binary of Standard English versus black dialect posed special problems for black writers, making it difficult for them to use the speech of the black folk they wished to represent. This tension is evident in Douglass's novella *The Heroic Slave* (1853): Douglass's protagonist, a rebel slave, speaks a highly literate English and declaims fluently, but rather improbably, in grandiloquent periods.

We do not, any of us, own the language we use. It comes to us from others, from ancestors and contemporaries with values and purposes different from our own. Mikhail Bakhtin explains:

> The word in language is half someone else's. It becomes "one's own" only when the speaker populates it with his own intention, his own accent, when he appropriates the word, adapting it to his own semantic and expressive intention. Prior to this moment of appropriation, the word does not exist in a neutral and impersonal language (it is not, after all, out of a dictionary that the speaker gets his words!), but rather it exists in other people's mouths, in other people's contexts, serving other people's intentions.[11]

For no one in Western culture was this predicament more acute than for black writers. The language they would use to demonstrate their humanity and defend their rights was the language of those who had enslaved them. American English comes to African Americans freighted with the residue of history. Three hundred years of conquest and enslavement powerfully shaped the English language's denotative opposition and its connotative echoes.

The "divided consciousness" Du Bois described reflects this linguistic entrapment. His veil metaphor is a textile reference; so also is "text," our word for a verbal construct. Both the veil and the text are woven from pre-existing materials whose colors and dimensional characteristics the weaver only partially controls. To extend Du Bois's metaphor, the "veil" through which Americans view themselves and the world is not transparent; it already has a pattern printed on it, a pattern that both conceals and reveals. It is not possible to summarily destroy or ignore the veil, for the world is always mediated by language. We can rend it in places and we change the pattern, but that commits us, initially at least, to working with the veil as it is.

Black writers have understood this fatal paradox and, as a result, have stood in a distinctive, ironic relationship to their language. Here is Henry Louis Gates Jr.'s explanation:

> To attempt to employ a Western language to posit a black self is inherently to use language ironically. The relation of the speaking black subject to the self figured in these languages must by definition be an ironical relation, since that self exists in the "non-place of language," and since these languages encoded figuratively the idea that blackness itself is a negative essence, an absence. [12]

No black writer before the Harlem Renaissance more fully embodied this ironic and skeptical attitude toward language than did Charles Chesnutt. Few American writers of Chesnutt's generation, black or white, surpassed him in his interest in and mastery of languages. The obsession was lifelong, and his journals record his struggles, through self-instruction, to master Latin, French, German, and Greek. He was largely successful in these efforts, and his daughter records that in his later years his display of linguistic erudition could try the patience of his friends. Perhaps even more important for the presentation of spoken language in his fiction was Chesnutt's daily professional activity. He trained himself in Pittman shorthand, painstakingly recording the speech of others. His journals again record his careful transcription of many different forms of discourse from many different individuals. Chesnutt later read law and passed the Ohio bar, but because of race prejudice, he was unable to earn his living in this profession. He became instead a court stenographer. He listened to daily and recorded carefully—perhaps with a wry smile—the logic, rhetoric, and casuistry that fixed the identities, rights, and obligations of white and black citizens.

We will explore Chesnutt's use of black vernacular more fully in chapter 4, but here I would like to illustrate his skeptical attitude toward a signifying system based on binary opposition by discussing "Baxter's *Procrustes,*" a story Chesnutt published in the *Atlantic Monthly* in June 1904.[13] The story's narrator, a bibliophile named Jones, belongs to the Bodleian Club, a group devoted to books and book collecting. The narrative is his account of one of the club's most unusual publications, a volume produced by a member of the club named Baxter and entitled *Procrustes.* Baxter, it turns out, has played an elaborate prank on his fellows. He has personally supervised the publication of a volume he authored, and the product is so handsome that the other members of the club immediately recognize the value of their personal copies. In fact, the volumes will be even more valuable if the pages are left uncut, and this poses a temporary dilemma for Jones and two other colleagues who have been asked to review the book for other members of the Bodleian. None of these reviewers wishes to reduce the value of his copy by cutting its pages, so each uses the elaborate rhetoric of literary criticism to praise a volume he has not actually read. Baxter's trap is sprung when a naive visitor actually opens the book and reveals that its pages are blank.

The story is, in the first instance, a satire on upper-middle-class cultural pretensions. No authorial commentary is necessary for this satire; the narrator's obtuse remarks suffice for the story's comic purposes. He prattles inanely about the "cap-and-bells border" and "blind-tooled design" (416) of a book with blank pages, oblivious or indifferent to the elaborate joke of which he is the butt. The satire is at its most delicious when the narrator and his fellow reviewers deploy the rarefied vocabulary of the book critic to praise a text that does not exist. Davis—apparently a philosophical critic—avers that Baxter's work "squints at the Spencerian view, with a slight deflection toward Hegelianism" (418). The narrator claims to find sentiments "in harmony with those of Schopenhauer, without his bitterness; with those of Nordau, without his flippancy. His materialism is Haeckel's, presented with something of the charm of Omar Kayyam" (419). Their friend Thompson, who has been asked to comment on the poem's formal qualities, praises its "sonorous lines, of haunting melody and charm . . . so closely interrelated as to be scarcely quotable with justice to the author" (419). Chesnutt was justly praised for his accurate representation of rural black speech, but here he skillfully captures language spoken at the other end of the social and racial scale. In creating the voice of his narrator he gives us a satirical pastiche of upper-middle-class book talk. Language is, then, central to this humorous send-up of these obtuse aesthetes. But the story is also about language in a broader sense: it critiques the signifying systems by which we organize reality. More specifically, it deconstructs the oppositions upon which literary culture is based.

The Bodleian Club's distinctive values need to be seen in the context of the late-nineteenth-century American culture. The merchants and industrialists who made their fortunes in the Gilded Age frequently spent their wealth by surrounding themselves with artifacts gathered from Europe. Paintings, statues, libraries, and, when possible, European titles were brought to America to vest new wealth with Old World prestige. The veneration of Europe and the devotion to art in its highest forms were attempts by the recently rich to appropriate for themselves the comforting sense of stability and tradition represented by the Old World and its centuries of cultural achievement. Convulsive social and economic changes in America had, over a few generations, moved families from rural hamlets and immigrant slums to aristocratic drawing rooms. There was, understandably, a nervous fear among the newly arrived that the historical forces that had lifted them up could also cast them down. The priceless art objects that they collected were, for these parvenus, signs of membership in a permanent aristocracy, fetishes of a factitious stability.

There are, to be sure, no Vanderbilts or Fricks in the Bodleian, but these bourgeois bibliophiles are driven by the same social and psychological forces that directed those higher on the social pyramid. Aestheticism, in nineteenth-century Europe as in America, had behind it the need to create stability amidst the chaos brought by industrial and social revolution. After the decay of the Christian church, the veneration of art offered some of the stability formerly provided by organized religion. We ought not be surprised, then, that for the Bodleians, their literary gatherings take on elements of a cult. Their clubhouse, the narrator informs us, is "a sort of shrine for local worshippers . . . visited occasionally by pilgrims from afar" (413). Indeed, no pilgrimage church could display its relics with greater reverence than that of the narrator cataloging the club's prized possessions: Goethe's paperweight, Emerson's lead pencil, Matthew Arnold's autograph. The cult depends on a number of key oppositions, among which the following are particularly important:

| art | commerce |
| eternity | history |

We know nothing of how the narrator and his friends gain their bread, and indeed that is the point of the club—a release from days at the office, brokerage house, or law courts. The club rooms are a place to relax, smoke one's pipe, and contemplate the good, the true, and the eternal. But even here the bad faith on which this complacent aestheticism is based can be glimpsed. In the same paragraph in which the narrator imagines a rare publication "enshrined in a sort of holy of holies . . . forever sacred from the profanation of any vulgar or unappreciative eye" he must also concede that "a fine book, after all, was an investment" (417). The undoing of the oppositions of art and commerce, eternity and history hinted in this early paragraph is fully accomplished in the narrative's denouement.

These gentlemen of culture claim to value literature and art as ends in themselves; nonetheless, they forswear actually reading Baxter's work for fear of reducing its commercial value. Literature and business, clearly, are much more closely related than the Bodleians would openly admit. But the plot has a further twist. When Baxter springs his trap, most members angrily destroy the empty pages, which they deem worthless, either as art or as marketable product. But the narrator and others who keep their copies discover the value of the elegantly produced volume. "The paper is above criticism. The true collector loves wide margins, and the *Procrustes,* being all margin, merely touches the vanishing point of the perspective" (422). When one of the surviving volumes is brought to auction, it is knocked down at the highest price ever paid for a book published by the club. To summarize: a text announced as an art object becomes a commercial product, is judged worthless, and then becomes even more valuable than initially imagined. Moreover, these reversals happen with surprising rapidity. In light of these events, it is difficult to maintain the separation of art and business and to argue the isolation of either from history and economics.

We should not let the Bodleian Club members off the hook, for they are indeed the story's target, but at the same time we must say that, even if they were more self-aware and honest, they could not be faithful to their professed principles because these principles, and the oppositions upon which they depend, are themselves unstable. The bourgeois aesthetes profess that the literary values they venerate are outside time and commerce. This assumption flatters their own hopes that the social structure from which they benefit is not subject to historical and economic shifts. But artistic approbation is the product of social consensus, and thus it is inherently dynamic and evanescent. It changes as societies change, and indeed, as individuals change. Thus the value of a book goes up and down, like any other object in the market, according to how it is valued by consumers. The complication of these seeming opposites—art and commerce, eternity and history—is then perhaps not particularly surprising.

Consider, however, these additional oppositions, which are also at issue in this story:

printed	blank
language	silence
meaning	nonsense
plenitude	emptiness

According to the standards of the club and of traditional literary culture, the terms in the first column are opposed to and inherently superior to those in the second. But in the working out of the story, Baxter's empty pages and his evasive silence about them are powerfully significative: they eloquently communicate his amused contempt for the club and its values. His gesture, seemingly a nonsensical act of defiance, proves more incisive and cogent than the reviewers' windy verbiage. Baxter is quite aware of the witty paradox he has authored, as he shows with his reaction to the reviewers' effusions: "I am," he announces, "too full for utterance" (421). In the working out of Chesnutt's story, opposites are turned on their heads, and vacuity is plenitude.

The narrator, reviewing a work he has not read, stumbles on an insight that challenges two other familiar oppositions:

original   traditional
individual   social

Scanning the critique he has written, the narrator remarks, "I had a vague recollection of having read something like this somewhere, but so much has been written that one can scarcely discuss any subject of importance without unconsciously borrowing, now and then, the thoughts and language of others" (419).[14] He finds himself, while composing his own response, recycling words he has heard or read elsewhere. The same thing is true in his different reactions to Baxter's book. In each instance—when he praises it, when he rejects it, when he embraces it again—he is responding to its market valuation, that is, to a particularly succinct, dollars and cents, social consensus about its worth. The narrator recognizes, dimly but pertinently, that he is inhabited by "the thoughts and language of others." In coming to this recognition, the character articulates an insight that is central to Chesnutt's vision. We, as individuals, see what our culture lets us see: we organize our perceptions according to the categories our society provides, and we articulate these perceptions in the language that our culture supplies. Sadly, these categories and this language are imperfect. To use the story's central metaphor, they are procrustean. To make sense, they divide what is continuous and set up oppositions where there are often affinities. These reflections lead us to a discussion of the story's title and a consideration of these contrasting pairs:

author   reader
text   reader

Procrustes—the Greek bandit who sought to cut or stretch everyone to the same dimensions—is introduced in the story by Baxter. The literal repetition of Procrustes' behavior, however, is the work of other members of the club. The Bodleians, aware of Baxter's attitudes, organize his life according to the familiar pattern of sentimental fiction, and they attribute his cynicism to "some disappointment in love or ambition" (415). Jones, extending this romantic narrative, speculates that Baxter is a sensitive artist wounded by an uncaring public. Acting on his "secret theory of Baxter's failure in authorship," Jones reassures his friend that limited publication of *Procrustes* within the club will protect him from the outside world's hostility. Baxter, we are told, is "visibly impressed" (416) by these reassurances, and he agrees to the Bodleian publication—the publication of a book without print. Baxter's blank pages can be "read" several ways. The prankster leaves empty what he knows will not be read. But he also leaves empty what he knows others will write, indeed, have already written. Jones and his fellows have already composed "Baxter, the Failed Artist," and they will write his text. And, in fact, they do so twice. They first compose the text they elaborate in their belletristic cant. However, when that text is undone by the revelation of Baxter's prank, they write *Procrustes* again. This is the text of infinite margins, broken only by a slim column of dollar signs down the middle of the pages. In light of the way Baxter and his book are written and rewritten, how do we separate author, text, and reader? Who or what controls meaning?

To fully understand the relevance of these reflections to Chesnutt's art, we must review his situation in the early twentieth century. Chesnutt wished from the beginning of his career to devote himself exclusively to his fiction, but he had also his responsibility for a growing family. In late 1899, after the initial success of his stories, Chesnutt abandoned his business interests and sought to support himself exclusively with his earnings as a writer. This proved not to be possible, however, and in 1902 he resumed his practice as a legal stenographer. "Baxter's *Procrustes*" appeared in 1904, and the story's ironic meditation on the tensions of art and commerce reflects his artistic and economic struggles during this period. Another occurrence was even more important for the story's genesis. In 1902 Chesnutt was proposed for membership in Cleveland's Rowfant Club, a prestigious group of upper-middle-class book collectors. His nomination, however, was voted down because he was a Negro.[15] Several years later he wrote this story spoofing a club very like the one that had rejected him. The story nowhere mentions race or Negroes, and yet it achieves a deeper, social level of meaning when these biographical facts are known. The narrative, with its playful tumbling of opposites, is about seemingly essential differences. The most important difference in American life, in Chesnutt's time as in our own, is racial.

Let us pursue our pattern of oppositions in the story a bit farther and consider these:

white	black
reality	appearance
essential	accidental

The pattern examined earlier privileged the printed page over the blank one, and presence over absence. Logically, then, black ought here to be the privileged term. But, of course, in American society it is not. In racial discourse, black, the presence of dark pigment in the skin, is read as emptiness, the absence of a power to signify socially, the "invisibility" of which Ralph Ellison's protagonist complains. White, the absence of skin pigmentation, is, paradoxically, the fullest and most potent social signifier. Chesnutt's personal fate was that of Baxter's book, valued always by his exterior—his putative skin color—rarely by his intellect or his character. In his case and that of other blacks, appearance was taken as the deepest reality, and the accidents of skin pigmentation were taken as essential identity. And yet, few members of the Rowfant were more "white" than Charles Chesnutt. Pictures of him and anecdotes about the social confusion he caused reveal a man indistinguishable in appearance from the typical European American. His parody of the Bodleians demonstrates his mastery of upper-class white speech and behavior. And yet he was, by social consensus, black. And this fact was for him, as for other African Americans, decisive for his social, economic, and personal identity.

Several paragraphs back the focus of this discussion shifted from Chesnutt's story to his personal experience, so we might appropriately reflect a bit further on this opposition:

author's life   author's text

The Bodleians assume that these terms name fundamentally different things and that, in the interaction of author and text, the author is privileged. Meaning originates with the individual whose name appears on the title page, and it flows from that individual to the text. Thus, the author's life can provide a stable point to which we can appeal in fixing a literary work's otherwise equivocal meanings. The Bodleian critics work from this assumption of authorial priority, and it provides an excuse for their intellectual indolence. "The style is an emanation of Baxter's own intellect" (418), one of the critics reasons, so he feels at liberty to gloss the uncut pages of Baxter's book with what he believes to be the author's life and opinions. The problem with the life-text opposition is that an author's life, at least what we know of it, is also a text. Frequently, as in this instance, our understanding and interpretation of a biography is as unstable and indeterminate as the literary text itself.

Equally important, the current flows both ways between these poles. The way we read the literary text can change the way we read the biographical text as easily as the reverse; and in fact, the club members understand Baxter differently after they encounter his booby-trap book.

This does not negate the importance of studying the context of literary production for understanding a poem or story. Text is not separate from context, and indeed context shapes meaning. It is just that contextual meaning is more problematic, and its interaction with an individual text is more complex than Jones and his colleagues imagine. What is true of the Bodleians' reading of Baxter's *Procrustes* is also true of our reading of Chesnutt's "Baxter's *Procrustes*." That is, the story grows in meaning when we know that it was written by an African American who had been rejected by European Americans. Chesnutt's humorous confounding of seemingly essential differences—art and commerce, language and silence, meaning and nonsense—takes on a deeper and more poignant reference when we recall the ultimate American marker: the color line. Similarly, the entity we denominate "Chesnutt" emerges as a more complex, ambiguous, and even contemporary personality than before encountering "Baxter's *Procrustes*."

The story is then, at its deepest level, about language, and more specifically, about the oppositions upon which language and literary culture depend. To make sense of the world, we break up what is continuous and mark differences where there are often important similarities. There is no escape from this: to make meaning we must disrupt a subtle continuum. In its comic meditation on the problems of meaning, the story hints at the postmodernist's troubled concern about our entrapment in language. Let me tie these thoughts together by cutting the uncut-cut distinction we introduced in discussing Baxter's title:

uncut	cut
preserve	destroy
construct	deconstruct

The titles of Baxter's book and Chesnutt's story allude to the Greek brigand who insisted that all humans be the same size. Those who were too tall, he brutally shortened; those too short, he stretched. The titles, then, prepare us to read cutting as destructive. But Chesnutt's story says something different from its title. The Bodleians err, not by *cutting,* but by *not cutting.*[16] The reviewers do not separate the pages of Baxter's opus, judging it instead by its sumptuous cover. They do not ask Baxter directly about his purposes, nor do they confront his text. Instead they content themselves with vague gossip and unsystematic surmise. The book's significance and Baxter's intention emerge only after the blade violates the volume, severing its leaves, exposing them to scrutiny.

The Bodleians fetishize Baxter's book, attempting to change it from a communicative act to an object with a clear exchange value. Their effort to reify the book is, as we have seen, futile, for its empty pages prove corrosively eloquent. The Bodleians' attempt to contain and preserve value is, in fact, hostile to their interests, even when these interests are understood in the narrowest commercial sense. For the Bodleians, market value attaches to objects that imitate models esteemed in the past. But value also accrues to objects judged unique for their bold innovation. Such works create new, often more marketable products by destroying old forms. One has only to reflect on the moment of the story's composition—the first decade of the twentieth century—and the aesthetic currents flowing at that moment to judge the relative acuity of the Bodleian Club's judgment about what kind of art would ultimately prove valuable in the market created by emergent modernism.

The relevant point here is not commercial value—although this is clearly the narrator's preoccupation—but meaning. We cannot fix meaning by locking the covers of a book; language continues its work without us. Nor can we evade the problems of language by a retreat into silence, for silence is itself a form of speech. It can signify, variously, acquiescence or repudiation of the speech of others. There is no solution to the problems of language except in and through language. We can attend to the words and distinctions that we use—and that use us—and we can intervene in them, unmasking their distortions and trying to reshape them. These seem to be the implications of Chesnutt's comic tale. Language, with its dependence on binary distinctions, is, to be sure, clumsy and inexact. But the greatest danger comes not from using it but from using it lazily and dishonestly. The critique of our signifying systems is simultaneously a deconstruction and an exfoliation of meaning. Charles Chesnutt was unquestionably a man of his times, embroiled in its concerns and enmeshed in its language. But he seemed to understand this condition in a strikingly modern way. He saw at the beginning of the twentieth century the philosophical dilemma we still face at the outset of the twenty-first.

The next two chapters continue the discussion of language and meaning by examining Chesnutt's journal and his most important essay. Before that, I wish to make clear my reasons for including these chapters in a book devoted to Chesnutt's fictions. Joseph McElrath, summarizing recent Chesnutt scholarship, remarks that "the tendency in literary criticism concerning Chesnutt's work dealing with race is away from the objective reading of the works as self-contained entities independent of their author's personality and toward the use of an autobiographical approach that promises the possibility of understanding the work's contradictory elements in terms of the conflicting impulses in, and the inconsistent intentions of, the originator of these works."[17] The recent editions of Chesnutt's journals, letters, and essays are important work to which McElrath has contributed significantly. These volumes will be invaluable to Chesnutt scholars for establishing the intellectual and biographical context in which Chesnutt worked. I think, however, that it is unlikely that Chesnutt's nonfiction can resolve the conflicts in his novels and stories. There are two errors to be avoided in considering the relationship between a writer's journal or article and the same writer's story or novel.

The first mistake is to assume that nonfiction and fiction are the *same* thing. They are not equivalent expressions, such that one can be superimposed on the other as a sure guide to the latter's meaning. An author's essay is not a template for understanding his story for the simple reason that each is a separate text. Each has its own autonomy, and each has its own distinctive and unique meanings. We cannot substitute one for the other, as tempting as that may be. It is precisely such a substitution, the reduction of Baxter's poem to what the Bodleians imagined to be his life and opinions, that Chesnutt's story mocks. The second mistake to avoid is to assume that nonfiction and fiction are *different*. Both, again, are texts. Both are acts of language. Both suffer the inadequacies of their verbal medium, as well as the conflicting pressures of the culture in which they emerge. To turn from one text to another cannot bring a sudden clarity or resolution, for to do so is to substitute one complexity for another. And this, for me, is the great value we derive from reading disparate texts by the same author side by side. They don't mean the *same thing*, but they often mean in the *same ways*. They provide analogous and complementary enactments, on adjoining territory, of the struggle for meaning. They offer fascinating further instances of a writer's work with, and within, his or her language and culture. Charles Chesnutt's journals, the subject of the next chapter, illustrate his struggle with his culture and its language.

2

Chesnutt in His Journals
"Nigger" under Erasure

Collective identities, in short, provide what we might call scripts: narratives that people can use in shaping their life plans and in telling
their life stories. —K. ANTHONY APPIAH, "Race, Culture, and Identity: Misunderstood Connections"

In 1875 Charles Chesnutt, then a seventeen-year-old schoolteacher, took a
summer job among rural South Carolina blacks. On August 20, he confided
to his journal about his pupils and their families:

> This is the doggondest country I ever saw to teach in. They say they'll pay
> your board, and then don't do it. They accuse you indirectly of lying, almost of
> stealing, eavesdrop you, retail every word you say. Eavesdrop you when you're
> talking to yourself, twist up your words into all sorts of ambiguous mean-
> ings, refuse to lend you their mules &c. They are the most suspicious people
> in the world, good-sized liars, hypocrites, inquisitive little ~~nigger~~ wenches &c.
> I wouldn't teach here another year for fifty dollars a month.[1]

Chesnutt, during the winter an assistant teacher at Charlotte's Peabody
School, had passed the examination for a first-grade teaching certificate in
North Carolina; thus he was entitled to a salary of up to forty dollars a
month. He was, however, obliged to take part of his salary in board and
to negotiate terms directly with the families of his pupils. These tenant
farmers, scarcely a decade out of slavery, were caught between the promises

of emancipation and new forms of exploitation. They were lucky—when not cheated by white landowners—to make half the salary the young teacher was asking of them. They had little knowledge of the world beyond their cotton fields, and naturally enough, they were suspicious of this light-skinned outsider and dubious of his services.

Chesnutt was the son of free blacks who left North Carolina before the Civil War and who returned afterward to participate in Reconstruction. Charles, born in Ohio, had imbibed his parents' reforming spirit and that of the Northern teachers who had come South to educate the former slaves. The teenaged teacher arrived at his summer post full of noble intentions, but his journal records his frustration with his pupils and their parents. We do not know the specific offenses of the "wenches" to whom Chesnutt refers, but we can imagine that some of his scholars were near his own age and that they had been influenced by their suspicious parents. They very well may have been nosey and insubordinate to the novice instructor. In exasperation at their behavior, Chesnutt writes the word "nigger" and then censors himself. However, he does not censor himself entirely, for the word is crossed out, not totally effaced.

This word with the line running through it foregrounds the central theme of this chapter: Chesnutt's difficulties with, and within, the American language in his earliest writings. The imperfectly erased epithet enacts, in capsule form, the problem with which Chesnutt struggled throughout his early journals, and indeed, throughout his literary career. Chesnutt attempts in this entry to articulate his feeling toward the most troublesome of his charges. But at the same time, he is also trying to work out his relationship to the community he serves and to which, by social custom, he belongs. This struggle is a key theme of these journals, and its pressures can be felt in Chesnutt's search for social, literary, and linguistic resources and in his first attempts at creative expression.

Although Chesnutt had black ancestors on both his father's side and his mother's side, he did not differ in appearance from most white citizens. On June 7, 1875, he records a well-intentioned white man's warning against teaching in a Negro school and his offer of a post in a white school. The offer was, in effect, an invitation to pass as white. Chesnutt declined the proposition and accepted a post among blacks. However, a month later, on July 31, after being taken for white twice in one day, he comments, "I

believe I'll leave here and pass anyhow, for I am as white as any of them"
(78). This is the only place in his journals where Chesnutt openly considers
giving up his African American identity. Three years later, in June 1878, he
married a woman darker than he. Chesnutt surely knew that in marrying
Susan Perry and beginning a family with her he was committing himself to
life as a black person, and he willingly accepted this fact. Nonetheless, the
theme of passing haunts his fiction, and Chesnutt's relation to the colored
community around him remained, in these early journals and in his fiction,
conflicted and ambivalent. No less conflicted was the community's attitude
toward him. His marriage did not fully settle the matter, for in 1888 he con-
fides, "I am neither fish[,] flesh, nor fowl—neither 'nigger', poor white, nor
'buckrah.' Too 'stuck up' for the colored folks, and, of course, not recognized by the whites" (157–58). This situation would never entirely change,
and Charles Chesnutt's position within America's rigid racial binaries would
remain, throughout his life, anomalous and liminal. The journals record
his earliest interrogation of these categories. In them, he attempts to discover or create—within the limited options offered by nineteenth-century
America—a narrative that would allow him to shape his life plans and tell
his story to himself.

Chesnutt was intellectually ambitious and wanted to prepare himself for
a literary career. But he lacked a community with whom he could test his
ideas and develop his voice. His contact with educated whites in North
Carolina, as Reconstruction crumbled and Jim Crow emerged, was fleeting
and superficial. During slavery blacks had been forbidden education, and
now, in the years immediately following emancipation, the vast majority of
African Americans in the South lacked the most meager elements of literacy.
Chesnutt wanted more resources than his community could provide. The
avatar whom young Charles invoked in his efforts at self-education was Benjamin Franklin, the archetypal American self-improver. But the social and
intellectual resources available to the eighteenth-century white man under
colonial rule and those available to a nineteenth-century black man in the
South were very different. Young Franklin grew up in one of the centers of
American intellectual life, and he had his Junto, his group of like-minded
peers, with whom he met weekly to discuss moral and philosophical ideas.
Chesnutt yearned for a comparable community, for he knew that a "harmonious, healthy mental development requires the friction of mind upon

mind" (137), but few possibilities for intellectual exchange were available to him.

In the intellectual solitude of these early years, Chesnutt turns to the friend he calls "my confidant, my Journal" (157). The notebooks he kept were a chance to speak and be heard—if only by himself. It was a sadly solipsistic expedient, for it could not provide a true dialogue. Chesnutt read voraciously, absorbing everything important that came beneath his eyes. After reading, he would carefully record his solitary reflections. This, of course, was not a true dialogue, for there was no possibility for Chesnutt to intervene, to influence the voice of his interlocutor. It would be better to describe this dynamic as parallel monologues; in it the second voice— Chesnutt's solitary journal—repeats the ideas and imitates the dominant voice—the canonical white texts he studied.

The journal that Chesnutt began in 1874 at the age of sixteen and in which he would intermittently make entries for the next nine years eventually filled three volumes, roughly 450 pages. Their purpose, Chesnutt tells us, is to record "the most important events" in his life "together with the reflections which were suggested by them at the time of their occurrence" (104). On balance, they record many more "reflections" than "events." In fact, what strikes us most about these jottings is the paucity of significant autobio-graphical detail. Chesnutt's parents, his brothers and sister are barely men-tioned; Chesnutt courts and marries Susan Perry, and these events are never mentioned. Susan gives birth to their first child, and we learn the fact only incidentally when Chesnutt records his discussion with the attending physi-cian. Reflections are rather more plentiful than events in these pages, but his thoughts are generally of a practical nature. Chesnutt lays out, for example, his schedule of activities for summer vacation 1879: an hour for each of the three languages he was studying, as well as another hour for composition in English. There was also time in his days for gardening, practicing short-hand, and the care of his child. Chesnutt can be coolly candid in assessing his weaknesses; he censures, for instance, his tendency toward what he calls "Aerial Architecture" (110), romantic plans of future glory. But there is little of what we would call deep introspection.

The notebooks contain much beyond that which is generally thought to be the province of the diary. They include his efforts in self-tuition: exercises in German, French, and Latin composition, as well as reactions to his readings of Homer, Gibbon, and Macaulay. The journals were also his personal account books, recording his earnings and his frugal expenditures. Richard Brodhead eliminated some of this in his edition of the journals—Chesnutt's exercises in shorthand, for example—but he wisely gives us a generous sampling, for the young scholar's pedagogical jottings are as revealing, in their way, as his self-conscious reflections. The notebooks are, Brodhead suggests, "The Journal of a Self-Made Man" (2), and they are the very workshop of Chesnutt's self-fashioning: the place where he assiduously seeks to equip himself for the world he wishes to enter, and the site where he struggles to assemble the persona he will present to it. The final result of Chesnutt's assembled identity is a social product as well as a personal one. K. Anthony Appiah's observation about the dynamic of self and society is relevant to the effort recorded in Chesnutt's journal: "We make up selves from a tool kit of options made available by our culture and society. . . . We do make choices, but we don't determine the options among which we choose" (96).

From the models proffered by his culture, Chesnutt particularly favors Benjamin Franklin and Horace Greeley, and he clearly means to place himself and his journal in the tradition they represent. It is the great American tradition of the success story, the narrative of one who, by fidelity to American middle-class values, rises to a position of respect and influence. The success-story genre had special importance—and poignancy—for the nineteenth-century African American, for both the means and the goal of the American dream were withheld from Americans of African descent. Blacks, in nineteenth-century science, were seen not as human but as a separate species, biologically and morally inferior to humans. They were, by this logic, incapable of the virtues that made bourgeois success possible. Chesnutt, of course, rejects this racial essentialism, but in so doing he seems close to a kind of racial subjectivism. He assumes that racial prejudice results from logical error or temporary ignorance. Whites believe blacks are inferior because they have not confronted blacks who can meet or exceed white standards of genteel behavior. Once blacks meet white standards, whites will recognize their error and accept middle-class blacks as their equals.

The strategy conceived here—to trump race with class—is one that would fascinate and frustrate Chesnutt and the characters in his fictions throughout his career. The strategy's appeal is easy to understand, for, in nineteenth-century ideology, racial categories were immutable while, in democratic theory at least, class distinctions were permeable. The problem with this strategy is that, in Western society, class has always been powerfully determined by birth. We have only to review the histories of words like "noble" and "genteel" to see how they are imbricated with assumptions of innate, inherited moral qualities. American democracy loosened this connection for those within its European-derived population, but not for those derived from African, Asian, and Native American ancestry. Social Darwinism reinforced the assumption that class hierarchies were grounded in nature, that groups that found themselves low in the social hierarchy were there because they were inherently less fit. Young Chesnutt naively assumes that whites will agree to the race-for-class swap. Chesnutt, taking American democracy at its word, imagines that whites will accept as their equal blacks who master the forms of genteel behavior. Booker T. Washington's *Up from Slavery,* the most famous story of post–Civil War African American success, was still decades in the future when Chesnutt was composing his journal, but it illustrates the contradictions in Chesnutt's project. In his memoir Washington made his own accommodation with the success genre. He proves the pattern's relevance for organizing his own life narrative at the same time that he forswears its appropriateness for most blacks. He could sit with the president and with white philanthropists, but most blacks would have to accept, at least provisionally, a status less than that of full gentility, a caste of artisans and small farmers, separate and unequal, beneath that of the white middle class.

Young Chesnutt ignores the obstacles to his success strategy as he begins his journals. No one could be more reverent than this young teacher in invoking and emulating the pieties of Victorian gentility. He expresses his faith in a just and provident deity, and he dedicates himself to a life of hard work and patient plodding. Confident that fair-minded Americans will grant him the respect his efforts deserve, he sets out to equip himself with the social tools essential to his struggle. The notebooks are as useful in the assemblage of his social self as they are to his academic formation. "If writing a lesson helps to learn it," he reasons, "why may not writing a good resolution help to keep it?" (104). Thus we find him copying in his journals laborious instructions about proper bathing, care of nails and feet, as well as change of clothing from *A Handbook for Home Improvement.* Conformity to the accepted rules of hygiene are key class markers, for they depend on resources—plumbing, plentiful linen, and leisure for grooming—beyond the reach of most members of the working class. Chesnutt accepts these rules as crucial elements in the middle-class self he is assembling, and he hopes that reverently transcribing them in his journal will fix them indelibly in his character.

His efforts are not wasted, and the life he records in these pages conforms, in many ways, to the success-story paradigm. By dint of his industry, he is, at the age of twenty-one, principal of the State Colored Normal School in Fayetteville, one of the best institutions of its kind in the South. Proficient in three foreign languages and widely read in the arts and sciences, he had equipped himself with an education equal or superior to that of the city's white, college-trained elite. And yet, despite all of this, he is denied the respect and influence that would be accorded a white man for similar achievements. In 1880, when local Republicans wish to nominate Chesnutt for town commissioner, prominent citizens warn him that a position of such importance cannot go to black man in the newly "redeemed" Southern political order. He gets an even more brutal lesson in Jim Crow from a local store clerk. The white man casually dismisses Chesnutt's achievements: "Well he's a nigger; and with me a nigger is a nigger, and nothing in the world can make him anything else but a nigger" (161). The *n* word, which Chesnutt struck from his diary six years earlier, returns, fourfold, applied to him. Young Chesnutt was probably no darker, and almost certainly better educated, than the white clerk. Notwithstanding, he was, in this white man's eyes, indistinguishable from the impoverished sharecroppers whose children he had taught in South Carolina. The young scholar's efforts at self-improvement seem, in fact, to have strengthened the white citizen's resistance, causing him to condemn Chesnutt to quadruple niggerhood. At this North Carolina shop counter, Franklin's success pattern collides with another archetypal American story—the narrative of niggerdom. The *n* word is more than an ugly epithet; it is a script, a prescriptive and preemptive account of a life *before* it has been lived. Kimberly M. Benston explains:

> Allotting black people the brand of "nigger" indicates a desire to void the possibility of meaning within the "blackened" shell of selfhood, thereby reducing substance to the repetitive echo of catachresis. "Nigger" is a mechanism of con-

trol by contraction; it subsumes the complexities of human experience into a
tractable sign while manifesting an essential inability to *see* (to grasp, to appre-
hend) the signified.[2]

Chesnutt does not hear the racist clerk's dismissal directly—it is reported
to him—but it is no less galling for that. We might compare the event with
similar incidents in Booker T. Washington's *Up from Slavery* and in W. E. B.
Du Bois's *The Souls of Black Folk.* Washington tells his readers how, traveling
as a boy in Virginia, he was refused a bed at a coach stop because of his race
and had to spend a cold night outside awaiting the next day's stage. Du
Bois, at about the same age, a schoolboy in Massachusetts, has his greeting
card returned by a white female classmate. Washington, alone and sleepless
in the frosty Appalachian darkness, suffers the sharper physical pain, but, he
tells us, he simply shrugged it off. Washington was on his way to Hampton
Institute, to education and a chance for service, and nothing could deflect
him. Du Bois's classmate's peremptory gesture cut more deeply, and, in
his telling, it became the occasion for his famous epiphany of the "veil."
The white clerk's brutal dismissal occurred later in Chesnutt's life than did
the youthful encounters with racism by the two black leaders, but all three
men narrate the devastating collision of self image with the white person's
othering gaze. Chesnutt's reaction, as recorded in his journal, more closely
resembles that of Washington than that of Du Bois. Chesnutt's position
on racial difference, throughout the journal, is that of an optimistic subjectivist. Racial prejudice, he believes, results from white misperceptions
of the black person's abilities. Once blacks achieve the signs of gentility,
middle-class white Americans will recognize their natural class kinship with
the evolved former slaves. The white clerk's insult—"nigger" four times
repeated—might seem devastating to Chesnutt's optimism, but it modifies
his thinking on racial barriers only slightly. To the barrier of class he adds
that of geography. He will move North and pursue his dream there.

Thoughts of migration northward are a recurrent theme in Chesnutt's
journals from their beginning. So also are thoughts of the literary career by
which he hopes to make his escape, and here again the journals are essential preparations. He reads voraciously and comments on these readings,
searching models for his own work. Chesnutt focuses, understandably, on
the works esteemed by the society that he aspired to enter. He reads Voltaire

and Goethe, Virgil and Byron with careful attention, and Charles Dickens, Robert Burns, Harriet Beecher Stowe, and Albion Tourgée inspire his literary ambitions. However, Chesnutt finds no models for his efforts in the nascent African American literary tradition. Against the background of the white canonical figures who are the basis of his education, the literary production of American blacks seemed primitive. In one entry he repeats Jefferson's judgment that Phillis Wheatley's poems are "beneath the dignity of criticism" (164). He also criticizes the presentation of facts in William Wells Brown's *The Negro in the American Rebellion: His Heroism and His Fidelity.* He remarks that the book reminds him of a gentleman in a dirty shirt. "You are rather apt to doubt his gentility under such circumstances" (164).[3] The comment is fascinating for the connection it establishes between hygiene and literature, between good grooming and good writing. The language and behavior by means of which blacks might demonstrate their human status were rigidly controlled; they were held to the most rigorous standards of the middle-class whites who judged them. Amiri Baraka (then LeRoi Jones) has written about the relationship of social and literary behavior among black writers:

> The Negro artist, because of his middle-class background, carried the artificial social burden as the "best and most intelligent" of Negroes, and usually entered into the "serious" arts to exhibit his familiarity with the social graces, i.e., as a method or means of displaying his participation in the "serious" aspects of American culture. To be a writer was to be "cultivated," in the stunted bourgeois sense of the word. It was also to be a "quality" black man. . . . It was, and is, a social preoccupation rather than an aesthetic one.[4]

Baraka accurately describes the social burden shouldered by earlier generations of black artists, but he seriously underestimates its weight. He contrasts these writers with black jazz musicians who created an art independent of white forms. The evocation of music in this context, however, calls attention to the much greater freedom available in that medium. American English came to black writers from whites, freighted with powerful and often hostile connotations that did not exist in the sound of a horn. Moreover, whites vigilantly patrolled their language, making literacy a crime under slavery, but they were more tolerant with music, allowing blacks to amuse themselves, and sometimes their white masters, with their improvised or borrowed instruments. Oddly enough, Baraka's ahistorical judgment on his black predecessors echoes an equally unfair comment by the young Chesnutt. "The mediocrity of what has been called 'Negro Literature,'" Baraka wrote in 1963, "is one of the most loosely held secrets of American culture" (105). Eighty-two years earlier, young Chesnutt ungenerously confided to his journal that "the Negro is yet to become known who can write a good book" (164).

In March 1881, when Chesnutt made this comment, Frances E. W. Harper's *Iola Leroy* (1892) and Paul Laurence Dunbar's *Oak and Ivy* (1893)— black publications that might have caused Chesnutt to modify this judgment—were still a decade in the future. Black writers were not numerous during this period, and Chesnutt's journal helps us see the obstacles they faced. We must count Chesnutt among the readers most likely to be interested in writings by blacks, and indeed he was.[5] But, in Chesnutt's case, we also have access to the literary education even the best-disposed readers brought to the reading experience. In his program of self-tuition the apprentice writer carefully studied and imitated G. P. Quackenbos's *Advanced Course of Composition and Rhetoric,* a text widely used in nineteenth-century American classrooms. Quackenbos was a neoclassicist who insisted on universal aesthetic standards. He strongly opposed the notion "that there is no such thing as *good* or *bad, right* or *wrong;* that every man's Taste is to him a standard without appeal; and that we can not, therefore, properly censure even those who prefer the empty rhymester to Milton." Quackenbos clinches his argument against aesthetic relativism with the following example. "The absurdity of such a position, when applied to extremes is manifest. No one will venture that the Taste of a Hottentot or an Esquimaux is as delicate as that of a Longinus or an Addison."[6] The "universal" human taste defended by Victorian arbiters did not include Africans or Inuits, for, in the nineteenth-century white consensus, the latter were not human in the same way and to the same degree as Europeans. Frederick Douglass, whose biography Chesnutt would later write, is not mentioned in Chesnutt's journals, nor are any of the slave narratives. These writings were powerfully relevant in the fight against slavery, but that battle was over, and a new story needed telling. These earlier African American narratives were, moreover, conceived for polemical purposes and reached a fairly narrow audience of morally earnest whites and free blacks. Chesnutt wanted to write differently, to create literary narratives whose artistic excellence would carry them to a white audience not reached by previous black writers. "I shall write for a purpose," he proposes in May 1880, "a high, holy purpose, and this will inspire me to greater effort. The object of my writings would be not so much the elevation of the colored people as the elevation of the whites" (139).

There is, however, one literary artist of African descent whom Chesnutt openly admired, but he is not an American. He is French—Alexandre Dumas. Dumas *père* was at the height of international success, on the stage as well as in popular novels, during the years of Chesnutt's literary apprenticeship. Dumas, son of a French general and a Martinique mulatto woman, was a quadroon, and, although his fictions do not treat the black condition explicitly, Chesnutt reads Dumas's post-Napoleonic romances as allegories of his own condition. Here is an entry from October 12, 1878:

> In some things I seem to be working in the dark. I have to feel my way along, but by perseverance I manage to make better headway than many who have the light; and besides, like the Edmund Dantes in Dumas' "Monte Cristo," I have become accustomed to the darkness. As I have been thrown constantly on my own resources in my solitary studies, I have acquired some degree of *self-reliance*. (92)

The identification with Dumas's hero leads Chesnutt, in the same entry, to one of his earliest and most grandiloquent statements of purpose. In it the North Carolina schoolteacher's voice blends with that of Dumas's defiant count, and the American success narrative modulates into French romantic revolt:

> I will go to the North, where, although the prejudice sticks, like a foul blot on the fair scutcheon of American liberty, yet a man may enjoy these privileges if he has the money to pay for them. I will live down the prejudice, I will crush it out. I will show to the world that a man may spring from a race of slaves, and yet far excel many of the boasted ruling race. If I can exalt my race, if I can gain the applause of the good, and the approbation of God, the thoughts of the ignorant and prejudiced will not concern me. (93)

There is more than Dumas's romantic power that secures his importance to the young Chesnutt. Dumas was a mulatto artist who had been received and hailed at the highest levels by the white artistic elite. This was the elite whose standards Chesnutt aspired to meet, and Dumas's example had value not only because he was black but because he had succeeded on white terms. The strange paradox of which Chesnutt's journal continually reminds us is that of the artist caught between two worlds. In the passage just quoted Chesnutt defiantly affirms his black identity and proclaims that he will bend every effort to exalt his race. He scorns the prejudice of ignorant men, but looks instead toward the approbation of a just God. Despite his proclaimed independence, the standards Chesnutt projects on his impartial deity are those of the white bourgeois culture to which he aspires. The paradox Chesnutt illustrates here was the dilemma of his time. To be accepted as fully human, blacks had first to prove themselves according to white standards.

This paradox can also be seen in Chesnutt's attitude toward Negro spirituals. The young Chesnutt, like most whites and many educated blacks of his time, is generally dismissive of black vernacular culture. But the impressive success of the Fisk Jubilee Singers performing spirituals before European and American white audiences—including the ultimate arbiter of Victorian taste, Queen Victoria herself—occasioned a new valuation of at least this one element of black culture. In April 1879 Chesnutt entered into his journal a letter he wrote thanking the editors of the *Christian Union* for their favorable attention to a Jubilee concert, and in March 1880 he considers editing a volume of Negro hymns and ballads for a Northern white audience. He concedes that "these songs are not of much merit as literary compositions," but, he reasons, "they have certain elements of originality which make them interesting to a student of literature, who can trace, in a crude and unpolished performance, more of the natural ability or character of the writer than in the more correct production of a cultivated mind. Burns and Bunyan rank, in literature, far above many inferior authors who could manufacture polished Alexandrines and heroic couplets, and who paid far more attention to the external graces of style" (121–22).

Chesnutt, in this passage, accepts the artistic products of black folk, but several things were necessary for this acceptance. First, he saw that the spirituals had been sanctioned by white approval and, second, he was able to assimilate them to canonical white models, in this case, Burns and Bunyan. There is also a third consideration. In this passage, a shrewd and ambitious young writer calculates the literary market. Chesnutt wishes to rise above the oppressive conditions in which he finds himself, and he has decided a literary career promises the surest means for escape. He surveys the cultural scene, notes the interest in spirituals, and discovers the profitability of the cultural materials surrounding him. He considers editing these materials as the first step in the literary career that will take him out of the South. Richard Brodhead catches the paradox in Chesnutt's complex relationship to black vernacular culture: "Chesnutt's coming to an appreciation of this local ethos is inseparable from the process by which he strives to secure a life apart from that ethos" (25).

The discussion of Chesnutt's relation to folk culture leads us to his relation to folk speech in his journals. Folk language was, of course, to be the basis for his early literary success with short fiction using rural black dialect. His attitude in the journals to black vernacular speech is as complex and conflicted as in the other areas of black life that we have explored. This is evident in that the word "nigger" is struck out in the first entry discussed. The American English word that he exasperatedly applies to his pupils bears racist implications, which he rejects: thus the line running through the epithet. But "nigger" is not, in every instance, a racist insult. The word comes frequently to the lips of Uncle Julius in *The Conjure Woman*, where it has a range of connotations. As used popularly by blacks among themselves, in Chesnutt's time as in our own, the word can be humorous, self-deprecating, even affectionate, as well as insulting.

Black American vernacular was the language of Chesnutt's students and their parents, and it would become the language of one of his most popular creations. But it was not yet the language of Chesnutt himself. Chesnutt's white Northern teachers would never have used the *n* word, nor would they have allowed Chesnutt to use it. Indeed, Chesnutt takes it as one of his chief responsibilities to correct his pupils' grosser departures from the standard American speech of his time. Chesnutt cannot use "nigger" as unlettered blacks might do; nor can he use the word as his white Southern neighbors use it. The word struck out calls attention to the young teacher's anomalous linguistic situation and his isolation from both the black and white communities surrounding him. Another entry from the South Carolina summer of 1875 further illustrates his linguistic and social isolation. Chesnutt writes of an encounter with a local black youth: "a high-headed young gentleman of considerable color accosted me by the venerable title of 'Uncle Chess.' I, in a most graceful and polite manner, informed him that I was unaware of sustaining that relationship to him" (77). The boy's greeting appears innocent, for "Uncle" combined with the diminutive form of Chesnutt's family name, in black vernacular, is familiar, but not necessarily condescending nor intentionally insulting. Nonetheless, Chesnutt responds to the vernacular salutation with elaborately high diction. He means by this diction—and by his emphasis on the boy's color—to emphasize that black vernacular is *black,* and to insist on the distance—racial, social, and linguistic—between himself and the boy.

What makes this entry particularly curious and revelatory of Chesnutt's linguistic ambivalence is the contrast between its self-conscious formality and the informality of the lines that immediately precede it in the notebook: "Hallo! Journal, How's your cromabomalopabus today? I haven't seen you in a coon's age" (77). Chesnutt greets his journal—greets himself, actually— in language even more colloquial than that of the boy whose salutation he refused. Chesnutt *does* use the vernacular and, in this passage, takes evident pleasure in its vigor and humor. But he does so privately, resisting the social stigma that would result in using dialect publicly. Acting in this fashion, Chesnutt was doing nothing more than what he had been taught. Chesnutt's formal training, Richard Brodhead reminds us, "was based on the systematic devaluation and even suppression of this vernacular" (22). The texts he followed in his course of self-tuition reinforced the same linguistic prejudice. One of his books was Hugh Blair's *Lectures on Rhetoric and Belles Lettres,* first published in 1783, but still used in American schools during the nineteenth century. Here, copied with the reverent attention devoted elsewhere to the text on personal hygiene, is Blair's advice on linguistic propriety: "Propriety is the selection of such words and phrases in the language, as the best and most established usage has appropriated to those ideas which we intend to express by them. It requires also the avoidance of vulgarisms or low expressions" (94). Style, for the eighteenth-century gentleman and for young Chesnutt, is not merely an aesthetic adornment; it is a crucial moral and social indicator, the outward sign of an inner gentility.

As fascinating as it is, Chesnutt's furtive lapse into dialect in the journal was momentary. It is a pleasure he allows himself only briefly and in private. His linguistic interest, at this early stage, is oriented in the opposite direction. It is the need to master literate English in its most sophisticated form that helps explain the existence of this journal. Chesnutt complains, during his South Carolina summer, of the limited vocabularies of the people with whom he interacts: "The people don't know words enough for a fellow to carry on a conversation with them. He must reduce his phraseology several degrees lower than that of the first reader" (82). The journal is not only his intellectual sounding board; it is his substitute linguistic community. He withdraws into his notebooks, fleeing the dialect speakers, to practice the language of Shakespeare, Cowper, and Macaulay.

Chesnutt's attitude toward black speech changes in the course of these journals in ways that parallel the changes in his attitude to black music. In May 1880, the same month he recorded his thoughts on spirituals, Chesnutt relates the experience of the Reverend Frederick Jones. This educated young black clergyman preached his first service to his congregation in highly formal language. The worshippers were not moved, and they called for "Brudder Sam," an uneducated folk preacher. The latter succeeded where Jones failed, filling the group with the spirit. Jones took the lesson and adopted, at least provisionally, the language and customs of his congregation. "It was a great sacrifice to the elegant Fred Jones, but he had an object in view. By going down to the people he gained their confidence" (132). The story of Frederick Jones had added authority for Chesnutt because it was told to him by Elder Davis, a prominent and politically influential black man whom Chesnutt respected.

In yet another journal entry from May 1880, Chesnutt considers the success of Albion Tourgée's *A Fool's Errand,* one of the period's most popular novels: "if Judge Tourgée, with his necessarily limited intercourse with colored people, and with his limited stay in the South, can write such interesting descriptions, such vivid pictures of Southern life and character as to make him rich and famous, why could not a colored man, who has lived among colored people all his life . . . write a far better book about the South than Judge Tourgée or Mrs. Stowe has written?" (125). In this passage, as with the passage discussing spirituals, we see Chesnutt discovering the literary potential of the material surrounding him. This material included the folk speech and customs he would exploit seven years later in his breakthrough story "The Goophered Grapevine."

Chesnutt in his journals was not yet at the level of literary skill he would later achieve, but his notebooks record his first efforts at creative expression. These early sketches and poems also reveal his ambivalence toward the racial community to which he belonged. "Lost in the Swamp," a five-hundred-word story, dated in his journal August 14, 1874, is an effort Chesnutt identifies as his "first real attempt at literature" (47). In it, the narrator, a boy named Nathan, recounts what happens when his father sends him on an errand to the farm of a neighbor named Bright. The boy's home and the Bright farm are separated by five miles and a large swamp. Nathan enters the marsh but quickly loses his way: "As the weather was cloudy, I could not divine my way by the sun, and I knew not which way to go. I was lost in the swamp. I wandered on for several hours, through blind roads. Night was coming on, and the tall trees and thick underbrush made my road particularly gloomy and somber" (47). Alone in the dark, the boy is haunted by fear of wolves and other dangers. Nonetheless, he keeps his courage, perseveres, and taking his direction from the polestar, he arrives safely at Farmer Bright's home.

It is easy enough to read this sketch as an allegory of Chesnutt's own situation as a teenage teacher-scholar in the South. His journal records his hunger for education and self-improvement at the same time that it records his fear of imprisonment in a setting without cultural resources. The symbolism of the dark swamp and Farmer Bright's property is fairly obvious, suggesting the contrasts of ignorance and knowledge, obscurity and renown. An untitled poem composed four years later presents another version of the same allegory. The poem describes the growth of a seed buried "deep in the dark damp womb of the earth" (99). The young plant strives mightily, draws strength from the sun's bright rays, and eventually stands free and tall, crowned by "crests of golden hair" (100). The poem, like "Lost in the Swamp," represents in symbolic form young Chesnutt's struggle for education and recognition.

In both works, dark and light figure illiteracy and education, as well as anonymity and fame. Dark and light, of course, are also an important racial opposition in our culture. Read with the latter opposition in mind, the dark swamp and the soil represent the black community; Farmer Bright and the golden-haired tassels suggest the lighter skins and fair hair of white and mulatto Americans. Nathan follows the North Star to safety, and in this way "Lost in the Swamp" echoes the slave narrative, but with an important difference: the imprisoning force is not a white slaver but other, darker, blacks. The contrast of darkness and light is thoroughly conventional in our culture: Dumas used it, and Chesnutt copies it when he compares himself to the captive count yearning for freedom. Chesnutt exploits this opposition in these early creative efforts, but it is not clear that he consciously intends all of the racial connotations I have adduced. The consequences of Chesnutt's uncritical use of conventional symbols are also seen in a second sketch entered the same month as "Lost in the Swamp." The sketch's title, "Bruno," refers to a faithful "jet-black Newfoundland dog" (52) whose owner dies. Before dying, the dog's dissolute master addresses the animal: "Poor Bruno! You have stuck to me through thick and thin. You have accompanied me in all my rambles, shared my fortunes and misfortunes" (53). The dog's owner implores the physician who attends his last hours to care for the faithful animal. The physician does so, and the old dog lives out his life under the loving care of the physician's family. In the context of the racial concerns seen elsewhere in the journal, it is possible to read "Bruno" as an allegory on the New South. The black slaves, represented by the loyal Bruno, served the dissolute white masters faithfully, and the latter have expired as a consequence of their sins. It is the responsibility of the new governing elite, black and white, to care personally for the former bondsmen. Comparison with a faithful animal was one of the more benign representations of the black person in plantation fiction by white writers. Thomas Nelson Page's "Marse Chan," where the old black retainer and the master's dog together guard the master's property in his absence, is a case in point. At the same time, however, the linking of the black person with the pet expresses condescension toward dark-skinned people. They are, after all, represented in young Chesnutt's allegory by a dog, albeit a faithful one.

These early creative efforts raise a serious question: to what degree does young Chesnutt *intend* the negative connotations I have adduced in these readings? The question is a difficult one, but it can be addressed by another question, or rather, the same question from a different angle. To what degree could young Chesnutt *avoid* these negative connotations, granted the way our language is structured? Should we think of these meanings as the exclusive product of Charles Chesnutt, understood as an isolated consciousness, or should we consider these meanings as, at least in part, products of the language in which Chesnutt was writing and the culture within which he was working? These questions point to the conundrum in the chiasmic title of chapter 1, "Chesnutt's Language / Language's Chesnutt." What is the relation between speaker and language, possessor or possessed? In raising these theoretical issues, my purpose here is neither to condemn or excuse Chesnutt, but to explain him. We are witnessing, in these early creative exercises, another instance of the cultural and linguistic push and pull that we saw in the *n* word with a line drawn through it.

We do not, any of us, have sole proprietorship of the language we use. We inherit it from the lips and books of our predecessors, and we share it, at any given moment, with millions of contemporaries. It bears the ideology of the culture that formed and uses it. We can, if we have sufficient skill and resources, turn the language to new meanings and values, but this is always difficult and never more than partially successful. This was even more true for the young man we have been discussing. Avid of learning and desirous of serving others, he was forced to learn and create in isolation, without the chance for real dialogue. And he had to express his sense of personal and social identity in a language and culture hostile to the race to which he belonged. K. Anthony Appiah speaks for himself, but his words apply to Chesnutt and to all of us: "Dialogue shapes the identity I develop as I grow up: but the very material out of which I form it is provided, in part, by my society" (95).

The journals pass from 1874 to 1882. Chesnutt progresses from his teens into early adulthood, and the South devolves from Reconstruction into "Redemption" and Jim Crow. As we move through these pages, we watch Chesnutt mature. We discover a more critical attitude toward American culture and a more skeptical and sophisticated use of American language. One of Chesnutt's last journal entries, recorded February 1882, is a poem entitled "A Perplexed Nigger." The problematic *n* word occurs again in this title, but here it signifies on a particular cultural reference. The perplexed darky, scratching his head and trying to comprehend the complexities of the white world, was a familiar stereotype in post-Reconstruction America. He appears in the minstrel show and in white plantation fiction, such as in Joel Chandler Harris's "Uncle Remus at the Telephone." In this sketch, Remus is confounded by hearing his master's voice on a telephone. "How in de name er God you git in dar, Mars John?" the startled servant exclaims, to the amusement of his white mistress.[7]

Chesnutt's title signifies ironically on this stereotypical image of Negro confusion. Here are the opening lines of Chesnutt's poem:

> I'm "quite an intelligent nigger",
>   words
> As *the phrase* in our section go,
> And I live in the land where the rice,
> And the corn and the cotton grow. (175)

The speaker, as his educated diction makes clear, is *not* the confused bumpkin that the poem's title leads us to expect. But in frustrating these expectations, the speaker introduces another familiar cliché. The phrase "intelligent nigger" enters framed by quotation marks. Clearly, the phrase does not belong to the speaker but to his white neighbors, from whom the speaker has borrowed it. To the white North Carolinians in Chesnutt's community, a "nigger" was "intelligent" if he knew what he was supposed to know, and nothing more.

But the speaker frustrates this stereotype as well, speaking openly and critically on contemporary issues. His specific focus is the unjust treatment of Henry Ossian Flipper and Johnson C. Whitaker in the United States Army. Flipper, who managed to graduate from West Point despite constant harassment, was dismissed from service on trumped-up charges. Whitaker was expelled from the United States Military Academy on equally specious grounds. These two cases, as well as the growth of lynch law, were devastating to Chesnutt's faith in the success-story paradigm. Prejudice, in these instances, existed not merely in an ignorant Southern store clerk, but at the highest levels of white society: in the American military, whose efforts had helped to free the slave, and in the American courts, who were supposed to protect that freedom. The speaker in the poem returns to the key phrase introduced in the first stanza and announces a conclusion that is considerably more bold than what a contemporary white reader might expect. The poem is a direct challenge to the legal hypocrisy of "separate but equal" segregation:

> I'm quite an intelligent nigger,
> But I cannot exactly see,

> Why there's one set of laws for the white folks,
> And a different set for me. (178)

We see Chesnutt's growing sophistication in the use of the language of the dominant culture. The *n* word returns. Earlier his defense against the word was to strike it out, but here he finds another tactic: "double-voicing," using the language of others, but letting us hear both its original meaning and another meaning critical of the first. For the white Southerner, there were two options for the black person: to be a "perplexed" fool, or to be "intelligent" and submit to white rule. Chesnutt invokes this binary to open a space within it. The poem's speaker is neither "a perplexed nigger" nor an "intelligent nigger," but he is clearly a black man confounded by racial injustice and shrewd enough to understand its sources. This short poem also gives us Chesnutt's first conscious use of a technique important in his subsequent fiction, speaking through a persona, in this case, the "perplexed nigger" of the title. The narrative persona allows him to speak in a voice close to his own and at the same time to make it the voice of a character, and thus to dramatize it and separate himself from it. These techniques are crucial to the fictions discussed in the following chapters.

I have begun and ended this discussion of Chesnutt's journals with two moments separated by seven years and nearly one hundred pages. In both instances, we find the apprentice writer struggling with the *n* word. The two occurrences mark significant progress in Chesnutt's self-definition. He first uses the *n* word, then crosses it out, to mark his distance from the unlettered blacks around him. In the poem, however, he understands that he also is caught in the hateful epithet. He seems to understand that his literary work will be the dismantling of this ugly word, and that this effort will be undertaken for his own sake as well for his people. More is involved in the struggle with this word than semantics, for, as we have said, "nigger" is not simply a nominative, it is a narrative. Sterling A. Brown and Saunders Redding have cataloged the narrative's dramatis personae—the buffoon and the beast, the contented slave and the wretched freedman, and so forth.[8] The narrative is a fiction, but it is no less real—no less powerful in defining horizons—for that. The Chesnutt we meet in these early personal reflections is not yet a professional writer, but he has already taken a crucial step. He has begun to criticize and manipulate the language and fictions of his culture.

3

—◦◦((◦))◦◦—

"The Future American" and "Chas. Chesnutt"

> Chesnutt should print his picture with his book in order to allow his
> readers to know whether he is a white man or a negro. This is said with
> all seriousness. After reading the work it is impossible to tell. —From
> a contemporary review of *The Marrow of Tradition*

The year 1900 marks the midpoint in Charles Chesnutt's sequence of book-length compositions. He had completed one novel and two short story collections before this date, and he published another novel in that year; three more novels would follow later in his career. As the new century dawned, Chesnutt was at the peak of his reputation. In his forties, he was a respected man of letters and an accredited spokesperson for the Negro cause. It is not surprising, then, that the august *Boston Evening Transcript* opened its columns to an extended expression of his opinion on the race question. Chesnutt's three-part essay, "The Future American," was published by the *Transcript* in August and September 1900.[1] The essay, in keeping with its title and its date of publication, is boldly prophetic. In it Chesnutt tries to predict the future course of American social history, and thus the essay may be read as a kind of utopian narrative of America's racial future.

This fact alone would justify including these articles in a discussion of Chesnutt's narratives of race. But there is an even more specific connection between "The Future American" and Chesnutt's fiction. Chesnutt's novels and stories are often proleptic: they frequently conclude with an explicit exhortation or a prayer for the time to come. These moments when Chesnutt tries to look over the horizon are key junctures in his narratives, for they reveal crucial antinomies in his, and America's, thoughts on race. The difficulties Chesnutt encounters when he attempts to join present and future in these essays prepare us for similar moments in his fictions, problematic moments when he attempts to gesture toward a better future.

An additional reason for taking up this essay in the second chapter of this study is that it allows further study of an issue considered in the previous chapter. In the journals, Chesnutt began his self-fashioning, the assembly of a personal identity within and against American cultural narratives. Part of the strategy he devised was the creation of an ironic mask, which allowed him to intervene in the discourse of his time and still distance himself from it. The result of this strategy in Chesnutt's fictions is a notoriously elusive authorial presence. Lorne Fienberg writes of the "strategies of veiling" in Chesnutt's stories, and Charles Duncan explores the "absent man," the enigmatic implied author within them.[2] "The Future American" is a polemical piece written during Chesnutt's maturity. It presents its author's prescription for America's social problem directly and at length. It would seem, then, an ideal place to unveil the individual who concludes his essay with the signature "Chas. Chesnutt." This signatory will prove, however, to be as complex and contradictory as any of the fictional characters we meet in later chapters.

"The Future American" begins by raising a question of considerable moment in 1900: the future of the American race. During the second half of the nineteenth century, America had absorbed unprecedented waves of European and Asian immigration. The century climaxed with the annexation of Spain's ethnically mixed colonies in the Caribbean and Asia. These important demographic shifts naturally elicited speculation about the American society that would emerge in the new century. Much of this speculation was dire: the inevitable product of American xenophobia and racism. Other predictions were more optimistic. Herbert Spencer, perhaps the most influential English-speaking philosopher of that time, offered the following prophecy while visiting the United States in 1882:

> It may, I think, be reasonably held that, both because of its size and the heterogeneity of its components, the American nation will be a long time in evolving

its ultimate form, but that its ultimate form will be high. One great result is, I think, tolerably clear. From biological truth it is to be inferred that the eventual mixture of the allied varieties of the Aryan race forming the population will produce a finer type of man than has hitherto existed, and a type of man more plastic, more adaptable, more capable of undergoing the modifications needful for complete social life. I think that, whatever difficulties they have to surmount . . . the Americans may reasonably look forward to a time when they will have produced a civilization grander than any the world has known.[3]

Chesnutt's article enters this debate on America's future from the optimistic side. He does not mention Spencer, but Chesnutt's theses are essentially those quoted above—with one major difference.[4] For Chesnutt, the new amalgam must also include African Americans and Native Americans. Chesnutt bases his speculations on contemporary physical and social science. Recent scientific research, Chesnutt tells his audience, has refuted theories of essential racial difference, and there are no longer any barriers to assimilating all communities in North America into a new type. The result will be "The Future American" of his title. What is more, Chesnutt argues, this amalgamation is already well begun. He devotes much of the article to demonstrating by census data, historical and literary evidence, as well as personal observation, that the European and African derived communities have already interbred to a greater degree than is usually acknowledged. The resulting mulatto population has distinguished itself in business, religion, and the arts; thus, he argues, Americans have nothing to fear from further interbreeding. Given the greater number of whites entering this synthesis, the ultimate product will be a general population of light-skinned Americans. Physical differences between the races will gradually disappear, and with them, the marks upon which racial discrimination have been based. The Future American will live harmoniously in a country devoid of racialstrife.

Chesnutt's article, which begins as scientific speculation, has important social implications. The assimilation he predicts is crucial for future domestic peace. But the natural and the social create a contradictory tension in his argument. Here is the article's penultimate paragraph:

That [racial amalgamation] must come in the United States, sooner or later, seems to be a foregone conclusion, as the result of natural law—*lex dura, sed tamen lex*—a hard pill, but one which must be swallowed. There can manifestly be no such thing as a peaceful and progressive civilization in a nation divided by two warring races, and homogeneity of type, at least in externals, is a necessary condition of harmonious social progress. (135)

The assimilative process, Chesnutt insists, is inevitable. The assertion of this natural principle is given the reinforcing strength of a Latin dictum. But this reference to natural law is at odds with the medical metaphor that follows it. Natural law controls us: we submit to gravity and to the movement of the tides, not they to us. Medicine, on the other hand, influences nature: we take a pill to contravene, redirect, or palliate nature's processes. The use of medicine requires a choice, in this case a bitter one. So the working of Chesnutt's seemingly inexorable process actually depends on our assent and complicity.

Chesnutt identifies for us the principal obstruction to nature's meliorative progress: "The main obstacle that retards the absorption of the Negro into the general population is the apparently intense prejudice against color which prevails in the United States. . . . this prejudice in the United States is more apparent than real, and is a caste prejudice which is merely accentuated by differences of race" (132). Chesnutt acknowledges, and then minimizes, the obstructive power of white prejudice. Prejudice is not based on antipathy to an ethnic group as such, but rather on disdain for a lower social class. Chesnutt does not explicitly state that social segregation is justified economically, but he seems to share the common assumption that such economic stratification is the inevitable product of the Spencerian struggle for survival. America's negative attitudes toward its black citizens are, in Chesnutt's analysis, economically based. As black Americans prove themselves in this economic struggle, they will rise socially, and racial prejudice will fall away:

> the steady progress of the colored race in wealth and culture and social efficiency will, in the course of time, materially soften the asperities of racial prejudice and permit them to approach the whites more closely, until, in time, the prejudice against intermarriage shall have been overcome by other considerations.
>
> It is safe to say that the possession of a million dollars, with the ability to use it to the best advantage, would throw such a golden glow over a dark complexion as to override anything but a very obdurate prejudice. (133)

The *lex dura* invoked in the passage quoted earlier is natural law, but here it is economic law. The African American community's accumulation of capital will gradually assure its full integration into American society. Chesnutt in this essay, as in his journals, continues to believe that class can trump race, but his analysis ignores several crucial questions. Do blacks suffer discrimination because of their impoverished economic conditions, or do they suffer impoverished economic conditions because of discrimination? A more plausible explanation is that racial prejudice exists to justify economic exploitation. If this is so, we cannot expect black economic progress until this prejudice is first removed.

There are other problems. Chesnutt equivocates about the length of time assimilation will require. At one point we are told that the new racial type will emerge "within a measurably near period" (125). But elsewhere in the article Chesnutt reassures us that "the process by which this will take place will be no sudden and wholesale amalgamation—a thing certainly not to be expected, and hardly to be desired" (124). Utopia will not arrive soon, and it is hardly desirable that it should. Perhaps the most troubling question posed by Chesnutt's analysis is the following: if economic development will solve the problem of black integration into white society, why is physical assimilation necessary? If the glow of money will lighten a dark skin in a white eye, why must that skin be physically bleached by intermarriage? These questions lead to another crucial equivocation in the article: Chesnutt's definition of race. At the outset of his essay Chesnutt summarizes the scientific discussions that have discredited racial essentialism, and he tries to be clear about his own understanding of the key term "race." Here are passages from his first and fifth paragraphs:

> a future American race, or, to put it perhaps more correctly, a future ethnic type. (121)

> I use the word "race" here in its popular sense—that of a people who look substantially alike, and are molded by the same culture and dominated by the same ideals. (123)

In the second passage quoted above, Chesnutt lists three distinguishing features of a "race." The second and third features—culture and ideals—are clearly social rather than biological. The first characteristic—"people who look substantially alike"—is more complex, for it depends on two things:

physical features and the way those features are read in society. It is not clear which is crucial for Chesnutt, whether phenotype marks something inherent in character and intelligence, or whether skin color and hair texture are neutral elements whose meaning is pure social construction. If the latter is the case, why must they be changed? Why not simply change the interpretation assigned to these elements?

Chesnutt seems to distance himself from racial essentialism by insisting that the term "ethnic type" is more accurate than "race." Nonetheless, it is the latter term he most often uses. In the first five paragraphs, "race" or "racial" appears twenty times; "type" appears only six times. More important, it is not always clear in which sense—biological or cultural—Chesnutt intends this key term. Here is the essay's final sentence: "The white race is still susceptible of some improvement; and if, in time, the more objectionable Negro traits are eliminated, and his better qualities correspondingly developed, his part in the future American race may well be an important and valuable one" (135). This important sentence raises a number of questions. What are the nature of the "traits" and "characteristics" mentioned here? Are they cultural, as Chesnutt implies in his definition of race? If so, why is physical assimilation necessary for their improvement? One can surely change one's culture without changing one's skin color. Or is he referring to physical characteristics? If so, which elements of the Negro's appearance are objectionable? And to whom? Chesnutt repudiates biologically based racial essentialism—what he calls "the vulgar theory of race" (122)—and yet he does not seem to entirely escape its shadow.

Perhaps pushing these questions in this way unfairly ignores the rhetorical circumstances in which Chesnutt's essay was conceived. He wrote his article for a newspaper with a predominantly white readership. The article informs his readers of an important trend in American demographics and seeks to persuade them to accept its social implications. One might well hold the conflicting pressures in this rhetorical situation responsible for the article's ambivalences and contradictions. Chesnutt argues the inevitability of racial amalgamation, while at the same time he seeks to placate white fears about this mixing. He personally believes race is a social construct, but he knows most of his readers still cling to biological definitions; thus he reassures them about the bleaching out of "objectional" black traits. The assimilative process will, it is true, bring profound social change, but, in Chesnutt's account, there will be no convulsive revolution: economic progress will quietly and painlessly do the work for us. Racial amalgamation is coming, he tells his readers, but don't worry, it is still safely in the distance.

This rhetorical discussion seems to account for some of the problems in the text, but it raises others. Chesnutt's placative purposes require that he adopt a reasonable, even ingratiating tone. And yet the essay is shot through with flashes of caustic irony. These comments seem unmotivated by the strict logic of his argument and come in gratuitous, biting asides. Note in the following passage his swipes at European American presumptions of superiority:

> This perfection of type—no good American could for a moment doubt that it will be as perfect as everything else American—is to be brought about by a combination of all the best characteristics of the different European races, and the elimination, by some strange alchemy, of all their undesirable traits—for even a good American will admit that European races, now and then, have some undesirable traits when they first come over. (121–22)

These comments seem designed to provoke, rather than placate, the "good American." So also do the following remarks about American imperialism:

> if certain recent tendencies are an index of the future it is not safe to fix the boundaries of the future United States anywhere short of the Arctic Ocean on the north and the Isthmus of Panama on the south. (122–23)

> The popular argument that the Negro ought to develop his own civilization, and has no right to share in that of the white race, unless by favor, comes with poor grace from those who are forcing their civilization upon others at the cannon's mouth. (133)

In the next two instances Chesnutt directs his sarcasm at lynching:

> The present generation has, however, brought to a high state of development one distinctively American institution, for which it is entitled to such credit as it may wish to claim; I refer to the custom of lynching, with its attendant horrors. (133)

> the penalty of extra-judicial death not extending so far North. (135)

The reason for calling attention to these passages is not that Chesnutt's irony is unjustified, for chauvinism, imperialism, and mob violence are certainly worthy occasions for sarcasm. The point is rather to call attention to the way this mocking tone works against the persuasive purposes hypothesized above. Chesnutt attacks popular attitudes that, although deserving attack, are not germane to his demographic, economic, and social arguments. As a result, rhetorically considered, Chesnutt fails to establish the tone that would win his readers' confidence in his judgments about the future. Consider also the conflicting purposes in the first paragraph of the essay's second installment.

> I have said that the formation of the new American race type will take place slowly and obscurely for some time to come, after the manner of all healthy changes in nature. I may go further and say that this process has already been going on ever since the various races in the Western world have been brought into juxtaposition. Slavery was a rich soil for the production of a mixed race, and one only need read the literature and laws of the past two generations to see how steadily, albeit slowly and insidiously, the stream of dark blood has insinuated itself into the veins of the dominant, or, as a Southern critic recently described it in a paragraph that came under my eye, the "domineering" race. (126)

The first sentence in this passage reassures the reader that amalgamation is simply another of nature's healthy changes. The third sentence, however, suggests something very different. Arlene A. Elder perceptively comments on the metaphorical implications of the sentence's syntax and diction: "The serpent-like movement of Chesnutt's own image of amalgamation suggests the power of cultural and, especially, religious symbolism; the recurrent sibilants, 'steadily,' 'slowly,' 'stream,' 'insinuated itself,' 'veins,' and 'race' are auditory reminders of Mather's 'black man' transforming Himself into the 'angel of light' in an earlier Edenic manifestation." Nature's healthy change has become a diabolical corruption. Elder also notes the similarity between this sentence and one that occurs in a Chesnutt letter of September 27, 1900. In this correspondence, Chesnutt refers to an editorial of August 18, 1900, which warned that "the white race was becoming insidiously and to a large extent unknowingly corrupted with negro blood."[5] The editorial appeared the week before the second installment of "The Future American," but the letter implies that Chesnutt read the editorial after the full publication of his own essay. Moreover, Chesnutt does not say he is quoting directly from the *Times*. Rather, it appears that, in both instances, Chesnutt is ironically mocking the language of racial alarmists. This ironic mimicry, like the gibe at the "domineering race," is at cross-purposes to the placative tone established in the first sentence.

Indeed, the entire article, read in the context of racial attitudes prevalent at the time of publication, seems a deliberate provocation. Chesnutt must have known that his blithe assertions that "the conception of a pure Aryan, Indo-European race has been abandoned in scientific circles" (122) and that "the unity of the human race has been proved" (122) overstated the actual scientific consensus in 1900. Chesnutt cites only one scientific source, William Z. Ripley's *Races of Europe: A Sociological Study*. Ripley does provide evidence that supports several of Chesnutt's assertions, but his study— six hundred pages of data and analysis—is much more cautious than Chesnutt's summary suggests. Nowhere, for instance, does Ripley make a claim as bold as Chesnutt's assertion that "the secret of the progress of Europe has been found in racial heterogeneity, rather than in racial purity" (122). Ripley focuses on Europe, and he does not directly address the American situation. He does, however, discuss breeding between Europeans and Africans in Africa. In this context, he observes that "a cross between two races is too often to be a weakling, sharing in the pathological predispositions of each of its parent stocks, while enjoying but imperfectly their several immunities. Mulattoes in any climate lack vitality; and, unless a continual supply of white blood is kept up, they tend to degenerate."[6] Ripley clearly looked on the mixing of European and African populations in quite a different way than Chesnutt did. Today, modern scientific opinion supports Chesnutt on all major points, but the formation of that opinion and its full acceptance was, in 1900, still several decades in the future.

Most provocative of all, Chesnutt's article proposes as the twentieth-century's savior the nineteenth-century's nightmare.[7] The Future American is the mulatto. As Ripley's comment indicates, American physical and social science in 1900 still held that the product of black and white union was a degenerate hybrid. It is unfortunate, but Frederick L. Hoffman's *Race Traits and Tendencies of the American Negro* (1896) comes closer to articulating the actual white consensus on race—scientific and popular—at the turn of the century than does Chesnutt. Hoffman offered statistics that showed the mulatto had larger cranial capacity than the pure Negro but had less lung capacity. The combination meant greater intelligence but less "vital power."[8] Hoffman did not have to spell out the frightening implications. His white readers would immediately sense the danger posed by a Negro with increased guile and diminished physical and moral strength. This mythic nemesis was the individual Chesnutt provocatively asks white citizens to hail as "the Future American."

Chesnutt did not make his assertions naively, nor was he ignorant of contemporary scientific debate. Few laymen of Chesnutt's time were better informed than he on scientific discussions of race. Neither scientific ignorance nor rhetorical imperatives account for all of the tensions and contradictions in this text. Chesnutt also read the press assiduously and shrewdly, and he would have known that the *Boston Evening Transcript* had embraced the South's gradual imposition of Jim Crow segregation, a policy whose stated purpose was the prevention of racial amalgamation. Rayford Logan records, for instance, that the "erudite organ of the Proper Bostonians" supported Hayes's withdrawal of federal troops from the South, the Supreme Court's decision to leave civil rights to the states, and Booker T. Washington's accommodation with Southern segregation.[9] Chesnutt could hardly have expected the *Transcript*'s cautious editors and readers to welcome his predictions about America's amalgamated future. The reaction of a Boston audience to a lecture Chesnutt delivered in June 1905 suggests the likely response of many *Transcript* readers. In his lecture, "Race Prejudice: Its Causes and Its Cure," to the Boston Literary and Historical Association, Chesnutt repeated his theses about future race amalgamation. His daughter reports that the speech "brought much bitter criticism upon Chesnutt. He received abusive letters, many of them from illiterate and anonymous writers, and some unpleasant newspaper notoriety."[10] And yet, in both instances, Chesnutt told his readers and auditors what he must have known they would not want to hear. Read in the context of white attitudes on race at the turn of the century, "The Future American" is a perplexing text, shot through with conflicting purposes. To grossly simplify the article's complexity, it contains at least two voices, a voice that seeks to pursue a logical argument on a pressing question and a voice that recognizes

America's resistance to logic on this issue. In it one voice attempts to placate the reader, and another mocks both the reader and the speaker himself for engaging in a hopeless enterprise. "The Future American" is inhabited by an individual who signs himself "Chas. Chesnutt," but this persona is not one thing, a unitary block; it speaks in several voices and is pulled by conflicting intentions. The "Chas. Chesnutt" in this "nonfiction" is as complex as the characters or narrators in his "fictions."

Let us continue our examination of Chesnutt's predictions on race a bit further and then return to our sense of the article's implied author. Chesnutt's faith in the salvation of our society by the eventual arrival of the Future American is grounded on at least two assumptions. It assumes, first of all, that differences between white and black Americans are not based in genetic inheritance but in social and economic class distinctions. It further assumes that white and black Americans will recognize the illusory nature of these distinctions and choose to efface them through assimilation. As we have seen, Chesnutt's essay vacillates on both of these premises. The following chapters show that Chesnutt's fictions, written before and after this essay, provide numerous examples that undercut or belie his assumptions about white willingness to accept middle-class blacks. Characters Ben Green ("The Web of Circumstance"), Dr. William Miller *(The Marrow of Tradition)*, and William Nichols *(The Colonel's Dream)* are industrious Negroes whose achievements do not win them white acceptance; on the contrary, their success incites white resentment and resistance. John Warwick *(The House behind the Cedars)* is one mulatto who does assimilate, at least for a while, and he becomes successful in white society. But he does so only by hiding his origins and by cutting himself from his black mother. When his past is discovered, Warwick's position is compromised, and he must begin again. His sister, Rena, attempts to follow him into white society, but she is destroyed because she cannot callously cut her family bonds. The novel accurately reflects the bitter price exacted by assimilation in early-twentieth-century America. These narratives are all set in Chesnutt's present. When their narrators try to look forward from the events they have recounted toward a more promising future, they are unconvincing and contradictory.

SallyAnn Ferguson, who edited Chesnutt's article for republication, casts interesting light into its shadows.[11] She argues that in it

Chesnutt most clearly reveals the limited nature of his social and literary goals. . . . scholars have incorrectly presumed that this writer seeks to use literature primarily as a means for alleviating white color prejudice against *all* black people in this country. But, while the critics romantically hail him as a black artist championing the cause of his people, Chesnutt, as his essays show, is essentially a social and literary accommodationist who pointedly and repeatedly confines his reformist impulses to the "colored people"—a term that he almost always applies to color-line blacks or those of mixed race. [12]

Ferguson is mistaken on several points. Nowhere in "The Future American" does Chesnutt make special claims for light-skinned blacks over darker blacks. Nor does Chesnutt use "colored people" as a synonym for color-line blacks as Ferguson asserts. In the two-paragraph passage from page 133 quoted above, Chesnutt states that "the steady progress of the colored race in wealth . . . will, in the course of time, materially soften the asperities of racial prejudice. . . . the possession of a million dollars . . . would throw such a golden glow over a dark complexion." Clearly, in this passage, the "colored race" includes people with a "dark complexion." In his article Chesnutt uses three words to refer to African Americans: "Negro" is most frequent, occurring thirty-five times; "colored" occurs eighteen times; and "black" occurs five times. There are perhaps one or two instances where "colored" might be taken to mean light-skinned blacks, but for the most part in "The Future American," these three terms—"Negro," "colored," and "black"—are used interchangeably. [13]

Ferguson is mistaken on these points, but she is accurate and candid about a troubling strain in Chesnutt's essay. "Colored" *has* often been a code word for light-skinned blacks, and "colorism"—prejudice against dark blacks—exists among blacks as well as whites. Chesnutt mocked color prejudice in "The Wife of His Youth" and in "A Matter of Principle"; nonetheless, colorism is present in "The Future American." It exists in the references to "objectionable" black characteristics, and it helps to account for Chesnutt's curious blind spots. Because of his light color, Chesnutt did not personally experience the full force of race hatred directed by whites against dark-skinned blacks. As a result, he undervalues the depth and intransigence of this prejudice in his prognosis for the future. But his blind spot also causes him to misjudge his black brothers and sisters. He assumes they also see darkness as objectionable, and he refers slightingly to their use of lightening creams. As a result, he undervalues black pride and underestimates black resistance to assimilation.

Ferguson calls attention to Chesnutt's blind spot when she explains the inconsistencies in the future he proposes:

> the ends and the means of his plan are utterly inconsistent and would leave black victims the perverse task of joining white racists in devaluing an aspect of themselves in order to win societal approval. Thus, Chesnutt reveals an almost total disregard for the psychological needs and human aspirations of "genuine Negroes" living in a racist society, to whom he offers a cultural ideal from which they alone are effectively excluded. His preoccupation with the "Future American" ethnic type leaves him indifferent to the consequences for dark-skinned Americans who, as a practical matter, could not become "white," even if they wanted to do so. . . . When Chesnutt relegates "genuine Negroes" to the racial status quo, he simultaneously ignores the immediate obstacle of racism as well as undercuts the self-esteem they need to combat it daily. When he advises such blacks to restrict themselves to materialistic pursuits, he, by implication, also urges them to accept the self-hatred this compromise inevitably brings. (116)

In "The Future American," as in his journal, Chesnutt tries conceptually to move immediately from a society saturated by race to one from which race is absent. Put differently, he tries to move from racial essentialism to racial subjectivism, without adequately understanding the power, and potential value, of racial constructions. The Africans who were brought to America as slaves found themselves bound not only by chains but by negative white formulations of their identity. During slavery and after, they created a distinctive culture, which resisted these formulations and substituted more positive definitions of their black selves. After accomplishing this important cultural work, many blacks, understandably, were unwilling to abandon its fruit: they had made blackness a sign of resistance and triumph, a sign to be worn proudly, not a stain to be hidden or bleached.[14]

"The Future American" is not a novel, but it is a narrative. More specifically, it is a utopian narrative, an attempt to recount the story of the future. Looking at the essay with this in mind helps us to see continuities with the journal and anticipate tensions in the fiction. The utopian narrative, like the success story, is progressive: it assumes that each moment grows logically out of the preceding one, and that each epoch represents an advance over the previous one. The mechanism that assures this meliorative movement, in the personal micronarrative and in the national macronarrative, is the working of American social and economic democracy. The frustration in both narratives—and in the voice of the narrators of the journal and the essay—results from the collision of these assumptions with another potent construct, the narrative of essential racial difference. This construct was powerful in early-twentieth-century America, and it is not entirely absent in the narrator of the diary and the essay. The narrative of difference tells two separate stories. It endorses the narrative of progress for some at the same time that it denies its applicability for others. By the logic of essential difference, some racial groups are frozen by God and nature at a level beyond which they cannot ascend. The contradictions in "The Future American" result from the unresolved tension between two conflicting social narratives.

American culture and the American population are unquestionably more mixed at the beginning of the twenty-first century than they were at the outset of the twentieth but are still a long distance from the creation of a new, amalgamated American type. In fact, the current in American society today seems to be running the other way, with increased emphasis on difference and diversity. My point in mentioning these facts is not to mock Chesnutt as a historical prophet. The contradictory predictions occasioned by our recent millennial moment should remind us that long-term looks into the future are almost always futile. Rather, the focus throughout this chapter has been on the difficulties confronting problems that lie not only in society but within us. We try to look past the present with the lenses of the present, but we see not the object upon which we train our gaze but the lenses themselves. The lenses are the constructs—the language and the categories—we use to organize our experience. Chesnutt understood this difficulty, and his fictions capture the problems of his present more accurately than his essay predicted the future. His stories and novels discerningly dramatize the divisions and contradictions in America's racial thinking. W. E. B. Du Bois offered his own prophecy for the new century: "the problem of the twentieth century," he wrote in 1903, "is the problem of the color line."[15] Du Bois's incisive remark captures the guiding theme of the twentieth-century's first great black fictionist. The following chapters explore the ways that Chesnutt's stories and novels dramatize and deconstruct the color line in American language and culture.

4

———◦◉◦———

Black Vernacular
in Chesnutt's Short Fiction
"A New School of Literature"

The novelistic plot must organize the exposure of social languages and
ideologies, the exhibiting and experiencing of such languages. . . . In a
word, the novelistic plot serves to represent speaking persons and their
ideological worlds. —MIKHAIL BAKHTIN, *The Dialogic Imagination*

Charles Chesnutt used the dialect tale to become the first African American to win a national white audience for his fiction. Chesnutt's choice of
this genre was, of course, the product of a shrewd calculation of the literary market. But there was more: Chesnutt understood that the popularity
of stories featuring rural black speech offered an opportunity to introduce
a new understanding of the recently emancipated Americans. The historic
importance of Chesnutt's dialect tales and the cultural work that they performed is the subject of this chapter and the next.

Charles Chesnutt understood the unique moment in which he lived and
the challenges it posed. "I represent a new element, another generation,"
he told an assembly of Fayetteville's black citizens in 1882, "I never saw
a slave" (*Essays and Speeches*, 25). In the nearly two decades since emancipation, a new generation of blacks had emerged and was moving toward
maturity, blacks who had never worn iron on their ankles nor felt a whip
on their backs. Born in freedom in 1858, Chesnutt was chronologically in

advance of this group; nonetheless, he felt part of it, and he aspired to be its literary spokesman. At the moment of Chesnutt's speech, black North Carolinians had been without the protection of Federal troops for six years, but they would not experience the full suppression of their civil rights for a decade and a half. The young orator acknowledged the loss of gains realized during Reconstruction; notwithstanding, he defiantly asserted his faith in the American dream: "you may believe what I say or not, but *I* believe it—but, in every country, the men who have the intelligence, the will, the education, the money—will rule—by fair means or foul" (27). The bitter irony of the phrase "or foul" would be painfully apparent six years later in the 1898 Wilmington riot. This event, a massacre of blacks by whites, climaxed the brutal imposition of Jim Crow in North Carolina and inspired Chesnutt's most powerful novel.

Chesnutt was not wrong in sensing that he was poised at a unique historical juncture. Nor was he mistaken in locating the uniqueness of this moment, at least partially, in the extraordinary opportunities that the abolition of slavery seemed to promise. Sadly, the nineteenth-century's final decades witnessed the systematic abrogation of these promises. Indeed, the tension between anticipated citizenship and the dashing of these hopes provides this moment's distinctive character in black history, and it defines the special challenge faced by blacks trying to write during this time. Chesnutt, in an 1889 essay, looked for "the dawn of a new school of literature dealing with the Negro as a man, with hopes and passions and aspirations as other men" (64). The difficulty he faced in creating this new literature is made clear by this typical opinion from 1884:

> the public mind is no longer interested in the affairs of the negro race. A generation of controversy and four years of terrible war gave the negro in America freedom and the ballot. Now the common sentiment is that enough has been done for him, and that he should make his own way upward in the social scale. There is no demand for a constitutional amendment which will put the machinery of federal courts at work to secure him good seats at the theaters, good beds in hotels and sleeping-cars, and the right to be shaved in the fashionable barber-shops. People are content . . . to leave such matters to state legislation.[1]

This indifference to the Negro's plight is all the more dismaying in that it appeared in the *Atlantic Monthly,* a journal that had opposed slavery and supported Reconstruction. It is a significant indication of Chesnutt's literary cunning that he was able to place his breakthrough publication, "The Goophered Grapevine," in the pages of the *Atlantic Monthly* in 1887.

One might have expected a different spirit in America after a Civil War fought ostensibly to free blacks from slavery. But discrimination was rampant in the North, and at the conclusion of the war, only one state, Massachusetts, granted civil rights to blacks. Thus, at the moment of armistice, "the strong sentiments in the North against slavery were paralleled by equally strong sentiments against miscegenation and for segregation, preferably by colonization in Africa once they were free."[2] The Civil War had settled only one issue regarding the identity of black Americans: they were not slaves. They also were not, in most American minds, the equal of America's white citizens. Before Chesnutt could tell the new story of the Negro as a human, he had to untell the dominant narrative of the Negro as subhuman.

From the beginning the effort to claim full human status for blacks had been, to an important degree, a literary effort. Slave narratives presented the black person's case eloquently and vividly; they were answered by the Southern plantation fictions of contented darkies within a benign extended family. The prewar literary struggle, aided significantly by Harriet Beecher Stowe, was won by slavery's opponents. However, "if *Uncle Tom's Cabin* triumphed in the ante-bellum 'battle of the books,' being widely remembered while its opponents are forgotten, the plantation tradition was to score a signal victory in the Reconstruction. Although no longer needed to defend a tottering institution, it was now needed to prove that Negroes were happy as slaves and hopelessly unequipped for freedom, so that slavery could be resurrected in fact though not in name."[3] Southern white writers of the "plantation school," apologists for the antebellum order, presented an idealized version of life under slavery. Joel Chandler Harris and Thomas Nelson Page were both best-selling authors in the 1880s and 1890s; the characters they created professed loyalty to their former masters in rich dialect. It was no coincidence that this literary movement developed simultaneously with the defeat of Reconstruction and the birth of Jim Crow, for these stories were a conscious attempt to justify the old order and reassure the North about the African Americans' situation in the redeemed South.

Charles Chesnutt's fictions intervened significantly in the postwar efforts

to narrate black identity. The specific feature of the intervention that is
explored in this chapter is Chesnutt's representation of rural black speech in
his short stories. Portraits of dialect-speaking former slaves figured prominently in the literature of the late nineteenth century, and they were of crucial importance in the period's competing cultural narratives. Language, as
we have seen, had from the very beginning been central in white attempts
to fix black identity. During slavery it was the test by which the abolitionists
sought to demonstrate black membership in the human family; under Jim
Crow, literacy tests would be used to withhold full American citizenship
from blacks. Representations of uneducated former slaves speaking their
distinctive variant of American English were abundant in post–Civil War
literature and entertainment. These images ranged from well-intended condescension to libelous caricature. Albion Tourgée and Frances E. W. Harper
represent two of the more benign instances. Tourgée's *A Fool's Errand* (1879)
strongly denounces America's abandonment of its black citizens. It also provides a moving portrait of black courage in the character of Uncle Jerry, an
uneducated former slave murdered for speaking "with sweet-voiced bold-
ness" against the Ku Klux Klan.[4] Jerry is, however, only a small detail in a
novel that accepted the premise that Southern blacks needed further white
tutelage before assuming full citizenship. Chesnutt admired Tourgée, and
in his journal he specifically invoked Tourgée's best-selling novel as a model
for his own writing (124–25); nonetheless, Chesnutt believed that he could
represent Southern blacks more accurately and effectively than the white
writer had done. Probably the most positive images of dialect-speaking
African Americans in the novel at century's end were those of an African
American writer, Frances E. W. Harper. Several of Harper's characters in
Iola Leroy (1892) show the vigor and eloquence of black vernacular speech.[5]
Nonetheless, these dialect speakers are subordinate characters in a work—
and, by implication, in a black community—where leadership was assumed
by mulattoes articulate in Standard English.

More important than any literary text for popular images of the American black person was the minstrel show. These performances reached their
greatest popularity in the decades immediately preceding and following the
Civil War and were in decline when Chesnutt began to publish his fiction.
Roughly one hundred minstrel companies toured during the 1860s, but in
the 1880s the number had dwindled to about thirty and by 1900 was less

than ten.[6] Nonetheless, the images of black folk disseminated by these entertainments were still powerful at the end of the century, and they deserve
some attention here. Minstrel shows, as performed before white working-
class audiences, including many recent immigrants, conveyed many different meanings.[7] Here the focus is on two aspects of minstrelsy: the representations of blacks as speaking subjects and of black language. These
representations were crucial in the black person's attempt to meet the linguistic test Europeans and European Americans had set as proof of human
status.

Minstrel comedy depended heavily on verbal humor. Typically, shows
included a raucous exchange between an interlocutor, speaking Standard
English, and Tambo and Bones, the dialect-speaking end men. The latter
were performed as fun-loving and irresponsible darkies who confounded
the interlocutor's attempts at sense and order. In another minstrel show
staple, the stump speech, a blackface performer would discourse on a learned
topic in dialect: the result was a comic combination of mispronunciation,
malapropism, and tangled meaning.[8] Blacks, as represented on the minstrel
stage, were either linguistic anarchists mangling standard speech by their
indifference to its rules or, at the other extreme, comic pedants attempting
to discourse in language beyond their understanding. This binary should
remind us of the paradox discussed earlier. Blacks were assumed to be incapable of nuanced communication, but when they confounded this expec-
tation by writing accomplished poetry, as Phillis Wheatley did, they were
reproached for parrotlike imitation of white speech. The dilemma blacks
faced in meeting white standards can be represented by two iconic characters
from the minstrel show: Jim Crow and Zip Coon. The rubber-limbed Jim
Crow, a precursor of the end men Tambo and Bones, was portrayed in play-
bills and on the stage wearing his white master's worn and ill-fitting hand-
me-downs. Zip Coon, a specialist in the stump speech, was a dandy whose
exaggerated elegance offered a comic parody of white fashion. In either case,
the point of these visual representations was that a black person in white
clothing—that is, a black person who aspired to equality with whites—
was in and of itself comic and incongruous. In the matter of the minstrel
show's comic representation of the black person, we ought also to note
the deliberate distortion of the organs of speech—the grotesquely fat lips,
the gate mouth, the dazzling teeth, and the flapping tongue. This stylized

representation was meant to suggest the absurd inadaptation of Africans for human utterance.[9] Black mastery of white language was thought to be an absurdity. Either blacks deformed it comically—black vernacular being the linguistic equivalent of Jim Crow's torn breeches—or alternatively, they imitated it extravagantly—the linguistic equivalent of Zip Coon's sartorial display. White assumptions of black linguistic inadequacy did not originate with blackface performance, but these entertainments reinforced stereotypes that denied blacks full human status.

Burntcork comedians claimed to have learned the language they spoke from rural blacks, and William J. Mahar confirms that minstrel show dialect reflected many features of Southern black vernacular. Mahar, however, defines minstrel speech as a literary dialect:

> Because it was a stage language, the dialect used by the early minstrels would not normally be considered a legitimate brand of American English. It is, technically, a "literary dialect," compiled, created, and presented by blackface actors who borrowed some of their material from black culture. More important, the fascination with BEV [Black English vernacular] found in the antebellum minstrel shows reveals a deep interest in the differences between white and black attitudes toward work, family life, recreation, and society, differences crucial to the whole comic apparatus of the minstrel stage.[10]

Mahar makes two important points. Minstrel show dialect resembles black speech, but it is different from it; it is a representation, a construction that borrows from black speech, exaggerating certain features and eliminating others. This representation, moreover, is not ideologically neutral; it is the vehicle for a particular view of the world. These are important points to bear in mind when considering another literary representation of Black English, published dialect humor.

Although minstrel performance declined in the nineteenth-century's last decades, the printed dialect sketch prospered. Important Northern publications, such as the *Atlantic Monthly, Harpers, Scribners,* the *North American Review,* and *Century,* published hundreds of dialect stories and sketches during this period.[11] Chesnutt, a shrewd judge of the literary market, noted the success of plantation writers and dialect humorists and turned these tastes to his own purposes. Published humor featuring dialect-speaking blacks has a long history. Henry Louis Gates Jr. reproduces two British comic broadsides, entitled "A Black Lecture of Phrenology" and "A Black Lecture on Language," in *The Signifying Monkey* (93, 95). From the early nineteenth century, these publications function in the same way as the minstrel show's stump speech, mocking a black speaker's efforts to discourse on serious topics. Printed dialect humor was also popular in the United Sates, and Wade Hall's study of Southern humor gives us several instances of white efforts in this vein. Sam W. Small's *Sayings of Old Si,* originally published in the *Atlanta Constitution* and collected in 1886, features a Negro who combines plantation school loyalty and the minstrel end man's comic indolence. Here is Si's disgusted reaction when he learns that, as a free and equal citizen, he will be required to pay full admission to the circus: "I tole dem niggers dey was spilin' de horn when dey wanted dem sibil rights, an' hyar's de truf of it, p'int blank . . . twixt us I say dam de sibil rights, speshilly when de circus is 'round." Other dialect sketches exploited the black character's misunderstanding of educated English. Jeannette Walworth created a comic black man describing his service on a Reconstruction-era jury: "It were when ol' Dave Rooney kilt his wife. The jedge he try mek we bring en a verdic uv manslaughter in de fus' degree, but we wur'n big 'nough fools to call killin' a woman manslaughter." [12] The political implications of these stereotypes, and the implied connection between linguistic competence and citizenship, are evident even in these brief extracts. Old Si cannot even pronounce "civil rights," let alone appreciate their value, and the fact that the black man does not understand the word "manslaughter" implies that he is unfit for jury service.

These printed versions of dialect humor call attention to basic problems in the written presentation of black dialect. Black vernacular evolved as an effective and nuanced form of oral communication in a slave community where literacy was a crime, but it had no written form of its own. It was transcribed by literate whites and blacks as a deformation of Standard English, with apostrophes calling attention to absent letters and altered spellings indicating distortions of Standard English phonemes. In the passages cited above, the reader decodes the message by recognizing the standard form beneath the dialectal utterance and working back and forth between the two codes. Dialect humor exploits this double reading; laughter emerges from the incongruity of the dialectical utterance and the Standard English palimpsest beneath it. Humorists often intensified this effect with "eye dialect," misspellings that are not caused by mispronunciation. The spellings of "dam" and "uv" in the passages by Small and by Walworth are examples.[13]

The phonemic and graphemic systems of English do not map perfectly one on top of the other. No one, not even the most educated speaker, pronounces English precisely as it is written: there are always dropped consonants and blurred vowels. Dialect humor notes these discrepancies selectively, calling attention to them in the speech of one group of speakers, but not for others. A Northerner at the turn of the century listening to a conversation between a white and a black Southerner might note that the speech of both speakers differed from his or her own, but plantation writers and dialect humorists do not usually allow readers to make this discovery. The speaker of standard "white" English in comic sketches is usually a straight man, a neutral surface to set in relief the distortions of the black speaker. These reflections call attention to the fact that black vernacular dialect was yoked in a powerful cultural binary where standard "white" English was the privileged term. Any attempt to imply that black speech was the equal of the "white" standard was instinctively seen as presumptuous and absurd.

It is with this binary that Chesnutt struggles in his attempt to represent black Americans and their language. The product of these efforts can be described with Mary Louise Pratt's term "autoethnography." Here is her contrast between this form of representation and conventional ethnography. "I use these terms to refer to instances in which colonized subjects undertake to represent themselves in ways that *engage with* the colonizer 's own terms. If ethnographic texts are a means by which Europeans represent to themselves their (usually subjugated) others, autoethnographic texts are those the others construct in response to or in dialogue with those metropolitan representations."[14] Both Thomas Nelson Page and Joel Chandler Harris prided themselves on the accuracy of their renderings of rural black speech, and their stories were taken as faithful portraits of black behavior and attitudes. These stories were ethnographic in the sense defined by Pratt, but these portraits were, of course, heavily oriented by the white Southerners' own cultural assumptions. Chesnutt's autoethnographic attempts to rewrite these representations fall into two categories. The first group self-consciously exploits plantation school and dialect humor stereotypes to turn these images against the ideology they conventionally support. Two stories, "Appreciation" and "The Fall of Adam," illustrate this group. Both were published in the 1880s in mainstream "white" periodicals. "Appreciation" signifies on the plantation school, while "The Fall of Adam" tropes on the stump speech of the minstrel show and the printed comic sketch. A second group of Chesnutt's dialect stories uses vernacular speech to reveal the positive features of rural black culture. "The Partners," published in a journal with a mixed, black, and white readership in 1900, illustrates this second group.[15]

"Appreciaton" relates the meeting between Dixon, a white man, and Pilgrim Gainey, a black man who left Missouri for the North after emancipation, but who has now returned. Dixon is surprised to see the Negro back in the state where he was once a slave. He asks Gainey about the North and the higher wages, voting privileges, and civil rights that he enjoyed there. Gainey admits that these advantages existed but insists that he cared little for them. Dixon presses further in his questioning, and this is the sketch's conclusion:

> "I don't see why you don't like the North, Uncle Pilgrim?"
>
> "Well, I tell yer jes' how it is, Mistah Dixon. Yer kin git plenty wu'k, an' big pay, an' yer has all de privilege yer wants: but de rale fac' is, dat cullu'd people ain't 'preciated at de Norf. Dat's what's de mattah!"
>
> Just then, young Tom Macmillan came up behind the old man, knocked his hat off, and saluted him with a playful kick.
>
> "Look a 'heah, Marse Tom, you stop dat now!" said Pilgrim with a delighted grin, which displayed all his wealth of ivory. "Is yer got any terbacker, Marse Tom?"
>
> Tom tossed the old man a half-plug of chewing tobacco.
>
> "Now dat's what I call 'preciation," said Uncle Pilgrim, filling his mouth with the savory weed. "I nevah had dat much terbacker give ter me all de time I wus at de Norf!" (64)

William Mahar's comments on minstrel show dialect can be applied to black speech in the comic sketch as well and are pertinent here. The comic sketch represents black speech from a distinct ideological perspective. Mikhail Bakhtin argues that this is always the case with literary representations of languages and speaking subjects. "The speaking person in the novel is always, to one degree or another, an *ideologue,* and his words are always *ideologemes*. A particular language in a novel is always a particular way of viewing the world, one that strives for a social significance."[16] From Bakhtin's perspective, discussion of dialect in fiction cannot limit itself to phonological, semantic, and syntactic features; it must engage the values implicit in a distinctive linguistic perspective. For Bakhtin, scrupulous attention to the ideology in languages or dialects in a narrative takes us to the conflict of values that that narrative dramatizes. Here is Bakhtin's understanding of plot's function, and the important recognition to which it can lead: "The novelistic plot must organize the exposure of social languages and ideologies, the exhibiting and experiencing of such languages. . . . In a word, the novelistic plot serves to represent speaking persons and their ideological worlds" (365).

Pilgrim Gainey's speech in "Appreciation" can be considered in light of Bakhtin's definitions of language and plot. While the phonological and semantic features resemble those attributed to uneducated rural blacks, Gainey's utterances reveal values many blacks would reject. Gainey's values are essentially those propounded by white apologists for the antebellum order. Chesnutt's sketch echoes several details of one of the most famous products of the plantation school, Thomas Nelson Page's story "Marse Chan."[17] In Page's sentimental tale, the white narrator meets Sam, an elderly black man who tells of his devotion to Marse Chan, whom he served for most of his life. His master is now dead, but Sam has stayed on after his own emancipation to guard his former owner's property. The story ends with the narrator, moved by the former slave's loyalty, rewarding him with several small coins. In Chesnutt's sketch, Gainey, like Sam, remains faithful to the Southern white order and earns a plug of tobacco for his loyalty. Gainey's language and behavior—the deferential "Marse" and the servile grin—are stylized to support a specific ideology. This representation of black vernacular might be called "plantation speech" because of its distinctive, socially conservative, ideological orientation.

It is important to recognize not only the values in Gainey's speech but the way they are handled within Chesnutt's sketch. The attitude in Page's story toward Sam is sentimental approval, but the attitude in "Appreciation" is critical satire. This satire is conveyed by the interaction between Gainey's speech and the narrator's Standard English. This brief narrative mocks a black person who foolishly trades economic opportunity and political rights for white paternalism. The story's meaning turns around the dialect words " 'preciated" and " 'preciation" in the sketch and their ironic translation into Standard English in the story's title. Gainey's " 'preciation" depends on two things: immediate sensory gratification—the half-plug of tobacco—and physical abuse. His " 'preciation" actually appreciates (increases) with a kick in his rear. He addresses Dixon as "Mistah," but he rewards his tormenter with a broad grin and the title "Marse."

The meanings of the dialect words are judged and criticized from outside the narration by their translation into Standard English in the story's title. Viewed from this perspective, "Appreciation" is ironic in all three of the word's common meanings. In the sense of gratitude, Gainey's is foolish and his forbearance is met by no true gratitude from the whites. In the sense of increase in value, there has been no appreciation in the black person's situation in the decades following emancipation. This Pilgrim has made no progress; Gainey has made no gains. Finally, in the sense of appreciation as an overall assessment, the judgment on Southern whites and servile blacks is bitterly condemning. As in many dialect sketches, the story features an encounter between a white straight man and dialect-speaking fool. The white interlocutor's Standard English represents a perspective from which to judge or mock the vernacular speaker. The crucial difference in Chesnutt's instance is the dialect and the ideology that is criticized: Chesnutt's satirical target is the plantation school representations of black values and language. A black who trusts white paternalism, the sketch implies, is indeed a fool.

A similar strategy is at work in "The Fall of Adam." In this story, Br'er Gabe Gainey, a rural black preacher—and, perhaps, Pilgrim Gainey's near relative—is visited by a member of his congregation. The parishioner asks his pastor to explain two problems he has encountered in reading the Bible: if Adam fell, where did he fall from, and why are Negroes black? The preacher cannot immediately respond, but he promises to meditate, pray, and provide an answer in Sunday's service. Gainey gives himself to "ras'lin' in pra'r" (179) and on the next Sabbath delivers a dialect sermon, which is the story's comic centerpiece. In Gainey's account, Adam, after his original sin, fled God, jumping over the oceans, Jupiter, and the moon. He could not quite clear the sun, however, and he fell to earth. This explains both Adam's fall and the African's color: "When Adam jump' ovuh de sun, de fiah wus so hot, it scawched 'im black as a crips, an' curled up his ha'r so he nevuh couldn'n't get it straight agin" (181). As a result, "all Adam an' Eve's chillun bawn fo' de Fall wus white, and dey wus de fo'fathers ob de white race o' people— all Adam an' Eve's chillun bawn aftuh de Fall wus black, an' dey wus de fo'fathers ob de black race of people" (182).

The unnamed narrator invites our amusement at the sermon by alerting us early on that Bre'r Gabe's "pulpit powers were developed under circumstances somewhat unfavorable to a thorough knowledge of the Scriptures or to any acquaintance with the rules of grammar" (177). The narrator's elevated diction and his elaborate understatement increase the ironic distance between his voice and that of the dialect speaker. We should also note the narrator's equation between linguistic competence—"acquaintance with the rules of [standard white English] grammar"—and general knowledge and intelligence. The latter equation is crucial to racist ideology. For the racial essentialist, differences in dialect are not neutral linguistic phenomena but signs of inherent mental inferiority. Brother Gabriel's sermon supports the same ideology because it offers a biblical explanation of racial difference: Africans are black because of ancestral guilt. In the more familiar biblical account of black origins, blacks are "sons of Ham," punished for Ham's sin of looking on his father, Noah, while Noah was naked. In Gainey's sermon, Adam substitutes for Ham, but the implications are the same: black difference results from divine punishment.

Gainey's sermon resembles the minstrel show stump speech: a dialect speaker expatiates comically on a topic beyond his competence, in this case, biblical exegesis. It should be clear that we are, with this preacher, in the familiar ideological landscape of plantation fiction and the dialect sketch. But this is the point where Chesnutt's story, once again, breaks from traditional patterns. Chesnutt's story mocks the biblical justification for racial difference. This doctrine, central in the South's resistance to black equality, is ridiculed by being put into the mouth of an ignorant fool. And even more damning, its refutation—and the refutation of the equation between intelligence and Standard English—comes out of the mouth of a black man speaking dialect. At the end of Gainey's sermon, Brother Isham rises from the amen corner. He points out that if Adam's children born before the fall were white and Adam continued to live with Eve after the fall, "unduh all de sarcumstances ob de case dem chillun bawn aftuh de Fall oughtah be'n mullatahs" (182). Isham (is Ham) deconstructs Gainey's biblical exegesis and, in so doing, invokes the racial essentialist's ultimate nightmare: miscegenation. Isham's subtle point—that racial mixing was already well advanced in the South—was made earlier by Frederick Douglass, who also saw the implications of this fact for biblical justifications of racial essentialism: "a very different-looking class of people are springing up at the south, and are now held in slavery, from those originally brought to this country from Africa; and if their increase will do no other good, it will do away with the force of the argument, that God cursed Ham, and therefore American slavery is right."[18]

In Chesnutt's sketch, the subordination of Gainey's voice and his perspective, established by the narrator's ironic comments at the outset of the story, find unexpected support from a dialect speaker at the story's conclusion. Thus, although Gainey is mocked, the status of the dialect speaker as such is subtly adjusted upwards by Isham's pertinent rejoinder. All the more so in that the narrator, describing the congregation's murmurous reaction to Gainey's sermon, comments that "it was not at all certain that the murmur was one of unqualified approval" (182). The narrator suggests that Isham is not alone among these rural blacks in rejecting Gainey's argument, and in this way the story distinguishes between the minstrel versions of rural black values and other, more authentic voices among the South's former slaves.[19]

In addition to the stump speech, it is also possible to view Gainey's sermon in the context of black folklore's etiological tales. Such narratives try to explain how the world came to be as it is and how blacks acquired their physical characteristics and their social condition. These tales, like Gainey's sermon, frequently feature divine punishment for black failings, such as disobedience, pride, or laziness. Daryl Dance challenges the view that blacks who told these stories accepted the negative white stereotypes these stories seem to embody.

> In their very effort to supposedly give some logic to the prevalent attitudes towards the Black man, the creators of these tales make those beliefs so ridiculous that one must conclude that the views and attitudes of the white man are positively ludicrous. An additional bit of irony may derive from the Black narrator's use of the white man's God to explain most of these situations, especially considering the fact that the white man has used his religion to justify

some of his most hypocritical and sacrilegious actions towards the Blacks. The unavoidable conclusion is that these tales are not myths — they are only parodies of myths. They are indeed *jokes* and the butt of these jokes is only ostensibly the Negro — the real target is often the white man or America. [20]

Chesnutt's version of the etiological tale makes explicit the covert parody implicit in its folk predecessors.

Chesnutt's strategy in representing dialect-speaking black folk is, in these two stories, primarily defensive. In both stories, he identifies and repudiates the ideological implications of white representations of black dialect speakers. In other stories he takes a different approach, revealing the positive strengths in the distinctive rural black worldview. This is preeminently the case with the stories Uncle Julius McAdoo tells to his white employer. These stories, some of which are included in *The Conjure Woman,* are among Chesnutt's best-known fictions and are addressed in the next chapter.

Chesnutt again challenged racial and linguistic binaries in "The Partners," a story published in 1901. The story is set in the South during Reconstruction. It tells of two former slaves, William Cain and Rufus Green, who decide to work together and share the fruits of their labor. The story is, then, a parable about the importance of black solidarity and mutual aid in meeting the challenges of post–Civil War America. However, it is also a narrative about languages and the values they embody. A central character in the story is a text, a partnership agreement between the two men. This agreement is cited early in the narrative and again at its end, and although it remains the same, we respond differently to it and the values it embodies at the second reading. What happens between the two readings is that William's text has been tested by events and by interaction with the narrator's comments in Standard English. A challenge such as this lies at the heart of Bakhtin's concept of dialogic narrative. "The idea of testing the hero, of testing his discourse," Bakhtin writes, "may very well be the most fundamental organizing idea of the novel" (388).

Here is the contract's first appearance in the story, framed by the narrator's comments:

The scribe and the paper were found, and William dictated the following agreement, the phraseology of which is reminiscent of certain solemn forms which

he had heard used from time to time, being town-bred and accustomed to the
ways of the world:

"William Cain and Rufus Green is gone in partners this day to work at whatever their hands find to do. What they makes shall belong to one as much as
the other, and they shall stand by each other in sickness and in health, in good
luck and in bad, till death shall us part, and the Lord have mercy on our souls.
Amen."

This was written in a doubtful hand, on each of two sheets of foolscap paper,
and signed by the partners with their respective marks. (253–54)

The most striking feature of this text is its hybridization. Generically,
the document confounds legal contract, wedding vows, and burial prayers.
Linguistically, it mixes Standard English and dialect. The scribe to whom
William has dictated the agreement has smoothed away the rougher elements of rural black speech, but substantial traces of William's uneducated
voice remain. Note the absence of the subject-verb agreement required in
Standard English—"William Cain and Rufus Green *is* gone." Note also the
shift from third to first person—"*they* shall stand by each other . . . till death
shall *us* part"—and the simple syntax. On our first encounter this hybridization creates a comic effect. Indeed hybridization—the presentation of a
form of discourse normally reserved for educated English in uneducated
vernacular—is, as we have seen, a staple of dialect humor.

The racist's ear notes the difference of black dialect from standard speech
and hears in that difference an audible sign of inherent mental inferiority.
Thus, by this logic, the black's attempt to articulate sophisticated concepts—
in this case a legal agreement—in his own dialect must necessarily be comic.
There is a homology in the racist mind between such linguistic hybridization and racial miscegenation. The attempt to join black and white—whether combining black speech and white ideas or by mixing black blood with
white—is an offense against nature. The result must, by the logic of racist
ideology, be comic or monstrous. The presence of an educated speaker in
the text sets in contrast the solecisms of the unlettered speakers and provides
a perspective from which to judge them. The narrator's Latinate diction and
his complex syntax contrast with the simple text it introduces. His ironic
description of William as "town-bred and accustomed to the ways of the
world" deliberately mocks the former slave's naive attempt to use the lan-

guage and genres of his betters. The contrast of black and white speech in this first instance is clearly invidious to the story's black characters.

The attitudes embodied in the narrator's comments illustrate Bakhtin's assertion that the presence of dialect in a story alongside standard speech can set in relief the ideological assumptions of both languages. That is the case here, for the story turns on a series of oppositions:

Standard English	dialect
written	oral
European American values	African American values

In the course of the narrative these oppositions modulate into additional contrasts:

individual ownership	communal ownership
positive law	natural justice

A key turn in the narrative occurs when a meddling white philanthropist persuades William and Rufus to dissolve their communal arrangement in favor of private property and free-market individualism. Rufus, the less gifted of the two, falters under the new arrangement and then bitterly turns against his former partner in an ill-conceived lawsuit. Rufus's entry into the white man's legal system leaves him vulnerable to a conniving former slave owner who uses this system to seize Rufus's remaining property. These events subtly shift our sympathies in this contrast of black and white cultures. The narrator's irony, previously directed against William, turns against the white meddler. He calls our attention to the mistaken assumptions of the educated but foolish philanthropist: "A thoughtful student of history might have suggested to the philanthropist that the power of highly developed races lies mainly in their ability to combine for the better accomplishment of a common purpose" (254). The narrator also uses the language of the white legal system to narrate the unjust seizure of Rufus's farm: "Upon certain plausible representations the surveyor procured, for a small sum, a quit-claim deed of all the right, title and interest of the philanthropist's heir in the land occupied and improved for many years by Rufus. Armed with this document he returned home and began an action in ejectment" (258). Chesnutt, a lawyer and a legal stenographer, knew that he did not have to exaggerate legal language to obtain a satirical effect. It was enough to accurately transcribe the language of the American courts to achieve his comic purpose. The opaque diction and the stringy syntax of the narrator's description heighten the contrast between white and black language in this story. But now the contrast works less to the disadvantage of blacks and more to their advantage. If the world of the unlettered dialect speakers seems naive, that of the white courts seems perversely complicated. Even more important, the agreement composed in dialect works for what we recognize as justice, while the white courts work for its opposite.

The reversal of the contrasts existing at the beginning of the narrative is accomplished by a second presentation of the partners' agreement at the end of the narrative. William discovers Rufus's misfortunes and goes to his former partner with the original document. This is the story's conclusion:

> "An' now Rufus," said William . . . "does you reco'nize dat paper?"
>
> "No, William, you 'member I never l'arned ter read."
>
> "Well I has, an' I'll read dis paper ter you:
>
> "William Cain and Rufus Green is gone in partners this day to work at whatever their hands find to do. What they makes shall belong to one as much as the other, and they shall stand by each other in sickness and in health, in good luck and in bad, till death shall us part, and the Lord have mercy on our souls. Amen."
>
> "Ou' old podnership paper, William," said Rufus sadly, "ou' ole podnership w'at wuz broke up ten years ago!"
>
> "Broke up, who said it wuz broke up?" exclaimed William. "It says 'in good luck an' in bad, till death shall us part,' an' it means w'at it says! Do you suppose de Lord could have mussy on my soul ef I wuz ter fersak my ole podner at de time er his greates' trouble? He wouldn' be a jes' God ef he did! Come 'long now, Rufus. . . . I've seen my lawyer, an' he says you got plenty er time yit ter 'peal you' case an' take it ter de upper co't, wid eve'y chance ter win it. . . . I've got money in de bank an' w'at's mine is yo'n till yo' troubles is ended, an' f'm dis time fo'th we is podners 'till death shall us part.' " (260)

The text that William reads to Rufus is identical to the text at the beginning of the story, but now it reads differently. Its naive mixing of law and religion, of partnership and prayer, seem a sapient attempt to ground their relationship on values deeper than those of positive law. Even the grammatical mistakes reflect this perspective. The disagreement between plural subjects and singular verbs—"William Cain and Rufus Green *is* gone"—acknowledges that the two now stand as one. The shift from third person to first person—from *"they"* to *"us"*—expresses a wish to engage themselves deeply and personally. These ex-slaves may be without letters, but they are not without values. The black American's survival in captivity instilled faith, perseverance, and solidarity. The dialect text asserts these values, and the narrative affirms them and their importance for the new order. The linguistic interaction in this text produces a situation where the two languages and value systems stand as equals. This new relationship is solidified by the translation of a key term. The black men see themselves, in their dialectical speech, as "podners." The narrator mocks their claim, referring ironically to "what they called partnership" (254). The story's title, however, is not ironic; it translates the key term and recognizes the men, as "partners" in the fullest and most meaningful sense of the Standard English word.

Chesnutt's story affirms the old oral culture of dialect speakers and at the same time opens to a new order. William has learned to read and write, and he will use his new skills in the courts to recover Rufus's property. The partnership that the story calls for exists on several levels: between the two men, between the old and the new, between the oral culture and the written one, and potentially, between blacks and whites. By exposing the rich values present in the world of the dialect-speaking blacks, the story argues that the blacks have a right to full partnership, for they do not come empty-handed. They bring their own valuable contribution—their religious faith, their patient endurance, their communal responsibility—to the new civil partnership. The echoing of this key term in the story and in its title—in both dialect and standard speech—confirms the new relationship between the cultures. This story, published the year after "The Future American," also looks toward amalgamation, but the mixing is cultural rather than biological. Neither William nor Rufus has any desire to leave the black community. This story shows the importance of an independent and self-sustaining black community. However, it also argues strongly for the distinctive contributions blacks can make in creating a new American society.

It is true that earlier white writers recognized the deep moral wisdom of unlettered blacks. Harriet Beecher Stowe describes Uncle Tom as "all the moral and Christian virtues bound in black morocco."[21] The old slave can barely read the Bible, but he embodies its teachings more fully than does

Senator Bird, for whom the "idea of a fugitive was only an idea of letters that spell the word" (86). Stowe challenges the traditional privileging of written white culture over oral black culture on a moral level, but she does not do so on an intellectual or a juridical level. For Stowe, Tom and other emancipated slaves would remain wards of benevolent, educated whites. Chesnutt departs from this pattern. It is not incidental that his story focuses on a legal document, because a crucial issue in post-Reconstruction America was the legal standing of black Americans. Could they serve on juries? Could they bring suit against white citizens? The racist answer was that illiterate blacks were incompetent to participate actively in the enactment and enforcement of American justice. Chesnutt's story refutes this assertion. William has adapted very quickly to freedom; he has educated himself, and he asserts his partner's claim in the courts.

Chesnutt's story is about black American language and culture, but it also helps us to see "white" language and the assumptions it harbors more clearly. The story bears out Bakhtin's assertion that different languages in the same text illumine one another. What is realized, he tells us, in fictions such as the ones we have been considering "is the process of coming to know one's own language as it is perceived in someone else's language, coming to know one's own belief system in someone else's system. There takes place within the novel an ideological translation of another's language, and an overcoming of its otherness—an otherness that is only contingent, external, illusory" (365).

5

———◦◉◦———

The Julius and John Stories
"The Luscious Scuppernong"

What would deliver [the New World Negro] from servitude was the forging of a language that went beyond mimicry, a dialect which had the force of a revelation as it invented names for things, one which would finally settle on its own mode of inflection, and which began to create an oral culture of chants, jokes, fall-songs, and fables. —DEREK WALCOTT, *Dream on Monkey Mountain and Other Plays*

Chesnutt's best-known fictions are the stories based on North Carolina folk culture and narrated by an illiterate ex-slave named Julius McAdoo. Chesnutt collected seven of these stories in *The Conjure Woman* (1899), and between 1889 and 1904, he completed another seven stories, featuring the same characters, that were not included in the collection.[1] Critics refer to these stories variously as Chesnutt's "conjure tales," "dialect stories," or "Uncle Julius tales."[2] However, not all of these stories include conjuring, and Chesnutt used dialect in fictions other than those featuring Julius McAdoo. Moreover, Julius is not the only narrator in these stories, nor is he their only important character. I prefer to describe these fictions as the "Julius and John stories," for this designation calls attention to the presence of two narrators, two languages, and two views of the world. Most important, it reminds us of the dynamic between two contrasting perspectives, which lies at the heart of the stories' form and meaning. The dynamic interaction of the two perspectives in these stories represents a potent challenge to important binaries in our culture. The fruitful and deconstructive dialogue of Julius and John is the principal topic of this chapter.

The Julius and John designation also helps us see the connection between Chesnutt's stories and the John and Old Master trickster tales. The latter tales, conceived orally in slavery and collected afterward, narrate the continuing battle of wits between an ingenious slave named John and the slaveholder to whom he belongs. Chesnutt's stories are most often viewed in the context of the white Southern dialect fiction, which Chesnutt quite deliberately evokes and revises.[3] But the stories also draw on an African American narrative tradition of black and white intellectual contest, which is discussed later in this chapter.

In Chesnutt's stories, John, an Ohioan whose last name we never learn, has come South with his wife, Annie, to improve her health and to exploit a new economic opportunity. Their resettlement in the former Confederacy echoes several important political and literary narratives of the 1880s and '90s. The first is "The New South," an account of the postwar South's social progress given by Henry W. Grady. Grady, an editor of the *Atlanta Constitution,* addressed the New England Society in New York on December 22, 1886. In his speech, which was widely reported, Grady reassured his Northern listeners that the prejudices of the past were dead and that Northerners might safely and profitably invest their energies and their capital in the creation of the new Southern economic and social order. "We have learned that one Northern immigrant is worth fifty foreigners, and have smoothed the path to southward, wiped out the place where Mason and Dixon's line used to be, and hung our latch-string out to you and yours."[4] The late decades of the century also saw the flowering of "the novel of reconciliation." These fictions of North-South healing frequently recounted a Northern family's move to the South and a reconciliation of the two regions through intersectional marriage.[5] John and Annie's new life in North Carolina climaxes in "Hot-Foot Hannibal" with Annie's sister's engagement to a prominent member of the local aristocracy. Thus the narrative that develops across these stories follows the pattern of regional reunification—but with an important difference. In the other instances of literary reconciliation, the new order is negotiated by Northerners and *white* Southerners, often on the backs of black Southerners. Chesnutt's Julius and John stories enact dialogue between a white Northerner and a *black* Southerner. Julius initiates John into Southern history and folk belief, assisting his commercial success, and Julius contrives to unite the white lovers.

John is Julius's employer, and it is he who introduces each of Julius's stories. All of these tales are elicited by John and Annie's interest in the lore of their new home, and the Northerners react variously to the stories Julius spins. What distinguishes these stories from other fictions presenting rural black speech is the way these narratives bring educated white speech into the fictional frame. In "The Fall of Adam" and "The Partners" both languages are present, but the narrators are nondramatized; they and their speech stand outside the universe inhabited by the dialect speakers, commenting on these speakers from above. The narrators in "Appreciation" and in Page's "Marse Chan" are in the frame, but they are only minimally present. They listen and record, but they keep an amused distance from the black speaker, with whom they do not interact in any significant way. Joel Chandler Harris's Uncle Remus tales are more complex in this respect. The animal tales are told by Remus, but an omniscient narrator, outside the story world, feels free to interject and direct our attitudes toward Remus and the society that produced him. John F. Callahan's metaphor for this strategy is apt; he remarks that Harrris's "narrative voice and his frame act as a literary picket fence around the black folktales."[6] The stories in *Legends of the Old Plantation* (1881) include an attentive white listener, the grandson of Remus's former owner. This seven-year-old boy is, by implication, the appropriate interlocutor for the childlike Negro. The boy interacts minimally, setting the narratives in motion with his simple questions. The young auditor allows white readers to be both imaginatively engaged by the stories and distanced from their own emotional response—relegating these responses to the nursery, so to speak. There is also another auditor, the child's mother, who listens in. She *overhears* rather than *hears* the dialect speaker, never interacting, except to call the child away, keeping a suspicious distance between herself and the former slave. John and Annie are different. They are white adults who listen, initially with skeptical amusement, but with increasing avidity and seriousness, to an uneducated black man. They hear the voice of a former slave in its own accents and rhythms. They react and raise objections; more important, they learn and subtly modify their opinions. As a consequence, white speech loses its privileged status: it is brought into dialogue with the speech of the other, and it is challenged and relativized by this contact. This is most obvious in the progressive interactions between Julius and his auditors in *The Conjure Woman,* but it is true of all the Julius and John stories. In the Julius and John tales, the "plot of bilingualism," upon which the conventional white dialect sketch is based, becomes the narrative of dialogism.[7] Chesnutt adds to the complexity of this dialogue by adding the presence of two, quite different, white auditors. John is more rational and practical in a dollars-and-cents way; Annie is more intuitive and more sensitive to emotional nuance. John is the man, and thus nominally in charge, but he clearly loves his wife and often accedes to her judgment. These tales—both in their creation and in their reception—are the product of a collaboration between male and female. Julius relays the folk wisdom distilled from the actions of conjure women. The white couple exchange reactions across gender lines, even as they exchange views across the racial line with Julius.

Authentic black and white dialogue was rare in late-nineteenth-century America. Black political leaders who emerged during Reconstruction were rudely pushed aside at its end. Booker T. Washington did not step onto the national stage until 1895. In the meantime, white America was content to allow the black Americans' former masters to speak for them. Chesnutt 's story "The Dumb Witness" allegorizes the problem of black speechlessness and its consequences during these years.[8] In this story John learns from Julius about an atrocity committed by a slave owner named Malcolm Murchison. Murchison cuts the tongue of Viney, his slave mistress, after she speaks to Murchison's white fiancée. Murchison's cruel act turns against him, however, for his uncle, who secreted the family treasure during the war, dies after having confided its hiding place to Viney. Viney cannot convey this information to Murchison; her maimed tongue conveys only a "meaningless cacophony" (*Short Fiction,* 155), and she has never been taught to write. Murchison is gradually driven to insanity and death by the tantalizing presence of wealth he cannot reach. After Murchison's death and Viney's emancipation, the former slave reveals that she had retained her ability to speak, but that she had hidden this fact to punish her brutal master. She reveals the secret to Murchison's much more sympathetic nephew, and the nephew recovers the family wealth.

The silence imposed on blacks by violent intimidation is an important chapter in white America's denial of black personhood.[9] Before Ellison's invisible man, there was Chesnutt's inaudible woman. Chesnutt's story argues that this black silence actually worked against white interests, for it prevented blacks from sharing their knowledge and experience, information that could aid all members of the community. The story's title, "The Dumb Witness," is ironically inaccurate in both senses of the word "dumb." Blacks are neither speechless nor stupid; they need only a sympathetic hearing in order to make their distinctive and valuable contribution to American society. "The Dumb Witness" shows that Chesnutt clearly understood what was at stake in the language problem that blacks faced in post-Reconstruction America.

The problem of black speech after Reconstruction was not simply freeing the black person to speak but deciding how he or she was to speak. An early Chesnutt sketch, ironically titled "An Eloquent Appeal," provided an example of how *not* to proceed. By negative implication, it points to the approach in the stories that Julius narrates in rural dialect. In "An Eloquent Appeal" a black man arrives at the white narrator's door and addresses him sententiously: "Sir . . . you see in me the representative of a despised and down-trodden race. For centuries the race with which you are identified held my people in a bondage more cruel than death, and lived lapped in luxury while their black bondmen toiled beneath the burning sun" (*Short Fiction*, 66). The orator continues in this vein for several more paragraphs, but this is enough to illustrate Chesnutt's rendering of the race reformer's moralistic rhetoric. The language is educated English, and the strategy is lecturing to the white man about his guilt. This lecture, it turns out, is actually the prelude to a sales pitch for a "Magic Corn Cure." The narrator listens and then gives the black man a quarter; in return he gets a "bow that would have done credit to any headwaiter in America" (67). The consequences, for black-white understanding, are not greatly different than those that resulted from the encounter in "Appreciation." The twenty-five cents collected by this black salesman exceeds, to be sure, the value of the chewing tobacco earned by Pilgrim Gainey, but there is no difference in the level of respect accorded to the black men in the two instances.

William L. Andrews explains that in the last quarter of the nineteenth century "a black writer could no longer expect to get a hearing simply by rehearsing the familiar horrors of antebellum southern life in the manner of abolitionist literature."[10] After the collapse of Reconstruction, white ears were inured to oratory appealing to high moral principle. Chesnutt understood the new literary climate, and his strategy in the Julius and John stories was more subtle. His character speaks in the colorful dialect already familiar and attractive to white audiences from the minstrel show and white plantation fiction. In Chesnutt's instance, this black voice actually dialogues with white voices and broaches subjects previously untreated in popular fiction. The purpose was gradual transformation of white readers from within— metamorphosis, or conjure. Julius, like the corn-cure salesman, is a trickster, but there is a significant difference in what he accomplishes. He offers more than a patent medicine of dubious value; for his appeal, in the final analysis, is based not on guilt but on white self-interest.

The white presence in the John and Julius stories is central to Chesnutt's purpose. That purpose, as framed in Chesnutt's journals and practiced in these stories, was "not so much the elevation of the colored people as the elevation of the whites" (139). John and Annie stand as surrogates for the white reader, and the couple's metamorphosis would, Chesnutt hoped, also be that of many other literate white men and women. The white couple's education proceeds simultaneously on a number of levels—historic, moral, aesthetic, and linguistic. These levels are closely interdependent, but for purposes of analysis we can begin with the historical. The white Southerner's view of the past was so dominant in the 1880s that John, a reasonably well-disposed Northerner, has been caught in its spell. Thus he professes at one point that he finds Julius's view of the past "very strange," for the old Negro apparently feels no nostalgia for the "Arcadian joyousness and irresponsibility which was a somewhat popular conception of slavery" (*Short Fiction*, 133).

Details about life in bondage are less abundant in these stories than in the slave narratives, which were so powerful in the abolitionist struggle, but they are carefully chosen, and they strike at the heart of the former slave-owners' defense of the "peculiar institution." Central to the Southern case for slavery, during its practice as well as in posthumous attempts at justification, was the claim of paternalism. In this view, the Negro was by nature an intellectual and moral child, and the white slave owner was the providentially provided parent. The plantation, black bondspeople included, was an extended family, directed by a benevolent patriarch. The fictions of Harriet Beecher Stowe, Frances E. W. Harper, and William Wells Brown exploded this myth by emphasizing one of slavery's worst abuses, the sep-

aration of black families. Again and again, Julius, in the course of his narratives, recounts instances of lovers being separated, of children torn from
their mothers, and most daring of all, of the slave owner's sale of his own
mulatto sons and daughters. The significance is not missed by Julius's inter-
locutors. Annie exclaims after one of these tales of tragic separation: "What
a system it was . . . under which such things were possible!" (*Conjure Woman,* 60).

Annie and her husband are educated, not only about Southern whites,
but also about Southern blacks. Plantation writers presented idealized portraits of selfless retainers sacrificing even their freedom for their masters.
Thomas Nelson Page's Sam and Joel Chandler Harris's Remus offered
models of black fidelity to white masters before, during, and after the Civil
War. Chesnutt, in an 1890 letter to George Washington Cable, expressed
his distaste for representations of "the sentimental and devoted negro who
prefers kicks to half-pence" (*"To Be an Author,"* 66). Chesnutt's Julius
McAdoo is clearly at some remove from the plantation school's guileless servant. Julius, Sylvia Lyons Render comments, "is obviously self-serving and
has no scruples about practicing chicanery when it suits his purpose." But,
she continues, "he is not altogether selfish or mercenary. His concern for
those he cares about transcends gain, and his friendship cannot be bought"
(*Short Fiction,* 24). He is, in short, a full human being with human needs
and loyalties, with whom, John discovers, he can collaborate to their mutual
advantage. This is the important difference between the less than eloquent
appeal made by the salesman-orator considered above. Chesnutt believed
that if whites were to be brought around, it would not be by moral abstrac-
tions but by a practical demonstration of their own interest.

Southern nostalgia for the "old Negro," the selfless servant of plantation
myth, had his negative counterpart in Southern disparagement of the "new
Negro." This phrase from Alain Locke's Harlem Renaissance manifesto has,
as Eric J. Sundquist has shown, an earlier history, which is directly relevant to Chesnutt's stories.[11] Southern apologists for white supremacy used
this term—or more crudely, "the new nigger"—to criticize the black personality that had emerged with emancipation. The postwar black was, in
contrast to the sentimentalized version of his antebellum predecessor, indo-
lent and insubordinate. Chesnutt directly engages this cultural narrative,
and he considered entitling one of the Julius and John stories "De Noo

Nigger" (*"To Be an Author,"* 105). The story appears in *The Conjure Woman* as "Mars Jeems's Nightmare," but its relevance to representations of post-Reconstruction blacks is still evident. Julius tells of a slave owner, James McLean, "Mars Jeems" in dialect, whom a conjurer turns into a black slave, and who becomes the "new Negro" on his own plantation. But Mars Jeems has his double, for there is also a "new Negro" in the frame story. John had recently introduced a new employee on his property, Julius's grandson Tom. Tom has proven lazy and irresponsible, and John has just fired him. Julius tells a story that demonstrates, among other things, the white slave-owner 's difficulty adjusting to the changed circumstances he finds in being transformed into a slave. The slave's transition to a freeperson, after the brutal effects of bondage and after the supports of Reconstruction were removed, was also difficult. Julius's story implies that Tom and his generation deserved sympathy and patience. Annie takes the lesson and rehires Tom, and John does not interfere.

To continue the contrast of old and new: the "old white," the plantation paterfamilias of legend, has his counterpart in the South's "new white." We catch a brief but telling glimpse of James McLean's grandson, red-faced with anger, furiously whipping his horse. It does not take much to see this same figure, shrouded in a white hood, applying the same whip to human flesh. The point of these parallels is that, if there has been a historical decay, it has not happened only on the dark side of the color line. John, if he is to judge the black man, must also judge the white. He is given two models of white behavior: on the one hand, cruel James McLean before his transformation and his abusive grandson; on the other, James McLean rendered generous and forgiving by his own experience as a slave.

John gradually sees that patience and tolerance with Julius and his family are in his own interest. He has come South with his capital and his energy, but he does not know the country from which he would extract wealth. Julius, born on the land, has learned from working it and listening to the lore of others who worked it before him. John quickly discovers that Julius was "familiar with the roads and the watercourses, knew the qualities of the various soils and what they would produce, and where the best hunting and fishing were to be had" (*Conjure Woman,* 64), and thus he retains him and treats him with respect. More important than this practical instruction is the philosophical education that Julius imparts. It is an introduction

to a different cosmology with different ethical, epistemological, and aesthetic assumptions. The worlds of Julius and John, which these stories bring
together, are in dramatic contrast: two different languages, two different
views of the world. Among the differences that emerge in these stories, the
most obvious are the following:

North	South
white	black
literate	oral

Beyond these, but related to them, are these additional contrasts:

human	natural
matter	spirit
empiricism	imagination

The stories challenge the privileging in our culture of the first terms in each
of these pairs. Perhaps more important, these stories also show that our
dependence on binary signification often obscures and distorts subtle continuities in our experience.

John and Annie's education in Julius's language and worldview begins
shortly after their arrival when they hear an unfamiliar word from his lips:
"goophered" (*Conjure Woman,* 11). John enquires as to its meaning, and
Julius offers several synonyms—"cunju'd, bewitch'" (11)—for this word of
African origins, but it is still mysterious to the Northerners.[12] The word's
full meaning and the worldview it implies—a world where familiar distinctions like those listed above are blurred—emerge only through a sequence
of stories. To begin with the conjure woman herself: in Julius's telling she
has strange powers, but are they supernatural or natural? She does not
invoke God or the Devil—nor gods and devils—and she makes no appeal
to saints or ancestral spirits. On the other hand, she freely uses fragments of
nature—plants, herbs, and roots. Are her powers occult or psychological?
They make possible strange transformations, but they are facilitated by their
subjects' predisposition to believe. Not the least of the conjurer's powers—
and this refers to Julius as much as to Aunt Peggy—is the power to narrate,
the ability to weave phenomena into a convincing tale.

To continue with the puzzles these tales pose: are the forces they reveal
under the exclusive control of a few individuals, or are they at work generally

in the world? Aunt Peggy and Uncle Jube are famous for their goophers, but Tenie, in "Po' Sandy," and Phillis, in "The Marked Tree"—neither previously known as conjurers—cast potent spells. Furthermore, the strange events in "Lonesome Ben," "A Deep Sleeper," and "Dave's Neckliss" occur without magic intervention by anyone. The questions we have been asking are deliberately left vague in the stories, and they call into question common assumptions about the separation of the supernatural and natural, spiritual and material, divine and human. Several things are clear, however: these forces are not moral, and they are not transcendent. The conjurers create goophers for good purposes or bad, for blacks and for whites—whoever will pay their price. And these conjurers are not invincible. Aunt Peggy and Uncle Jube compete in "The Grey Wolf's Ha'nt," and Hannibal outsmarts Chloe despite her use of Aunt Peggy's goopher in "Hot-Foot Hannibal." The most that can be said about these forces is that they are in this world and of it, not radically separate and transcendent. We are some distance from the Judeo-Christian view of an omnipotent moral authority standing above humans and nature and controlling them.[13] No one, among the conjurers, has absolute dominion, and battles are won by shrewd collaboration. The conjure stories tell of a world in which the natural, the human, and the supernatural interpenetrate. Metamorphosis—the transgression of familiar boundaries—is commonplace. In Julius's world, birds speak and pine trees cry out; humans become grapevines, frogs, and wolves; and masters awake to find they are slaves on their own plantation.

Julius's view of a mysterious and protean world implies important differences in the relation of man to the land. John characterizes these different perspectives as "proprietary"—private ownership—versus "predial"—a communal sharing (*Conjure Woman*, 65). These views come into conflict when John discovers vines bearing delicious grapes on property he plans on buying. He assumes that these fruits "were the undisputed prey of the first comer" (6), that is, they were his for the purchase of the property. The question his naive formulation misses is, who, in fact, is the "first comer"? John has just arrived, but Julius has spent a lifetime on the plantation. His light color and his family name suggest that he may, in fact, be a blood relative of its former owners. And legal title is, from Julius's perspective, irrelevant, for in his view, the land does not belong to humans at all, but humans to the land; men and women do not live on nature, but in it.

There is throughout these stories an interpenetration of the human and the natural. For Faulkner these levels were powerfully connected: human presumption against nature, or the appropriation of the wilderness to private ownership—what John calls the "proprietary" view—was prelude to the further sin of slavery. Similarly, in the Julius and John stories man and nature are intimately related, and sins frequently occur simultaneously on the human and natural levels. In several stories slaves suffer as a direct result of the white man's wish to extract more wealth from the land. Dugal' McAdoo uses a conjurer first to keep his slaves from sharing his grapes, and then to extract greater profit from buying and selling his slave Henry. McAdoo's greed finally perverts everything, destroying both the vineyard and the slave. The South's sins, in these stories, are often figured in natural terms. In "Po' Sandy" the whine of a saw blade ripping into a pine tree is, for Julius, the mournful complaint of a slave separated from his wife, and in "The Marked Tree" the rot in an ancient oak stands for the decay of a cruel plantation dynasty. John takes these lessons, but he does not give over to a primitive communism. Nor is he asked to do so. It is too late for such idealism, in Chesnutt as in Faulkner. John does allow his black employees to take their share of his grapes, and he provides work and shelter for those who have lived on the land before him.

The sequence of stories in *The Conjure Woman* marks the regular progress of the Northerners' education. The first three stories—"The Goophered Grapevine," "Po' Sandy," and "Mars Jeems's Nightmare"—explain the blacks' right to nourishment, shelter, and employment on the lands they have worked. The third story, in which the white master becomes a black slave, marks a key moment in John's philosophical and linguistic education. John remarks that the story's miraculous transformation "was powerful goopher" (101). His use of the dialect word shows that he now understands the concept that had puzzled him in the first story. More than that, the suppression of the definite article, which Standard English would require in this construction, shows that he can express this understanding in the blacks' own dialect. In the fifth story ("Sis' Becky's Pickaninny"), the couple's moral growth is figured on the physical level. Annie's health, fragile at their arrival, is restored by the edifying tale of a mother's reunion with her child. The final tale, "Hot-Foot Hannibal," climaxes this sequence with the joining of lovers, both in Julius's conjure story and in John and Annie's family. In the latter context, Julius facilitates the union of Annie's younger sister, Mabel, with Malcolm Murchison. Young Murchison is very likely the grandnephew of the slave owner who took Viney's tongue in "The Dumb Witness" and the son of the more compassionate Roger Murchison, who listened to Viney and benefited from her speech. The union of Malcolm and Mabel joins an enlightened member of the old Southern aristocracy and a representative of the newly arrived Northern capitalists. Their union is facilitated by a freed black slave who is offered employment by both white families. The healing proposed here is more comprehensive than in other reconciliation narratives of the period: North and South, as well as black and white, come together and cooperate in a model for the new South.

Parallel to the moral and social instruction we have been tracing is an epistemological and aesthetic education. One of the strongest oppositions separating the newly arrived Northerners and the former slave is the contrast between what John calls "reason and common sense" and "childish super-stitions" (135). John and Annie, educated members of the middle class, are empiricists; they are, moreover, European Americans, and thus inclined to regard the African American as a mental child. However, despite their prej-udices, they repeatedly fall silent and give attention as the unlettered black man spins a tale. The ambivalence of their reaction to Julius's story world is suggested by John's comments at the outset of "Tobe's Tribulations."

> His [Julius's] views of life were so entirely foreign to our own, that for a time after we got acquainted with him his conversations were a never-failing source of novelty and interest. He had seen life from what was to us a new point of view—from the bottom, as it were; and there clung to his mind, like barnacles to the submerged portion of a ship, all sorts of extravagant beliefs. The simplest phenomena of life were to him fraught with hidden meaning—some prophecy of good, some presage of evil. (*Short Fiction*, 98–99)

John's response mixes repugnance and fascination: he tries to distance him-self from Julius's world at the very moment that he and his wife prepare, once again, to submit to its spell. Julius's universe is "foreign," and thus vaguely unsettling, but at the same time, it is new and fascinating. Implic-itly invoking class privilege, the white man consigns the black man's view to the lower social depths from which it emerges. However, his intended metaphors of dismissal—"the bottom" and barnacles on a submerged ship—

say more than they intend. The black man's tales, in John's metaphor, float up from repressed depths: strange visions fraught with intimations of good and evil, subdued but never entirely conquered by the Northerners' commonsensical empiricism.

The sequence of stories in *The Conjure Woman* dramatizes the couple's shifting attitude toward the black man's stories and the world they evoke. The first half of the collection is punctuated by expressions of incredulity, such as Annie's or John's claims that Julius's accounts are "absurd" (61, 106), "quite improbable" (100), and "ridiculous nonsense" (107). In the collection's fourth story, "The Conjurer's Revenge," Annie adds an additional criticism: not only is the story implausible, it is without purpose. Julius's story, Annie tells him, "is n't pathetic, it has no moral that I can discover, and I can't see why you should tell it" (127). The white woman, a solid member of the middle class, feels that if she invests time in a story, she has earned payment in the form of a moral or an ennobling sentiment. But this focus on explicit moral instruction misses one of fiction's important functions. Julius's tales often carry a lesson, it is true, but they don't always, and "The Conjurer's Revenge" is an instance. The conjurer-storyteller's deepest work, prior to any explicit ethical message, is release from the imprisoning limits of the familiar. As "The Conjurer's Revenge" begins, we find Annie "wearily but conscientiously ploughing through a missionary report," while John tries to follow "the impossible career of the blonde heroine of a rudimentary novel" (104). Both happily abandon their readings when Julius arrives and the possibility of one of his tales presents itself. The Northerners do not lack conventional sentiment or moral edification in the publications they brought from their former home. What Julius's narratives offer is the chance to be caught in the spell of a world radically different from any they have known before. Julius answers Annie's reproach of implausibility by pointing out that a young black scholar had told him that the earth revolves around the sun. For Julius, such an idea clearly contradicts the senses, and "ef a man can't b'lieve w'at 'e sees, I can't see no use in libbin'" (128). Thus is John's "common sense" turned against his trust in science. But finally the old black man is not interested in empirical or scientific notions of truth, for they are not the object of his tales. "Dey's so many things a body knows is lies," he says, "dat dey ain' no use gwine roun' findin' fault wid tales dat mought des ez well be so ez nought" (128).

These discussions are prelude to the next story, "Sis' Becky's Pickaninny," which as we have said, is crucial to Annie's recovery. At this tale's conclusion, deeply moved by the miraculous reunion of mother and child, Annie remarks that "the story is true to nature, and might have happened half a hundred times, and no doubt did happen, in those horrid days before the war" (159). Annie's phrase, "might have happened half a hundred times, and no doubt did happen" is an acceptable paraphrase in Standard English of Julius's utterance in dialect, "dat mought des ez well be so ez nought." Both formulations approximate Aristotle's assertion that, in literature, a probable impossibility is preferable to an improbable possibility. Julius's stories enact a complex release from the familiar on one level and a return to it on another. The stories violate accepted notions of what is physically possible, but they precipitate an encounter on a deeper level with what is morally probable. Given certain acts, and given human psychology, these are the likely consequences of those acts: what "mought des ez well be so ez nought."

Annie is deeply stirred by the tale and, John tells us, she is restored to health by it. The exact nature of Annie's illness is never stated, but we know that she was already suffering in the North and that she experienced some relief during her first year of residence in her new home. However, she has recently had a relapse and fallen into "a settled melancholy" (132). Her illness seems less physiological than psychological, although its actual sources are unclear. One possibly significant fact is that the couple is childless. An earlier miscarriage or a frustrated wish to conceive might well account for Annie's melancholia. Julius's tale is about a mother's love for her child and the return of the child to the mother. This story could have helped Annie to confront fears or frustrations about motherhood. After Annie's restoration to health, John acknowledges that "even the wildest" of Julius's fictions "was not without an element of pathos,—the tragedy, it might be, of the story itself" (168). Earlier John dismissed Julius's tales as children 's literature, but here he remarks a feature of tragedy—the evocation and purgation of powerful feeling. Annie, it seems, has experienced a catharsis, the discharge of strong and troubling emotions.

It was intended from the beginning that nature would play a part in Annie's therapy. The couple moved to their new home in search of a climate and a setting more congenial to her recovery. We might then, in this context, note the phrase "true to nature" in Annie's characterization of Julius's fictions. The notion of "nature" in this instance is considerably more elastic than the one implicit in her earlier criticisms. She now opens herself more generously to Julius's story world, and there are no protests of incredulity, from either Annie or John, during the telling of the collection's last two tales. Annie's phrase "true to nature" links Julius's cosmology with his aesthetics, connects nature and narrative. Often, in these stories, a peaceful rural setting is the prelude to a tale. The first story in the collection begins with the couple wrapped in "cloistral solitude" beneath "solemn aisles of the virgin forest" (7). It is from this atmosphere, from nature itself, that these tales seem to emerge. And it is to nature—understood as a fusion of the physical, spiritual, and human—that they return. The collection's penultimate tale ends with the white couple and the black man silently attending to the rising wind, "a long, wailing note," epitomizing the story's "remorse and hopelessness" (192–93). Julius's leisurely narrative style requires that his auditors submit to the slower rhythms of the South and of nature. When Annie presses for an explanation to a supernatural occurrence, Julius answers simply, "It's all in de tale, ma'm. . . . It's all in de tale" (203). In the last story in the collection, "Hot-Foot Hannibal," Julius, driving the rockaway, wants to take his employers on a route that is considerably longer than necessary, and when forced to take the shorter path, he deliberately stalls their progress. The delay gives him time to tell his story, and more important, it permits the headstrong lovers, Mabel and Malcolm, to cool their tempers and heal their quarrel.

We have mentioned above how Annie's remark that Julius's tale "might have happened half a hundred times, and no doubt did happen" renders in Standard English an idea we earlier encountered in Julius's dialect, "dat mought des ez well be so ez nought." This movement of an idea from one idiom to another highlights the interaction between black vernacular and educated English in these stories. The result of this interaction is a reduction of the distance between these languages and the social communities they represent. This linguistic interaction takes a number of forms. An ironic instance occurs when John quotes the following passage from his philosophical reading:

> " 'The difficulty of dealing with transformations so many-sided as those which all existences have undergone, or are undergoing, is such as to make a com-

plete and deductive interpretation almost hopeless. So to grasp the total process of redistribution of matter and motion as to see simultaneously its several
necessary results in their actual interdependence is scarcely possible. There is,
however, a mode of rendering the process as a whole tolerably comprehensible.
Though the genesis of the rearrangement of every evolving aggregate is in itself
one, it presents to our intelligence' "— (163–64)

We should note parenthetically that, although these tales are praised for
their rendering of rural black speech, Chesnutt was also concerned about
capturing the educated white man's voice. "The introductions to the stories," he explained, were "written in the best English I could command"
(*Essays and Speeches,* 543). In this case, he is quoting for ironic purposes
a singularly opaque instance of educated English. Annie characterizes the
passage as "nonsense" (*Conjure Woman,* 164)—a term she applied earlier to
Julius's tale (107). Julius's fiction may be implausible, but John's philosophy
is impenetrable. Thus the distance between high and low is diminished. To
the degree that meaning can be glimpsed in this philosophical thicket, it
seems to be something like this: reality is multifaceted, dynamic, and inter-
connected, and for these reasons it does not yield easily to rational understanding. But these are essentially the cosmological assumptions implicit
in Julius's protean story world. John's philosophical reading provides the
occasion for a contrast between the language in the frame and the language
in the tale, a contrast between the discourse of educated whites and that of
illiterate blacks. The juxtaposition is not invidious to the unlettered former
slave.

The source of the philosophical passage is not identified in the story; it is
taken, ironically, from Herbert Spencer's *First Principles.*[14] Spencer was one
of the nineteenth-century's most ambitious system builders. He aimed in
his projected ten-volume *Synthetic Philosophy* to unify the physical, biological, and social sciences in a single system governed by a set of universal principles. Spencer thus represented the rationalist, generalizing tendency in
Western thought to its fullest degree. This trust in universal "natural" rules
had, of course, significant social consequences. Social Darwinism, which
was derived from Spencer's teaching, led to a laissez-faire approach to society. Nature's laws, the Social Darwinists argued, should be allowed to do
their work unimpeded in society. Needless to say, by this logic, those groups

at the bottom of society should be left there, whence they would eventually be eliminated by nature's wise workings. Julius's voice in these stories contradicts Spencer on virtually every point. Julius also embraces nature, but a nature more mysterious and less mechanical than that of the British philosopher. The old black man instinctively prefers pragmatic adaptations over appeal to abstract principle. And he sees the connections between humans and their shared need to cooperate. The title of the chapter from which John quotes, "The Instability of the Homogenous," provides another level of irony. One of Spencer's cardinal principles held that on every level—physical, chemical, biological, and sociological—"the more homogenous must tend ever to become less homogenous" (416). He was willing to argue on the basis of this principle that America's ethnic diversity was its great strength and that the eventual mixture of these ethnicities was a reason for great hope. Spencer, rather illogically, did not include African Americans or Native Americans in this new race; his universal law of inevitable and salutary heterogeneity apparently did not go that far. But Chesnutt's notion of American dialogue and interactions among cultures did, and his text's linguistic interpenetration and Julius's mixed blood make this point.

Another kind of contact between white and black dialects results from the fact that Julius's stories include white characters. When these whites speak, their speech is necessarily rendered in the narrator's language. The effect can subtly mock the whites and their attitudes. In "Sis' Becky's Pickaninny" a sententious planter deploys the clichés of Southern honor to escape a bad horse trade:

> " 'My conscience,' sezee, 'has be'n troublin' me 'bout dat ringbone' hoss I sol' you. Some folks 'lows a hoss trader ain' got no conscience, but dey doan know me, fer dat is my weak spot, en de reason I ain' made no mo' money hoss tradin'. Fac' is,' sezee, 'I is got so I can't sleep nights fum studyin' 'bout dat spavin' hoss; en I is made up my min' dat, wiles a bahg'in is a bahg'in. . . .' "
> (*Conjure Woman*, 156)

The planter's pompous hypocrisy would be evident in any case, but giving his protestations in the accents of his social opposite adds to their comic incongruity.

In "Tobe's Tribulations," one of Mrs. McSwayne's slaves has escaped North and then written her former owner a taunting letter. Julius renders the slave mistress's reaction in dialect and, in the process, pokes fun at the white woman's self-righteous indignation: "how ongrateful dat nigger wuz, not on'y ter run 'way, but to write back sich wick'niss ter w'ite folks w'at had alluz treated 'im good, fed 'im, en clothed 'im, en nussed 'im w'en he wuz sick, en nebber let 'im suffer fer nuffin' all his life" (*Short Fiction,* 99). In another context, white science, in this case agronomy, is made to seem quite different when we hear it in black vernacular; a fertilizer recipe—a "mixtry er lime en ashes en manyo" (*Conjure Woman,* 29)—sounds like a conjure potion when it is presented in dialect. Throughout the Julius and John tales, dialect has a deflationary effect on white titles, names, and institutions. Colonel Pendleton becomes "Kunnel Pen'leton," Marlborough McSwayne becomes "Marrabo McSwayne," the Old Dominion is "Fuhginny" (*Conjure Woman,* 137, 41, 137), and the Scotch-Irish house of worship is the "P'isbytay'n Chu'ch" (*Short Fiction,* 118).

A comparison of a passage in John's educated English with a passage in Julius's dialect will further clarify the different values in the stories' two languages. The passages occur within a few pages of each other, and both are about the grapes that are the occasion for the first contact between the white man and the former slave. Here is John's two-sentence description early in *The Conjure Woman*'s first story:

> The vines—here partly supported by decayed and broken-down trellises, there twining themselves among the branches of the slender saplings which had sprung up among them—grew in wild and unpruned luxuriance, and the few scattered grapes they bore were the undisputed prey of the first comer. The site was admirably adapted to grape-raising; the soil, with a little attention, could not have been better; and with the native grape, the luscious scuppernong, as my main reliance in the beginning, I felt sure that I could introduce and cultivate successfully a number of other varieties. (6)

The first sentence describes the vineyard in a way that suggests its current underdevelopment and the potential it offers an individual willing to seize the initiative. The first independent clause of the second sentence concisely states the Northerner's judgment: "The sight was admirably adapted to grape-raising." The next two clauses support this conclusion with additional data. The second sentence concludes with a confident assertion of eventual success. What John provides in these two sentences is, in essence, a miniprospectus for the enterprise he is about to launch. The carefully constructed sentences develop his argument logically and coherently, and they provide a synoptic view of past neglect, current promise, and future prosperity.

An important reason for John's confidence is the presence of a local grape whose hardiness will assure success in this setting: "the luscious scuppernong" (6). John's phrase brings together two words: a Latinate adjective and a substantive derived from the Indian name for a local river. The literate and the vernacular, the human and the natural, stand side by side in this locution. They are held together by the regular rhythm of stressed first syllables and by the lushly sibilant alliteration of *s*s and *c*s. This description occurs early in the collection's first tale, and it is a prelude to the narration that follows. But it is also its product. John is narrating retrospectively, recording stories he has heard from Julius over several years. The understanding between the white man and the black man that the stories enact has already occurred; Julius has his share of the scuppernongs, and John benefits from Julius's experience. John's evident satisfaction in these first pages indicates that both the agricultural and social experiments have succeeded.

But what is the nature of this success? What is the shape of the social arrangement produced by the interaction of black and white pursued through these tales? The key, as several critics have noted, is contained in John's picture of the vineyard. "The vines—here partly supported by decayed and broken-down trellises, there twining themselves among the branches of the slender saplings which had sprung up among them—grew in wild and unpruned luxuriance" (6). The description, given the complex time frame of narration, is both prospective and retrospective. It captures John's hope on seeing the property he was going to buy, but it is also flavored by several years of working that land with Julius's help. The vines, trellis, and saplings symbolize the complex interweaving of nature, whites, and blacks in a new, emerging South. Henry B. Wonham characterizes this new relationship as "blending and hybridization," but this reading does not accurately capture what has occurred, either horticulturally or socially.[15] What is described is not one thing, a blend or hybrid, but three things—vine, trellis, and sapling—which remain separate even as they interact. Insofar as this description figures racial relations in this new order, there are separate but interdependent elements held together in a dancelike dialogue. Joined by common interests and circumstance, John and Julius warily watch, listen, and cooperate.

John's discourse on the grape contrasts with Julius's explanation of his affection for the fruit given a few pages later:

> Now, ef dey's an'thing a nigger lub, nex' ter 'possum, en chick'n, en watermill-yums, it's scuppernon's. Dey ain' nuffin dat kin stan' up side'n de scuppernon' fer sweetness; sugar ain't a suckumstance ter scuppernon'. W'en de season is nigh 'bout ober, en de grapes begin ter swivel up des a little wid de wrinkles er ole age,—w'en de skin get sof' en brown,—den de scuppernon' make you smack yo' lip en roll yo' eye en wush fer mo'; so I reckon it ain' very 'stonishin' dat niggers lub scuppernon'. (13)

We are some distance from John's utterance here. Julius's diction is, of course, the most immediate contrast with John's description. John is educated and his vocabulary is frequently Latinate and polysyllabic; Julius is illiterate, and roughly half of his vocabulary, in this passage and elsewhere, is rendered as mispronunciations or transformations of Standard English words. And yet in the context, Julius's dialect words are more evocative than their standard counterparts. "Watermill*yums*" and "*suckum*stance" better express his gustatory pleasure than do their dictionary equivalents. "Scuppernon'" drops the word's final diphthong, leaving its last syllable open, allowing the word to linger in the mouth. Julius mispronounces "shrivel" as "swivel," but, in so doing, he describes the grape pivoting on its stem to catch the full force of the sun's warmth.[16]

Julius's syntax and his rhetorical purpose appear less complex than those of John. The Northerner develops his ideas with nearly syllogistic rigor. Julius, on the other hand, is content to state the same idea over and over—grapes taste good! But Julius's relish is so palpable—and rendered with such linguistic bravura—that the sequence is hardly repetitive or boring. He introduces the scuppernong as the last in a sequence of his other favorite foods, and he describes the fruit at the climactic moment of fullest ripening. John draws together vine, trellis, and sapling in a single picture, and he synthesizes past and present in the interest of future profit. Julius focuses uniquely on the succulent grape, fastening on the moment of sensual enjoyment, vividly rendered in a moment of lip-smacking, eye-rolling pleasure.

The comparison of these two passages, then, brings us back to the juxtaposition of values we discussed earlier: the contrast between the Northern capitalist, who sublimates immediate gratification in the interest of later profit, and the natural man of Africa and the South, who enjoys his senses and the moment. But before we give ourselves too easily and too completely to these contrasts, we ought to keep in mind that Julius is not ignorant of the past—he is John and Annie's historical tutor on slavery—and he is not indifferent to the future. Julius clearly stages the storytelling scene that follows in hopes of retaining his personal use of the grapes. In fact, the more we consider the scene, the more we suspect that Julius's lip smacking and eye rolling is contrived, part of a performance, based on real enjoyment, to be sure, but stylized for a particular audience. His language becomes the particular stylization of vernacular that we have called minstrel speech. In this conversation and in the tale that follows, Julius is staking his claim to a fair portion of the land's fruit, but he is doing so in a way that will not threaten John. In this performance, Julius reassures John that he is not his competitor—the stereotypical behavior signals his inadaptation for capitalistic sublimation and investment—so he can be John's helper.

Just at the moment when the story's oppositions start to sort themselves into a familiar pattern, they dissolve again. The protean Julius seems to settle into the shape of the conventional plantation darky only to announce the factiousness of this incarnation. Julius's pleasure in the instant becomes performance focused on the future. Then who is Julius? His comfort in nature and his delight in the moment seem genuine: the pile of grape skins at his feet, accumulated before John and Annie's arrival, proves his obvious affection for this fruit. But his trickster skills are also real and consummate, as this story and each subsequent story amply demonstrate. So, then, how much of his behavior in this scene is pure pleasure and how much is planned performance? Chesnutt, in creating the Julius and John stories, self-consciously used and subverted the assumptions of white plantation fiction; Julius, the artist within these tales, also exploits and transforms white fictions of black behavior.

Annie tries to get to the truth of Julius as he concludes his first tale: "Is that story true?" she asks. "It's des ez true ez I'm a-settin' here" (33), Julius answers. As straightforward an answer as one could want, it would seem, until the question is asked: *why* is Julius sitting there? John and Annie drive out from town, become lost in the woods, and eventually find their way into the gothic precincts of a decayed plantation. There they come upon Julius, alone, seated on a log, almost as if waiting for them. A romantic interpretation, in the spirit of Julius's supernatural tale, would encourage us to see him as an emanation of nature, like Henry the conjured slave, human kin to the vine. But if we choose to look at the scene from a less romantic perspective, we might surmise that, in a small town like Patesville, Julius would know that the recently arrived Northerners were interested in the vineyard from which he derived a significant income. Julius's surprising presence in the vineyard at the time of their visit would then be purposeful, and his response—"des ez true ez I'm a-settin' here"—offers a pragmatic definition of truth. The tale, he tells us, is like his waiting presence on the plantation, the response to a specific situation. Annie is an epistemological realist who assumes that there is a reality independent of the narratives we construct about it. Julius is a pragmatist: the truth of a story resides not in the ultimate ontological status of the events it describes, but in its usefulness in the present circumstances.[17]

I would like to conclude this discussion of the former slave and the white plantation owner by turning to the John and Old Master tradition evoked at the beginning of this chapter. There is considerable variety in this oral folk tradition. The slave often succeeds in outwitting his master, but not always. Sometimes he is caught out and pays with a severe beating or even with his life. In other instances, both slave and master are made to appear foolish. Nonetheless, there are several features that are fairly constant in this cycle, and they make a useful contrast with Chesnutt's stories. The first of these is the lack among slave tricksters of the "strong communal ethos" found in the analogous African folk tradition.[18] In the American stories, the nimble-witted slave most often acts for himself alone, and he may even cause another black person to suffer. Such individualism should not surprise us under a slave system that divided tribes and families and that exploited the division between field hands and house slaves. Julius, to be sure, shrewdly protects his own interest, but unlike earlier slave tricksters, he also looks out for his fellows, gaining employment for his relatives and a church for his community.

A second point to note in the antebellum encounters between the slave John and the white man who owns him is that they never effect a fundamental change in the relationship between the two men or in the social context of that relationship. Old Master will always try to force John to do his will, and John will always try to resist. There will be temporary victories and setbacks on both sides, but—barring death or escape—the same drama will continually replay itself against the same psychological and social background. A comparison between "Philly Me York," a John and Old Master story collected by Zora Neale Hurston, and Chesnutt's "Mars Jeems's Nightmare" will reveal Chesnutt's revision of this tradition. In Hurston's oral tale, the master leaves his plantation for Philly Me York, a city in the North, and he puts his slave John in charge during his absence. What follows is a comic carnival with John donning his master's clothes, smoking his cigars, and inviting the other slaves into the manor house for a party. Unfortunately for John, the master returns, his face dirtied to disguise his identity, to spy on his slave. The master quickly ends the party and prepares to punish John by hanging him from a persimmon tree. John's trickster skills rescue him once again. With the help of another slave he simulates lightning, frightening the master and gaining his own freedom. There are similarities between this tale and Chesnutt's story, and it is likely that Chesnutt knew a version of it.[19] Both narratives deal with metamorphoses: in the tale collected by Hurston, slave becomes master, and master becomes poor white; in Chesnutt's story, master becomes slave, then master again. However, in Chesnutt's tale, the transformations are more profound and consequential. The white man becomes physically and socially black, and, even after his return to his former status, he remains, to an important degree, "black," that is, capable of viewing the world from the slave's perspective. Mars Jeems, the white black man, stands as the emblem for the blurring of binaries, which is the work of Chesnutt's Julius and John stories.

Henry B. Wonham, concluding his otherwise perceptive and useful analysis of these tales, goes too far and then not far enough in characterizing the relationship between black and white figured in them. He sees "inevitable cultural synthesis" (54) in the grapevine twining among the saplings, recalling his earlier reading of this metaphor as "blending and hybridization" (16). Chesnutt does indeed anticipate racial amalgamation in his essays, but that is not described here. The hybridization of a grapevine with a sapling—

to say nothing of a grape arbor—is a botanical impossibility, and it is not anticipated, even metaphorically, in the Julius and John tales. Wonham then argues that the tales "begin and end with an affirmation of stark intellectual inequality, an affirmation inscribed in the very linguistic differences that clearly mark Julius as an illiterate speaker. Moreover, the permanent discontinuity between John's Latinate, bourgeois idiom and Julius's earthy black dialect implicitly nullifies the very range of social possibilities that the stories ostensibly seek to open up, social possibilities that exist somewhere between John's and Julius's mutually exclusive worlds, in a cultural space the dialect tales can only vaguely suggest."[20]

The range of options Wonham imagines is too limited: there are other possibilities between hybridization at one extreme and containment in mutually exclusive worlds at the other. Between harmony and cacophony, there is the possibility of polyphony; between unanimity and competing solipsistic monologues, there is the alternative of dialogue. In the case of Julius and John, two different voices speak in turn, each retaining its distinctive accent and perspective. Each voice listens and hears the other voice; each voice is altered by this contact, momentarily entering the other's world, and in the process, helping the speakers, and their modern listeners, overcome the illusion of essential racial difference.

6

Race in Chesnutt's
Short Fiction

The "Line" and the "Web"

Mulattoes, most certainly, are terms of mediation, partaking of two
fundamentally opposed forces. —HENRY LOUIS GATES JR., *Figures in
Black*

In 1887 when Chesnutt introduced Julius McAdoo to the readers of the
Atlantic Monthly, he described him simply as a "venerable looking colored
man."[1] However, in 1899 when he revised "The Goophered Grapevine" for
inclusion in *The Conjure Woman,* Chesnutt added to this description. Julius,
we are told in the revised version, "was not entirely black, and this fact,
together with the quality of his hair . . . suggested a slight strain of other
than negro blood" (9–10). With this retrospective clarification of Julius's
racial identity, Chesnutt created his first important mulatto character. The
fact that he has a white antecedent is of relatively little importance for Julius's
identity; his situation as a former slave, his poverty, and his lack of formal
education mark him as fully "black" within his community. In other short
fictions, several of which are explored in this chapter, Chesnutt constructed
his racial narratives around characters whose ancestry and identity were
more ambiguous. People of mixed blood, most of whom would be a good
deal lighter than Julius, were to be Chesnutt's enduring preoccupation, and

they were to provide the protagonists for all but one of his six novels and the central figures for many of his stories.

This chapter discusses Chesnutt's use of mixed-race characters in his short fiction to challenge America's racial binaries. Chesnutt's interest in Americans of mixed ancestry reflects, of course, his own status as a Negro who could easily be mistaken for white. This focus on light-skinned blacks was, however, more than an autobiographical indulgence. Chesnutt returned again and again to the world of the Anglo-African because it was the ambiguous area where the arbitrary, socially conditioned nature of racist thinking could be most easily exposed. Racist ideology insists on rigidly exclusive categories: blacks and whites are fundamentally and immutably different, biologically and morally. So great are these differences, the racist argues, there can be no mixing of the races, and where it has occurred, an individual with the slightest African ancestry must be treated as a full black. But the existence of people of mixed blood contradicted the assumptions of absolute racial difference; mulattoes were living proof that desire and love had drawn whites and blacks together in ways that revealed their essential similarity. Moreover, mulattoes—full Negroes under the law and in racist ideology— often differed little in appearance, behavior, and achievement from whites. Life along the color line, with individuals moving back and forth across a supposedly uncrossable gulf, is a world of slipping signifiers, a world where the artificial, socially and historically conditioned nature of our thinking about race is most evident. Charles Duncan explains that Chesnutt's fiction "does much more than place binary oppositions in conflict. Rather his fiction explores the shadings of the people he writes about; or, more metaphorically, it plays among the shadows that in large measure constitute human identity."[2]

People of mixed blood were central figures in African American political and literary history before and after the Civil War. Under slavery, planters believed their mixed-blood slaves to be intellectually superior to their darker property, and they often demanded higher prices for them at auction. Planters preferred light-skinned slaves as house servants, and when the mulattoes were their own offspring, they sometimes granted them freedom. During slavery, New Orleans, Charleston, and Richmond had substantial communities of free blacks, most of whom had some white ancestry. In the North before the Civil War, mixed-blood Americans, like Frederick Douglass,

William Wells Brown, and Frances E. W. Harper, were prominent in the abolitionist movement. In the South under Reconstruction, mulattoes occupied many elected or appointed government positions. Before the Civil War and after, light-colored African Americans frequently enjoyed educational and social opportunities not available to other blacks; thus they were disproportionately represented in the leadership of black churches, schools, and businesses during the second half of the nineteenth century. These facts had a tendency to produce, in addition to the white-black distinction, a brown-black demarcation within the African American community, with a real or perceived sense of superiority on one side and suspicion and resentment on the other.

Northern writers found that the image of a fair-skinned person in chains was an effective means to shock white sensibilities and mobilize sentiment against slavery. Thus abolitionist fiction from Richard Hildreth's *The Slave; or, Memoirs of Archy Moore* (1836) through William Wells Brown's *Clotel, or The President's Daughter* (1853) feature mulattoes as central figures. These protagonists were often shown as more intelligent, enterprising, and freedom loving than darker slaves, and these positive characteristics, either explicitly or implicitly, were held to be their inheritance from white ancestors. On the other hand, Southern writers who fought against emancipation and citizenship for blacks saw the mulatto as the symbol of all they opposed. After the Civil War, the opponents of Reconstruction viewed the person of mixed ancestry as an insidious figure committed to poisoning Anglo-Saxon racial purity. The rhetorical question continually raised by Thomas Dixon, the most influential antiblack novelist in American history, is this: "Shall the future American be an Anglo-Saxon or a Mulatto?"[3] Dixon was part of a long tradition of racial essentialism that held that Africans and Europeans were separate species. According to one etymological account, the word "mulatto" is itself a product of this tradition, for it derives from "mule," the sterile product of mating between a horse and an ass. The product of black-white union, this etymology suggests, was in its very nature flawed and doomed to extinction.[4]

These biological assumptions, which Werner Sollors calls the "topos of 'blood infusion,'" dominated both positive and negative representations of mulattoes from before the Civil War through the Harlem Renaissance.[5] The most important product of these representations was the "tragic mulatto."

The "tragedy" derived, first, from the fact that mulattoes could not be accommodated in America's black-white racial binaries. Even more fatally, they were often assumed to be the victims of "warring bloods," contradictory genetic inheritances that doomed them to sterility and decay. Sterling A. Brown deplored the importance of this "tragic mulatto," which he found stereotypical and nonrepresentative, in literary portraits of black America.[6] Brown's studies remain important, but recent critics have identified a countertradition in renderings of mixed-blood Americans. Werner Sollors argues that "literary representation of biracial characters . . . does not constitute an *avoidance* of more serious issues, but the most direct and head-on *engagement* with 'race.'" Similarly, Daphne Patai and Murray Graeme MacNicoll acknowledge that the mulatto figure was used to engage white attention and sympathy, but they warn that too strong an emphasis on this fact can cause us to miss the "deconstructive potentialities of the white-black character." In the same line of analysis, Henry Louis Gates Jr. describes the mulatto protagonist of Harriet E. Wilson's *Our Nig,* as "the functional equivalent within myth of the trickster figure."[7]

Gates's mention of the trickster returns us to Julius, the mulatto with whom we began, and it reminds us that Charles Chesnutt's mixed-blood characters are an important part of the countertradition to which Sollors refers. The title of Chesnutt's second short-story collection, *The Wife of His Youth and Other Stories of the Color Line,* concludes with a provocative phrase, "color line," which Chesnutt's stories challenge and deconstruct. The phrase assumes the existence of two distinct and containable categories. It further assumes that the boundary between these categories is clear and recognizable and that these boundaries are constant in time and space. None of these premises are true. Color, in the physical world, is not organized in discontinuous units but along a constantly blending spectrum. Any "lines" that arbitrarily break up this banding, dividing one segment from others, comes not from nature but from outside of it, from the choices made by observers. These choices, it follows, are not stable but vary as do all human choices. Moreover, in the matter of race, there is, in practice, not one line but several. The official black-white binary has proved unworkable, and it has unofficially been supplemented by other "lines." Among these are a variety of distinctions made between African Americans with varying proportions of white ancestry. This chapter considers the transgression of these "lines," the complication of racial identity, in five Chesnutt stories: "Her Virginia Mammy," "White Weeds," "The Wife of His Youth," "The Passing of Grandison," and "The Web of Circumstance."[8]

"Her Virginia Mammy" tells the story of Clara Hohlfelder, a young dance instructor who loves and is loved by Dr. John Winthrop. Clara has learned that the German couple who raised her are not her birth parents, and she feels that she cannot marry John until she is certain about her ancestry. She explains to John that the identity by which she has been known now "seems like a garment—something external, accessory, and not part of myself. It does not mean what one's own name would signify" (28–29). Clara's explanation displays a naive faith in language and genealogy. Words, for her, are not arbitrary signifiers attached randomly to things in the world; rather, some words give essential reality. Clara feels that family names are such words because they connect with biology and history. John Winthrop has such a name, and perhaps because of this, he is skeptical. Genealogy is a narrative, and like all narratives, it is selective and distorted. John realizes that his illustrious *Mayflower* ancestor may have been nothing more than a cook or a cabin boy; elsewhere, unrecorded, or conveniently forgotten, the family's history may contain thieves, murderers, and vagabonds. John sees the futility of Clara's search, and he advises her to abandon her morbid fixation on the past and live in the present and future of their love.

Clara's search ends in a conversation with Mrs. Harper, a mulatto friend of one of Clara's dance students. Mrs. Harper reveals that Clara's birth father, a member of one of Virginia's first families, died in a riverboat accident, leaving Clara an orphan. These events in Clara's life conform to one of the most popular patterns in nineteenth-century melodrama and sentimental fiction: the story of the orphan who discovers that she or he descends from distinguished forbearers. Clara exultantly embraces these facts and completes her personal narrative, but in the process she misses other significant details. The reader, and later John Winthrop, sees these elements and makes other deductions from Mrs. Harper's account. The mulatto woman is Clara's mother. She and Clara's white father could not live as a married couple in Virginia, and they were fleeing to France when the accident killed the father and separated the mother and the child. Clara, however, comes to an entirely different conclusion about Mrs. Harper's identity, as this exchange reveals:

"You were the colored nurse? — my 'mammy' they would have called you in my old Virginia home?"

"Yes, child I was—your mammy. Upon my bosom you have rested; my breasts once gave you nourishment; my hands once ministered to you; my arms sheltered you, and my heart loved you and mourned you like a mother loves and mourns her firstborn." (55)

Although Clara never realizes it, her reaction to this disclosure refutes her faith in language as an unequivocal guide to truth. Mrs. Harper gives Clara the facts of her birth, but she allows Clara to interpret her statements in a way that reshapes and evades the truth. This exchange between a mother and her daughter brilliantly illustrates the semantic slippage between different dialects and different levels—literal and figurative—in the American language. Crucial to this demonstration is the word "mammy." The word occurs in the story's title, and it is highlighted twice in the exchange quoted above: first by the quotation marks with which Clara encloses it and then by the dash indicating Mrs. Harper's hesitation before repeating it. The word "mammy" originates in black dialect, where it means "mother"; the word was borrowed by white planters to denote a black nurse, the surrogate mother for a white child. Clara poses the question in "white" English asking Mrs. Harper if she were her Negro nurse; Mrs. Harper answers truthfully but in dialect: she is Clara's mother.

Mrs. Harper assures her daughter that her "mother—also belonged to one of the first families of Virginia" (53), intending "belong" in its literal sense: Clara's mother was the property of the family in question. Clara assumes she is white, and since white persons cannot be property, she understands "belong" in a secondary sense, signifying membership in the family. She makes a similar assumption when she is told that her "mother's people" (57) opposed the marriage: the people in question were Mrs. Harper's owners, although Clara assumes they were her mother's legitimate blood kin. Mrs. Harper speaks the literal truth when she tells her daughter that she loved and mourned her "like a mother." The simile is equivocal: it could mean "like the mother she was" or "like the mother she resembled." Clara unhesitatingly selects the second option, for it follows the other choices she has made. From Mrs. Harper, Clara gains her family name; she is now "Virginia Stafford," but the identity she constructs around this name is no truer than that of "Clara Hohlfelder." Clara's mother and her future husband, both of whom know the truth, are complicit in Clara's self-deception. They know that their culture offers an alternative narrative for the facts of Clara's birth: the story of the tragic mulatta. But this narrative is no more a necessary or accurate account of who Clara is than the narrative she has chosen. John Winthrop and Mrs. Harper know that Clara's racial identity is a social construct and that it is irrelevant to her true worth, and so they allow Clara to embrace a white identity. Clara is a racial essentialist, but Mrs. Harper and John are subjectivists, for whom race has only that meaning we choose to give it.

Clara's conversations with Mrs. Harper and John are staged in the context of a ballroom dance lesson given by Clara to a group of middle-class blacks. Clara, who has had little previous contact with blacks, is pleasantly surprised to find that, in manners, dress, and professional attainments, these people are indistinguishable from middle-class whites. She is surprised also to note the variation in skin color among them: "From the few who were undistinguishable from pure white, the colors ran down the scale by minute gradations to the two or three brown faces at the other extremity" (35). As Clara hears her story in one room, white, tan, and brown dancers glide and spin in the next. Their graceful shifting of positions mock the assumption that human reality sorts itself into simple binaries of black and white. Clara's much more radical movement in the adjoining room—her unwitting passage from white to black to white—mocks her assumptions of a stable social order grounded in nature.

"White Weeds" is from a later period than "Her Virginia Mammy," but it also turns on a woman's problematic racial identity and the decision made about it by the man she loves; thus it provides a further elaboration of themes treated in the earlier story.[9] John Marshall Carson, a mathematics professor at a New England college, is engaged to Marian Tracy. On the eve of their wedding, Carson receives an anonymous letter telling him that his fiancée is of black ancestry. Carson shows the incriminating letter to his friend John Turnbull, president of the college where he teaches, and asks his advice about what he should do. Turnbull offers several suggestions, including the one he personally favors: simply dismissing the whole matter. Turnbull realizes, however, that Carson must decide the matter for himself:

"A gentleman of your character and antecedents can hardly fail to select a course consistent with—"

"With honor," murmured the poor professor. (394)

Carson descends from the Southern aristocracy, and he assumes that his actions will be guided by the innate ethical sense of his class.

Carson proceeds with the marriage, but on his wedding night, he presents his wife with the charge made about her ancestry and asks her to respond. Marian asks why he is concerned, and Carson explains that, although he lives and teaches in the North, he is a Southerner. "His father had been a planter, with wide estates and numerous slaves. His mother had suffered deeply in her pride and her affections, because of some poor unfortunate of color. With his mother's milk he had drunk in a deadly antipathy to the thought of any personal relation between white people and black but that of master and servant." "It is part of me," he tells Marian. "Nothing could ever make me feel that the touch of a Negress was not pollution." Marian dryly asks, "How white . . . must one be, to come within the protection of the code of Southern chivalry?" For Carson, a racial essentialist, there are no degrees: "men and women are either white or black. Those who are not all white are all black" (401–2). Marian coolly refuses to answer the charge, and their marriage is never consummated. Weakened in mind and body by harassing doubts, Carson dies shortly after the marriage.

Two sets of questions pose themselves. The first are about Carson's behavior, the second about Marian's. Carson's racial essentialism leads him to assume that certain people—well-born whites—are by birth morally superior to others. Marian's query about Southern chivalry pointedly calls this assumption into question. Carson insists that he is defending his mother's honor. But what, Marian asks, about the honor of the colored woman, presumably Carson's father's slave mistress? Two cultural fictions conjoin to prevent Carson from seriously considering the wrong done to the colored woman. First is the myth of the white aristocrat's innate sense of honor, and the second is the myth of the mulatto's equally innate treachery. The second myth corroborates the first in Carson's judgment on his father and his mistress. The guilt in this sexual transgression must fall uniquely on the mulatto woman. Carson's racial paranoia causes him to entertain the possibility that Marian has deliberately concealed an important part of her background. In the vacant space of Marian's silence, Carson inscribes the cultural narrative of the deceitful mulatta, which he has learned from his mother and from Southern culture.[10]

Marian's own actions require some discussion. Her closest friend's husband tells Turnbull that Marian's family's racial reputation is impeccable, so Marian's refusal to speak should not be taken as an admission of guilt, nor as an attempt to hide a secret. This is not to say that her friend's version is ultimately "true": neither her friend nor Marian herself can have absolute knowledge of all Marian's antecedents. Her family genealogy is a narrative, with all that implies about selectivity and bias. The point is, however, that her narrative is socially accredited, and this validation alone would be more than enough to crush an unsigned and unsubstantiated smear. But Marian refuses to invoke her family's social credentials or even to deny the allegation. She understands that Carson's problem is not in her past but in his mind: if Carson could not free himself from his racial fears, no answer she could give would help him.

Marian's behavior after her husband's death is even more singular. Mourners arriving at Carson's funeral are surprised to find the widow clothed entirely in white and her home bedecked with flowers as for a wedding. Equally surprising is the musical entertainment Marian provides. She has hired an orchestra, which performs three selections. One of these, Gustav Graben-Hoffman's "Der Shönste Engel" (1888), is a love song and, one would think, hardly appropriate for a funeral. Despite this fact, the narrator notes that, even among the mourners who did not understand the German lyrics, "there was a vague intuition that the song was of a piece with the other unusual features of the occasion" (397). Indeed, it is. Here are the lyrics, minus repeats, followed by my prose translation:

> Ich sah dich unter Blühten, doch kam dir keine gleich,
> die Lilien erglühten, die Rosen wurden bleich,
> Manch Sternlein schient herneider,
> du bist das reinste Licht,
> du bist von Gottes Liedern das lieblichste Gedicht;
> gehst du von den Mängeln der Welt zum Himmel ein,
> so wirst du unter Engeln der schönste Engle sein.[11]

* * *

I saw you among the flowers, none could compare with you,
The lilies glowed with color, the roses turned pale,
many stars shine down,
you are the purest light,
in God's song you are the loveliest verse;
when you leave the world's insufficiencies for heaven
you will, among the angels, be the loveliest angel.

The song is for a baritone voice, so normally it is addressed to a woman. But this performance has been commissioned by Marian, and it is her sarcastic tribute to her high-minded spouse. This chivalrous Southerner was an "angel." His pure light outshined that of the stars, and his story was a verse in God's divine story. Too pure for this world, he has fled it for paradise. Most relevant to Marian's situation are the song's first two lines. Her husband's pure beauty turned everything to its opposites: roses lost their hue and lilies took on color.

Marian's other "funeral" music is equally paradoxical; both selections are by Wagner: Wolfram's aria "O du mein holder Abendstern" from *Tannhäuser* and the wedding march from *Lohengrin*. Both, of course, are songs of love rather than death, but both are, in their Wagnerian settings, ironically relevant to John Marshall Carson. In the instance of Wolfram's song, Tannhäuser has violated his chivalric code by joining Venus's cult of profane love, causing Elisabeth, who loves him, to die of a broken heart. Wolfram, who faithfully watches over Elisabeth, prays that the evening star will guide her to heaven. In the instance of the famous wedding march, this music is performed at the nuptials of Lohengrin and Elsa. Lohengrin earlier has defended Elsa's honor against Frederick's calumnies, and he has agreed to marry Elsa, on condition that she never seek to know his name and history. Shortly after the wedding, Elsa, goaded by Frederick, breaks her vow and forces Lohengrin to disclose his identity. His secret known, Lohengrin returns to Monsalvat, his wedding unconsummated. Heard in their operatic contexts, these musical selections comment on the person reposing in the casket. Both operas sing of love that is frustrated and of honor that is betrayed.

These musical references form part of the profoundly paradoxical texture of the service Marian has constructed. She is, as Turnbull exclaims when he learns her story, "a widow, and yet no wife!" (403). This is only one of the ways her story confounds familiar oppositions. Marian was a wife who remained a virgin, a white woman who became "black." Carson is a mathematician controlled by irrational fears, a Northerner in thrall to Southern prejudice. Most important, he is an aristocrat whose code of honor causes him to dishonor himself and the woman he loves. Together, John and Marian entered a marriage that brought not love and life but suspicion and death. In the spirit of these paradoxes, Marian's service reverses important polarities: sorrow is expressed as joy, and black becomes white. The story's title, "White Weeds," refers to Marian's mourning attire, but it also alludes to the rancorous growth in the white man's mind. This "seed" produced "a harvest of suspicion and distrust" (403), destroying Carson's marriage and his health.

John Turnbull, the character through whom much of this story is focalized, contributes to its ironic texture. When Turnbull first sees Marian moving up the aisle on her wedding day, he murmurs, "Clothed in white samite, Mystic, wonderful" (395). The lines, from Tennyson's "Morte d'Arthur," seem as incongruous at this wedding as do Marian's musical choices at Carson's funeral. They refer to the arm of the Lady of the Lake handing the sword Excalibur to Arthur. In the poem, the description is retrospective. Camelot has fallen, and Arthur is mortally wounded. Arthur charges Sir Bedivere to return the sword to the lake whence it came, and in so doing he remembers the white-clad arm that emerged from the depths to give him the symbol of his power and responsibility. At this point, Turnbull knows only what Carson has told him: that Marian's reputation has been attacked and that Carson promises to act according to the honor of his caste. Turnbull's vision of Marian, then, is penetrated by a sense of the grave moral responsibility that she has placed on Carson, a responsibility to which he proves inadequate.

"Her Virginia Mammy" and "White Weeds" tell the stories of women whose personal histories contain mysteries about their racial origins. In both cases, these mysteries are explained by recourse to familiar cultural narratives: John Winthrop makes Clara Hohlfelder "white" by allowing her to believe herself the aristocratic orphan; John Carson's irrational fear of a black threat to white racial purity makes Marian Tracy a deceitful mulatta. In both instances these racial attributions are biologically inaccurate; nonetheless, these personal and social constructions have powerful consequences in the lives of the characters in question. Both stories challenge familiar racial categories. "White Weeds," in its numerous, ironic references to chivalry, also attacks the assumption of inheritable moral characteristics—aristocratic "honor"—which sustains racial essentialism.

"The Wife of His Youth," the title story in Chesnutt's *The Wife of His Youth and Other Stories of the Color Line,* has no white characters, but it also explores a color demarcation, the boundary between light and dark in the African American community. The story opens in the home of Mr. Ryder, a self-educated but highly literate member of the black middle class, as he prepares to host a gathering of the Blue Vein Society. This group of light-skinned mulattoes regularly congregates in genteel sessions that imitate the gatherings occurring in elegant white homes elsewhere in the city. We have met a member of this group, Mr. Simon Sadler, in "Her Virginia Mammy." Sadler was among the mulattoes learning fashionable dance steps from Clara Hohlfelder. Sadler explained to Clara Hohlfelder that members of his group deplored being categorized with darker blacks. "The more advanced of us," he complains, meaning those with the lightest skins, "are not numerous enough to make the fine distinctions that are possible among white people" (38), and so they must socialize with darker blacks. Thus these mulatto dance students mimic white society's color prejudice, just as they imitate white notions of genteel entertainment. Other blacks resent the Blue Vein Society's color prejudice, but the society members see themselves as leaders of their race. However, the language with which the club 's defenders articulate their group's purposes unintentionally satirizes their pretensions. The society was, in the minds of its members, "a life-boat, an anchor, a bulwark and a shield,—a pillar of cloud by day and of fire by night, to guide their people through the social wilderness" (2). This ill-assorted catalog of nautical, military, and biblical metaphors is an exaggerated and parodic instance of high literary English. This rhetoric tends to confirm rather than deny the assertion that the group has adopted the values and language of the dominant white culture.

As the story begins, Mr. Ryder is preparing to host a ball at which he will announce his engagement to Molly Dixon. His union with this cultivated, light-skinned widow will crown his ascent to the highest level of mixed-blood society. He turns to canonical white literature for words to articulate his feeling. He searches his beloved Tennyson for lines with which to toast his fiancée and comes upon these:

> At length I saw a lady within call,
> Stiller than chisell'd marble standing there;
> A daughter of the gods, divinely tall,
> And most divinely fair. (8)

His poetic research is interrupted by the appearance at his door of a stranger, a woman distinctly different from the one evoked by the English poet. His visitor is short and dark, so dark, in fact, that her toothless gums appear blue—an ironic trope on the blue veins upon which the mulattoes pride themselves. The stranger asks Ryder if he has "ever heerd of a merlatter man by de name er Sam Taylor 'quirin' roun' in de chu'ches ermongs' de people fer his wife 'Liza Jane?" (11). She tells Ryder her story in a heavy dialect that contrasts starkly with Tennyson's verse and Ryder's own polished diction. Liza Jane was separated more than twenty-five years ago from her husband when he escaped from slavery, and since emancipation she has sought him in the North and in the South. Ryder can offer her no information, but he takes her name and address, and she withdraws. Later that evening he tells her story to his assembled guests and announces that Liza Jane, who has returned, is the wife of his youth.

The story juxtaposes the different histories and social circumstances of two groups within the black community. On the one hand, there are the educated Northern mulattoes, many of whom were free before the abolition of slavery and able to benefit from the economic and social opportunities offered by Reconstruction; on the other hand, there are the masses of former slaves, uneducated and propertyless, trapped in the aftermath of Reconstruction's failure. The story also juxtaposes two different languages—the literate, highly rhetorical "white" English spoken by the mulatto elite and the black dialect of the masses. The coming together of these two languages in the story's denouement dramatizes the reconciliation of these two groups. After hearing Liza Jane's story, Ryder records her name and address on the flyleaf of his Tennyson volume. When Ryder tells Liza Jane's story to his guests, he abandons the rhetorical mode in which he has begun and tells it in "the same soft dialect" (20) Liza Jane had used. His audience is moved both by the story he tells and by the language in which he tells it, and they concur in his decision to recognize Liza Jane as his wife. When Ryder brings his narrative to a close, however, he returns to Standard English and he quotes Shakespeare. Thus at the end of the story, black dialect and Elizabethan English, the words of a former slave and those of our language's greatest poet, are granted equal stature in the same discourse.

The story is an allegory of the relationship between the black bourgeoisie and the recently emancipated black masses. Ryder, a member of the privileged minority, accepts his responsibility for one of the deprived majority. It is usually assumed that Ryder does this because he acknowledges his "true identity" as Sam Taylor, the slave husband of Liza Jane. Chesnutt himself seemed to support such an interpretation in a 1901 interview.[12] However, I would like to suggest that Ryder's identity within the story is less certain. He receives Liza Jane, listens to her story, and she withdraws, but there is no surprise, no consternation, and no overt sign of recognition by him or her during this encounter. A quarter of a century has passed, it is true, and it has surely brought changes in both individuals, but Sam Taylor and Liza Jane lived together in the closest possible intimacy, and so we might expect some startled spark of recognition during their reunion. But none is recorded. More significant, Liza Jane reports that Sam "wuz one er de triflin'es' han's on de plantation. I 'spec's ter haf ter suppo't 'im w'en I fin' 'im, fer he nebber would work 'less'n he had ter" (15). It is hard to find Ryder in this portrait; it is difficult to believe that the man who lifted himself to economic independence and social prominence by industry and thrift was ever "triflin." Can we imagine Ryder allowing himself to be supported by his wife? In fact, he does the opposite, supporting Liza Jane in her final years. Moreover, if Liza Jane really sees Ryder as Taylor, her unflattering description of her former husband would be a poor strategy for winning his compassion. There is some ambiguity about whether Mr. Ryder is Sam Taylor, about whether he was, in fact, Liza Jane's slave husband.

This ambiguity does not fundamentally change the story's meaning; in fact, it accentuates it. Regardless of his prior history, the man we meet in his drawing room at the beginning of the story *is not* Sam Taylor. That identity, if it ever existed for Ryder, is hundreds of miles and a quarter of a century distant. It was a name and an identity imposed on a slave by a master, and Ryder is under no legal or moral obligation to recognize it. Ryder accepts this identity in a singular act of generosity and solidarity. The man we watch at the end of the story *is* Sam Taylor because he chooses that identity and the responsibilities that go with it. Thus, in this way, Chesnutt extends his meditation on racial identity as a choice—made by the individual or imposed by others—rather than a biological or legal given. Clara Hohlfelder, with the tacit assent of Mrs. Harper and John Winthrop, chooses her racial identity. Similarly, John Carson imposes, in his own mind at least, an identity on Marian Tracy. Mr. Ryder, for his part, decides to stand with the ex-slave rather than the mulatto elite.

There is, in these stories, no "true" racial identity in the sense of a biological key to one's essential personhood. Nonetheless, certain identities are better than others in their personal and social implications. Clara's identity is good in that it allows her to love and share the lives of both her mother and John Winthrop. Her story is unusual in this regard, for "passing" in fiction almost always entails the sacrifice of one's family and some psychological suffering on the part of the one who passes. These difficulties are conveniently absent in Clara's situation. John Carson's choice is clearly bad in that it poisons his marriage and, finally, his own mind. Ryder's choice is good in that it saves not only Liza Jane, but it awakens his color-struck friends to their larger social responsibilities.

The story is usually read, correctly, as a ringing endorsement of racial solidarity and a repudiation of the color prejudice expressed by Simon Sadler. And yet, it is also the case that Ryder's decision widens the gap it means to heal. Ryder's story follows a pattern established in abolitionist and Reconstruction novels: the mulatto who remains true to the dark race, either by returning South to free slaves before emancipation, or by educating them afterward. This positive figure countered negative stereotypes of the mulatto scheming to pollute white America. "Far from social subversives, mulattoes become in these novels the best racial advertisement an apologist for black America could show to a skeptical and defensive post–Civil War white America."[13] To reassure white Americans, writers supporting black citizens were eager to prove their worthiness according to white codes. It should not surprise us, then, that the narratives they constructed resembled narratives already circulating within white culture. The story of noble-spirited mulattoes aiding uneducated former slaves echoed countless missionary reports of idealistic white evangelists assisting primitive Africans. The "white man's burden" became the "bright man's burden."

Ryder's noble gesture deserves our admiration, but it has paradoxical consequences. The paradox of noblesse oblige is that it separates what it purports to unite. The uniting obligation is accepted precisely because one of the parties is *noble,* that is, socially and morally superior to the other. For Ryder to be noble, he must sacrifice; for him to sacrifice, his union with Liza Jane must cost him dearly. And indeed it does. He will share his marriage bed with wrinkled, toothless Liza Jane, not lovely Molly Dixon. His evenings will be spent around the kitchen fire comforting the old woman, rather than in the drawing room discussing Tennyson with his educated friends. The extravagance of Ryder's gesture works against its healing import, calling attention to the real distance between the two black communities. The point here is not to denounce Ryder's choice, which is a good in its social effect. I simply wish to call attention to the fact that our control of the narratives we invoke, like that of our language, is only partial. There are always more meanings than we consciously understand and intend. Our language and our cultural narratives reflect the conflicted values of our society, and so inevitably do the identities we construct.

Ryder unintentionally illustrates this point with the Shakespearean verses he cites in introducing Liza Jane as his wife:

> This above all: to thine own self be true,
> And it must follow, as the night the day,
> Thou canst not then be false to any man. (22)

These are, of course, Polonius's words of counsel to Laertes in *Hamlet*. They were, in the 1880s as they are today, among the great truisms of genteel morality. Out of their context the lines seem to endorse Ryder's decision. But read within Shakespeare's play, Polonius's pompous advice is banal and useless, particularly if applied to the play's tragic hero. The problem for Hamlet is not truth to himself, but to *which* self? His father's avenger, his mother's protector, Ophelia's lover: these are among the numerous contending "selves" to whom Hamlet must somehow be "true." This is the complexity that Ryder and the story elide by recourse to Polonius's famous platitude. To which self is the story's protagonist faithful: Sam Taylor or Mr. Ryder? Is he a loving husband reunited with his mate, or a benevolent aristocrat bending to lift up one less fortunate? These are crucial differences because they imply different relationships between this man and woman and for the two communities they represent. Ryder's use of Shakespeare at this key juncture is as disjunct from his actual situation, as was his earlier quoting of Tennyson's "Dream of Fair Women." Liza Jane manifestly is not a fair woman, and Ryder's own condition more closely resembles Hamlet's fractured self than it does Polonius's fatuous complacency. Ryder is still attempting to read his situation through English literature. And this reading distorts as much as it clarifies.

There is another fiction in Chesnutt's color-line collection that sheds light on how identities are constructed for and by blacks. The story is about passing, or so its title—"The Passing of Grandison"—suggests. The narrative recounts a black man's passage from slavery in the South to freedom in Canada, but it can also be read as a commentary on "passing" in the sense of movement across established boundaries of racial identity. There is, indeed, a historical connection between these two meanings. Werner Sollors finds the first American use of "passing" as a synonym for racial concealment in reward posters for runaway slaves from the 1830s. These advertisements warn that the light-skinned fugitives might try to "pass" as whites.[14] Grandison, however, is dark, and he never attempts to imitate a white man: on the contrary, the further he goes in his passage to freedom, the "darker" he seems to get. It is in this ironic paradox that Grandison's story provides a surprising gloss on "passing" and a commentary on the construction of the black person's identity.

In this tale, Dick Owens, the son of a Kentucky slave owner, wishes to impress his abolitionist lady friend by assisting one of his father's slaves to escape to freedom. He asks his father's permission to take his personal servant, Tom, with him on a trip North. Dick's father, Colonel Owens, counts himself an expert on "the subject of negroes, having studied them . . . for a great many years and . . . understanding them perfectly" (176–77). The colonel suspects that Tom can read and that he would flee if given the chance, so he prefers that his son take Grandison. The latter is illiterate and, the planter believes, the very embodiment of black fidelity. And so Grandison seems. Before his departure, the black man loudly proclaims that a slave is happier than any free man, and he expresses his fear and contempt for abolitionists. After their departure, Dick continually engineers conditions for Grandison's escape, but the slave steadfastly refuses freedom. Finally, Dick has Grandison held captive in Canada until he can return home to

Kentucky without his black retainer. Dick is only temporarily successful, however, for a month after his return, Grandison shows up, claiming to have escaped his Canadian captors and to have fled South.

Colonel Owens is transported; his faith in the slave's love of his master, temporarily shaken by Grandison's disappearance, has been richly confirmed. He orders that Grandison's marriage to his slave fiancée proceed amid general rejoicing and feasting. However, a few weeks after his return, Grandison escapes with his new bride, his mother, father, aunt, brothers, and sisters. Grandison and his entourage are last seen crossing the lake to Canada. The black man, it turns out, had used his absence to prepare an underground rail route, and he returned to guide his entire family to freedom. After the slave's return, Dick had expressed reservations about Grandison's colorful account of escape from abolitionist kidnappers and his flight backward to the Kentucky plantation. Grandison's tale is an extraordinary *reversal* of the slave narrative: the black man craftily eludes abolitionists, and keeping the North Star always at his back, heroically wins his way back to slavery. Even dim-witted Dick finds this a bit much. "Nonsense," his father warmly protests; the tale is "the gospel truth!" (199), and, he feels, "Mr. Simms or some other one of our Southern authors ought to write it up" (199). And, indeed, they already had. William Gilmore Simms, the most popular antebellum Southern writer, was an ardent defender of slavery, and his novels present contented slaves within a benevolent plantation system. He was not alone among slavery's literary defenders. In the three years following the publication of *Uncle Tom's Cabin* (1852), Southern writers produced at least fourteen proslavery novels. Written to counter Stowe's powerful narrative, these Southern fictions tried to present a reality that contradicted hers at every point. They prominently featured slaves who loved their masters, slaves who feared abolitionists, and slaves who witnessed freedom in the North and either yearned for or returned to slavery in the South: in short, the essential ingredients of Grandison's elaborate fiction of servile loyalty.[15]

Grandison passes from Kentucky to Canada and from slavery to freedom. But this passage is made possible by another passing across the conventional racial typologies. Grandison's seemingly solid identity turns out to have been a hollow mask: he had been passing for many years as a "faithful nigger" (199). We are never given direct access to Grandison's inner life, and thus he remains something of a mystery, but it is apparent in retrospect that he was a freedom-loving black man, courageous enough to risk his life and freedom to rescue the ones he loved. He has kept this identity secret and has for many years performed the role of docile slave of plantation myth. Colonel Owens believes so deeply in this myth that he is blind to Grandison's plan to free his family. It is not that the colonel misses key facts; it is just that his cultural assumptions cause him to misread them. The planter is convinced that Grandison will never flee: "he's too fond of good eating, to risk losing his regular meals," he tells Dick, "besides, he's sweet on your mother's maid, Betty" (177–78). It is precisely Grandison's love of Betty that causes him to come back to free her—and to enjoy one final feast at Owens's table. Grandison's identity results not from anything intrinsic to his biological or moral nature, but from what others are able to see through their cultural filters. The story of Grandison's passing is, as Charles Duncan argues, "a sophisticated examination of identity formation."[16] Here is Duncan's commentary on the way the Kentucky planter interprets his slaves' behavior:

> Colonel Owens thereby devises a sliding scale for his slaves based on their relative abilities to "read." Ironically, he places Tom—who can *only* "read"—on the untrustworthy end of the spectrum while overlooking (or "misreading") the more potent threat to his ownership: Grandison can not only read, but in addition possesses a refined and subversive ability to *write* his own identity, albeit in code. (160)

Or to phrase it differently, Grandison *plagiarizes* a fictive identity, inscribing it within the existing codes of white Southern mythology. Grandison, like Julius McAdoo, is a trickster. He uses the white man's cherished stereotypes, creating an identity that allows him to manipulate and defeat his white adversary. In its consideration of "passing," this story asserts that it is not just the identity of mulattoes that is fictive, but that of many dark African Americans as well. The story calls attention to the fact that self-consciously acting according to expected forms of black behavior can, its own way, be as much an act of "passing" as pretending to be white. This is not to judge either behavior, for these stories show that both can be justified according to the situation. Rather, what Chesnutt's smudging of color lines shows is the artificiality of those lines, their susceptibility to erasure and transformation.

The final story in *The Wife of His Youth and Other Stories of the Color Line* recounts another, tragically unsuccessful attempt to move from one pattern of expectations to another. Ben Davis, the protagonist of "The Web of Circumstance," is an enterprising Negro blacksmith in a small Southern town after the war. He does not want to be a "nigger," and he has embraced, as piously as young Chesnutt in his diary, the premises of the American success story. "We colored folks never had no chance ter git nothin' befo' de wah," he explains, "but ef eve'y nigger in dis town had a tuck keer er his money sence de wah, like I has, an' bought ez much lan' as I has, de niggers might 'a' got haf de lan' by dis time" (293). Unlike Chesnutt's predictions in "The Future American," Ben's accumulation of capital does not "throw . . . a golden glow over a dark complexion"; rather it stirs white resentment against him, as in this comment from one of his less industrious neighbors: "'Pears ter me Ben gettin' mighty blooded" (292). Ben's faith in the American dream of success and acceptance through hard work collides with the narrative of niggerhood. The whip of Colonel Thornton is stolen and Ben is accused, tried, and convicted of the theft. The prosecutor argues that "men might lie, but circumstances cannot." The trial, however, proves the opposite, for "facts" have no meaning outside the narrative used to organize and interpret them. Ben is black, ergo he is a "nigger," ergo he is guilty. Even Ben's claims of innocence are interpreted as proof of the contrary: "I've tuck up more'n a hundred niggers fer stealin' . . . an' I never seed one yit that did n' 'ny it ter the las'" (302), explains the arresting constable. Most cruelly ironic is the way Ben's belief in justice is turned against him by the prosecutor:

> the defendant is a man of dangerous character, a surly, impudent fellow; a man whose views of property are prejudicial to the welfare of society, and who has been heard to assert that half the property which is owned in this county has been stolen, and that, if justice were done, the white people ought to divide up the land with the negroes; in other words, a negro nihilist, a communist, a secret devotee of Tom Paine and Voltaire, a pupil of the anarchist propaganda. (298)

It does not matter that Ben "could not have told the difference between a propaganda and a potato" (299); he is an ambitious black man, and this is a dangerous provocation to Southern racial doctrine. One might expect that Ben's industry would count for him at his trial, but to the contrary, the judge cites this behavior to justify the severe sentence he is about to impose:

> You are not an ignorant, shiftless fellow, but a man of more than ordinary intelligence among your people, and one who ought to know better. You have not even the poor excuse of having stolen to satisfy hunger or a physical appetite. . . . I can only regard your crime as a result of a tendency to offenses of this nature, a tendency which is only too common among your people. (311)

The final twist in the perverse misreading of Ben's character occurs when, after his release from prison, his innocent flight is misinterpreted, and he is shot down in the road by a white man.

The story, and the collection of which it is part, ends with the narrator's attempt to peer into the future.

> Some time, we are told, when the cycle of years has rolled around, there is to be another golden age, when all men will dwell together in love and harmony, and when peace and righteousness shall prevail for a thousand years. God Speed the day, and let not the shining thread of hope become so enmeshed in the web of circumstance that we lose sight of it; but give us here and there, and now and then, some little foretaste of this golden age, that we may the more patiently and hopefully await its coming! (322–23)

The narrative paradigm embraced here is not the one endorsed in the journals and in "The Future American." The narrator of "The Web of Circumstance" does not invoke the secular myth of inevitable democratic progress. The story thoroughly debunks the relevance of the American success story for the former slave, and it appeals instead to Christian eschatology. The narrator prays that a beneficent creator might, in the fullness of time, deliver his people from injustice. But even in this prayer there is a hint of doubt: "we are told"—the Christian promise of a harmonious golden age is also a narrative. Perhaps it also is a myth.

The final entry in the sequence of "stories of the color line" changes the controlling metaphor from "line" to "web." A line is one-dimensional; it offers a clear sequence of points to which one can apply an eraser, but a web has three dimensions. Almost invisible, it is, nonetheless, surprisingly resilient and enveloping. It is indispensable, for raw facts have no meaning without some connective tissue, a framework that organizes them. The web is an apt figure for ideology, the deeply imbedded system of representations within which we live and by means of which we define ourselves. Slavoj

Zizek's remark—"Ideology really succeeds when even the facts which at first sight contradict it start to function as arguments in its favor"—applies to many of the figures we have been considering.[17] The minds of Clara Hohlfelder, John Marshall Carson, Colonel Owens, and Ben Davis's prosecutor are enmeshed. Within ideology's coils, truth turns to falsehood, and falsehood to truth. Chesnutt's "web" and Du Bois's "veil" figure the complex meaning-making systems that hang within us and between us. Both metaphors remind us, however, that the veil and the web are woven. That which is woven can be unraveled by a patient widening of its gaps and pulling at loose threads. These figures also call to our attention the function of narratives. Stories are texts, the knitting together of effects and causes. The metaphor with which Chesnutt concludes this collection reminds us of the connections between our social lives and our literary lives, the interaction between master narratives and micronarratives. It encourages us to read Chesnutt's textual weavings as the unraveling of larger narrative patterns.

7

Mandy Oxendine
"Is You a *Rale* Black Man?"

Uncanny, foreignness is within us: we are our own foreigners, we are divided. —JULIA KRISTEVA, *Strangers to Ourselves*

Mandy Oxendine begins with the arrival of a man and woman at a rural rail station.[1] Both are well dressed, and both descend from the same first-class coach. The man and the woman boarded the train at the same point, and both now leave at the same terminus. There is no apparent social difference between them. The narrator describes a sign outside the station waiting room: "This Waiting-room for White People Only" (3). This is North Carolina after the failure of Reconstruction, and the man is a Negro—although this is in no way evident from his appearance. The white woman and the black man leave the station to enter entirely different worlds: she is led off to a stately mansion by the area's most important family; he is guided to a rude cabin by an elderly former slave. Chesnutt introduces in this way the arbitrary racial distinctions that governed life in nineteenth-century America. He will also show, in the course of this narrative, differences in class and gender, and he will demonstrate the way these distinctions reinforce and complicate one another. Even more fascinating, he will show how these distinctions, rather than separating groups of people, become the source of powerful and convulsive attractions between them.

The white woman at the station is of relatively slight importance in the plot that follows, but the seemingly white black male will be at the center of its complications. His name is Tom Lowrey, and he has come to find his former fiancée, also a light-skinned mulatto, named Mandy Oxendine. Mandy, impatient of Tom's two-year absence pursuing his studies, has left their former home and now passes as white. The separation of the two lovers—an ambitious young man, a young woman wanting the security of marriage—is a familiar plot device, and it might provoke a rather conventional sentimental romance. But Chesnutt complicates the plot with three additional passions: those of Bob Utley, a local aristocrat, and Elder Gadson, a white evangelist, for Mandy, and that of Rose Amelia Sunday, Tom's black pupil, for Tom.

Bob Utley seems a character borrowed from nineteenth-century melodrama: the handsome sexual predator stalking the young virgin. Chesnutt adapts this stock figure to the time and place: Utley is a member of the decayed Southern aristocracy, corrupted by his class privileges. As conventional as this character seems, there is something singular about his obsessive attraction to Mandy. Although he is cold-blooded and calculating, he is willing to risk a carefully arranged and financially essential marriage by pursuing Mandy on the very eve of his wedding. Rose Amelia Sunday, Tom's love-struck pupil, is, in most respects, the direct opposite of Bob Utley. Utley, white, male, adult, and an aristocrat, stands at the top of the local social hierarchy; Rose Amelia, a black daughter of a sharecropper, is at its bottom. To accentuate the reverse symmetry, Utley is classically handsome, while Rose Amelia's body is cruelly malformed. But the young black girl's passion for Tom more than matches Bob's attraction to Mandy. The origin of her desire is, however, less obscure; it is clearly driven by difference in color. "Is you a *rale* black man?" (15), she incredulously asks her teacher, whose light skin contrasts starkly with her own. Her "love" is a form of socially induced self-hate, an internalization of the loathing her dark presence incites in others in the racist community. When her desire is frustrated, it quickly becomes vindictive, nearly destroying Mandy and Tom, and finally destroying Rose Amelia herself.

Bob Utley and Rose Amelia Sunday's contrasting figures, as we have seen, provide symmetry in the schema presented above. We might wonder, then, why Chesnutt chose to disturb the pattern by adding an additional complicating figure midway through the narrative. But when Elder Gadson arrives in chapter 10, he introduces the novel's most convulsive emotion, complicating and intensifying the intrigue in important ways. Gadson comes into the community to lead a revival, where he delivers a stirring warning of God's wrath. When Mandy steps into the light surrounding his pulpit, Gadson is fatally caught in a passion that will lead him to kill another man and nearly precipitate a lynching. What, one might ask, is the source of the strange attraction Mandy Oxendine exerts over Bob Utley and Elder Gadson?

She is, to be sure, a romantically beautiful woman, but more seems to be involved. The answer is to be found in the nexus between race, gender, and religious doctrine. "There was," the narrator assures, "no external evidence of negro blood in Mandy, unless a slight softening of facial outline, a dreaminess of eye, a mellowness of accent, might have been ascribed to its presence" (27). Nonetheless, Mandy's dark sensuality dramatically sets her apart from the white women around her. Bob Utley judges Florence Brewington, his aristocratic fiancée, to be a "marble statue" (63) by comparison. Elder Gadson is struck immediately by the contrast between Mandy and the "pale and anemic" women with their "lank figures and sandy hair, lacklustre eyes and expressionless faces" (52) at the revival. A second feature setting Mandy apart in the community is her isolation. She arrives in the town with her mother, whom we glimpse only briefly and never outside of her home. Mandy is without father, brothers, or any male protection. She walks the country roads alone, and she appears at the revival unaccompanied. Her solitude marks her as a mysterious figure in this backwoods hamlet, most of whose inhabitants know one another and their antecedents. The local inhabitants might very well wonder: who is this enigmatic beauty? Where has she come from, and what is her secret? Although it is never stated, it must surely occur to at least some of the natives that her secret might be *the* secret in the South. The ultimate concealed truth among Southerners—universally known but seldom acknowledged—was black blood in the white population as a consequence of miscegenation under slavery. This suspicion may function only at a subliminal level, but it is likely that some of Mandy's erotic attraction derives from the suspicion of a violated racial taboo.

Mandy's physical attractiveness undoubtedly contributes to this suspicion. One of the most important features in American stereotypes of the mulatto female was her sensuous beauty. James Kinney, surveying antebellum literary portraits of the Negro, remarks that "no mulatto woman of any importance in a story gets away without at least two or three paragraphs on her slightly dusky charms."[2] In the racist imagination, "Negro blood means unbridled lust."[3] The strong sexual desires evoked by dark blood must be repressed; thus the mulatta's attraction is greatest when her black ancestry is only barely perceptible: "jest dark enough to be r'al purty" is how a white character in a 1856 novel puts it.[4] If we wish to account for Mandy's attractive power over two white males, we must note the ways her beauty and mystery feed into and are magnified by cultural narratives surrounding the female of mixed blood. For Bob Utley and Elder Gadson, Mandy Oxendine is the dark, sexualized other.

A revealing detail about Bob Utley is the name of his favorite horse—a black mare called "Satan." In the name Utley gives his prized possession is the homology between three important oppositions in his psyche and in that of his community:

white	black
male	female
good	evil

The oppositions undergirding these polarities are the oppositions between reason and passion, ego and id, recognition and repression. As in all workings of the subconscious, repression—racial, sexual, and religious—only increases the power of that which is sublimated. Utley—white, male, and, in his society's eyes, "good"—is clearly drawn to his opposite, represented by his mount and by Mandy. Utley on horseback, we are told, is "Satan ridin' Satan . . . drinkin', gamblin' an' rakin'" (7). Werner Sollors employs Freud's concept of taboo to explain the mulatta's erotic power in the white male imagination. For Freud, "taboo" evokes contrary meanings: "To us it means, on the one hand, 'sacred,' 'consecrated,' and on the other, 'uncanny,' 'dangerous,' 'forbidden,' 'unclean.'"[5] For whites, sexual contact with blacks was forbidden by law and custom—and it was all the more powerfully fascinating for that.

Utley is a conscious hypocrite, planning marriage to a white Southern belle at the same time that he tries to seduce her social opposite. Gadson, however, represents a more complex and therefore more explosive form of repression. Struggling to control his lust, he projects his guilt on Mandy. "She sings like an angel . . . she looks like an angel," Gadson admits as he secretly spies on her, "But alas! she is a po' sinner, a los' soul, a bran' to be pluck' from the burnin'" (66). The repressive Christianity Gadson preaches is riddled with similar contradictions. "God," he insists, "is no respecter o' pussons" (50); nonetheless, his worshippers are carefully segregated—whites on the right and blacks on the left. He preaches the salvation of Mandy's soul at the same time that he seeks the possession of her body. These contradictions finally drive him to murder Bob Utley for acting on the desires he himself tries to deny.

Rose Amelia is the most tragic of the novel's characters, for she has internalized most thoroughly the binaries upon which racist society is built. She fantasizes about having been born white and despises other members of her race "because they were poor and black" (80). Her obsession with punishment—her pleasure in imagining the "sharp swish of the hickories" (33) applied by Lowrey against her black flesh—very likely derives from this racial self-hatred. These strange attitudes fuel her desire for Lowrey, and when this desire is frustrated, it causes her to falsely denounce Mandy. The powerful emotions of Utley, Gadson, and Rose Amelia precipitate Utley's death and Tom Lowrey's near lynching. In working out the novel's denouement, Chesnutt complicates and overturns the conventional oppositions we have been discussing. At the revival meeting and afterward, when Utley, Gadson, and Lowrey follow Mandy, the four figures move in and out of the shadows, changing profile and color in the uncertain light. White and black, male and female, saintly preacher and evil seducer blend and lose their precise identity in the gloomy forest. In the aftermath of these desires, it is the mulatto couple who act nobly, while the aristocrat and the minister act immorally. The representative of law and stability—the sheriff—is prepared to rape Mandy and to hang an innocent Tom Lowrey.

This discussion of the drives animating secondary characters leads to a consideration of the forces driving the novel's protagonists. What are the attitudes of Mandy and Tom to the oppositions we have discussed? Mandy clearly does not feel bound by them. As William L. Andrews observes in his foreword to the novel, Mandy makes "a tough-minded assessment of her racial, gendered, and class-bound condition" (x), and she acts as she feels she must. Opportunity, she sees, comes with being white, so she will pass over the color line, leaving her former community and fiancé behind. Tom Lowrey's feelings, like those of Chesnutt in his journals, are more complex.

He comes to the Negro school because it provides the means for him to search for Mandy. He acknowledges that, unlike Mandy, "he had never felt the inclination to give up his people, and cast in his lot with the ruling caste." But this conviction derives less from a feeling of racial loyalty than from a personal sense of honor: "there was something repugnant to him in the idea of concealment" (46).

Despite their professed independence, neither Tom nor Mandy entirely escapes the color prejudice of their culture. Tom rebukes Mandy for disparaging blacks, reminding her that God made them. She answers, "He made 'em; an' he made 'em black, an' ugly an' pore" (23). Tom's own attitudes are more ambivalent, as we can see in his complex reaction to Rose Amelia. He represses a laugh at her droll accent, and the description of her smile narrated through his point of view—"a pleased display of ivory" (10)—is condescending and stereotypical. Note the play of disparate emotions in this response to the child's presence:

> As she stood before him he was struck by the contrast between the old and wizened look of her ugly little face, with its gleaming eyes, and the meager childish figure surmounted by it. She might have been a precocious child of ten or an older girl of stunted growth. This latter supposition was strengthened by the attitude in which she stood, with her shoulders thrown back at such an angle as to suggest a malformation of the spine. (14–15)

Tom admires the girl's evident maturity and courage; at the same time he is fascinated and repelled by her malformed body. The mixed emotions in this description recall the complex reaction to some of his students that Chesnutt recorded in his journal. He wrote down a racist epithet and then ashamedly struck it out. In addition to this personal memory there is another shadow, a literary reference, behind Rose Amelia. She resembles Topsy, a minor character in Harriet Beecher Stowe's *Uncle Tom's Cabin* who became, through the novel's theatrical adaptations, one of the most popular creations in American culture during the second half of the nineteenth century. Here is the description that introduces this little slave girl in Stowe's novel:

> She was one of the blackest of her race; and her round, shining eyes, glittering as glass beads, moved with quick and restless glances over everything in the room. Her mouth, half open with astonishment at the wonders of the new

Mas'r's parlor, displayed a white and brilliant set of teeth. Her wooly hair was braided in sundry little tails which stuck out in every direction. The expression of her face was an odd mixture of shrewdness and cunning. . . . Altogether, there was something odd and goblin-like about her appearance.

Topsy's odd, destructive behavior is as singular as her appearance, confounding her mistress's attempts to tame her. Topsy's explanation of her conduct is simple: "I's so wicked! Laws! I's nothin' but a nigger, no ways!"[6] In short, Topsy, like Rose Amelia, has internalized her society's negative reaction to her black self and acts out that identity in hostile and disruptive conduct.

Rose Amelia is Tom's pupil, a member of his race, one of those he has come to help, and yet she is strangely alien, even repellent, to him. Tom's reaction to Rose Amelia is not unlike white America's reaction to Topsy—a mixture of fascination and revulsion, affection and disapproval. Tom comes into the black community carrying some of the larger society's attitudes. His relationship to the group he serves is, as a result, confused. He regards himself as "white in fact and black in theory," and he confesses a "mingled feeling of pleasure and annoyance" (4) at being mistaken for white. He deliberately distances himself from Deacon Pate, who meets him at the train, introducing himself simply as "Lowrey," withholding his Christian name. The old Negro, to his credit, ignores the slight and addresses Tom familiarly as "Brer Lowrey" (4). In view of Tom's ambivalence, Rose Amelia might well ask him, "Is you a *rale* black man?" (15). Her straightforward query actually contains several questions. She raises, first of all a factual issue: does Tom Lowrey descend from African ancestors? Beyond this, Rose Amelia's question also raises another issue of concern to the blacks in this community. Their dialect word "rale," like its Standard English counterpart "real," can serve as an intensifying adverb. Rose Amelia's question thus also asks Lowrey: are you *really* black; that is, antecedents aside, are you truly committed to your black identity?

Lowrey equivocates on all points. "Not *real* black. I was left out in the rain an' got some of it washed off. But I'm black enough to teach you" (15). Unanswered within Lowrey's weak response is another question: how black is "black enough to teach you"? Without a satisfactory answer to this question, we are left to wonder what attitudes toward their black identity this young teacher inculcates in his pupils. These important questions—essentially, the cultural question of black identity—are left unresolved in this novel. Lowrey's—and his society's—failure to provide a positive answer to the crucial cultural issue bears directly on Rose Amelia's poignant tragedy. Her culture sees her as ugly, and it teaches her to do the same. Lowrey, her teacher and idol, does not escape these prejudices and offers a softened form of the rejection she suffered from others. The result is Rose Amelia's vindictive rage and self-destruction. Lowrey is moved by her tragic end, and he drops a sad tear on her grave. However, there is no indication that he fully understands the cultural attitudes that caused her tragedy or his own complicity in those attitudes.

Rose Amelia's question—"Is you a *rale* black man?"—is posed in dialect, and this linguistic feature is germane to the issues it raises. Her incredulity at Lowrey's blackness derives not only from the way he *looks*, but also from the way he *sounds*. Every member of her black community, including her preacher, speaks rural black dialect. Most of the white community—certainly most of the whites these poor blacks were likely to deal with—speaks a thick rural white dialect. Tom Lowrey arrives in Rose Amelia's classroom with his light-skinned face and speaks a cultivated language she may never have heard before. His education and language fascinate his pupil, but they also separate Lowrey from other blacks, and even from Mandy. Mandy has seen opportunity in being white, and she has stepped over the color line. Tom sees power in white culture, and although he does not pass, he eagerly seizes white cultural resources. It is his two-year educational pursuit of this culture—his "intoxification of learning" (29)—that has taken him away from Mandy and has precipitated the predicament they face at the beginning of the novel. Mandy lacks Tom's education, and although her speech is closer to the educated standard than is that of Rose Amelia, the solecisms and trite phrases in the letter she sends to Tom dramatize the differences in their educations.

Dear Tom,
I take my pen in han' to let you no that I am well an doin well an hope this will fine you the same. I got yor letter out of the postoffis yistiddy, an was glad to

hear that you was well an doin well. It is so lonesome sence you went away.
Make 'ase' an git thru school an come back to your own true love,

Mandy   (30)

The community's blacks speak a heavy dialect and express attitudes that reflect the figures of the minstrel show and the comic sketch. Here, for instance, is Deacon Pate on what, for him, are black folk's two passions: God "made 'em po' an' black, but he give 'em religion and chickens, de two things dey 'preciates mos'" (9). The same dialect speaker, however, can also slyly mock white people, as in this comment on the white community's plans to host a religious revival: "I reckon dey need's it, ef dey *is* white folks" (45). Chesnutt also uses white rural dialect to satirize white hypocrisy. "Gentlemen," the sheriff sanctimoniously intones to the lynch mob seeking keys to his jail, "I purtest agin' this outrage. Nothin' shell injuce me to tell you whereabouts in the cupboard in my settin'-room I keeps the jail keys" (102). Peebles, a former justice of peace, interrupts the lynching to insist that its perpetrators act in a Christian manner: "*Hol'* on a minute. . . . This here ain't no corn-shuckin' match. . . . Mebbe the nigger would like to pray. I sorter think we ought to ask the divine blessin' on the whole thing anyhow. It's a little onreg'lar, but the end jestifies the means. Who'll offer pra'r?" (103). The novel frequently patronizes poor blacks, but it is even less flattering to the white characters. Bob Utley, his aristocratic aunt, and his fiancée are cold and selfish; Elder Gadson, the sheriff, and the townspeople are hypocritical and brutal. Tom Lowrey and Mandy Oxendine are the only individuals who act decently or morally. They are both clear-eyed about the social odds against them. They can see the steel grip of Jim Crow tightening around black folk. At the same time they have no romantic illusions about white society. Nonetheless, the novel reserves the right for Tom and Mandy to choose for themselves, in terms of their own self-interests, their racial identity.

Mandy Oxendine, like earlier literary treatments of the mulatto woman, acknowledges the tragic potential in her attempt to cross the color line. Unlike earlier treatments, however, it locates the danger not in a "war of bloods," the supposed conflict of European and African inheritances within the mulatto subject, but in the attitudes of others toward her. It refuses to concede, moreover, that a transgression of racial boundaries must necessarily be destructive for Mandy and the ones she loves. *Mandy Oxendine* tries to uncouple the adjective and noun, "tragic" and "mulatta," which heretofore had been powerfully linked in the American literary imagination. The novel ends with Mandy and Tom's marriage and their departure from the small town in which their drama had been set.

> Whether they went to the North, where there was larger opportunity and a more liberal environment, and remaining true to their own people, in spite of some scorn and some isolation, found a measurable degree of contentment and happiness; or whether they chose to sink their past in the gulf of oblivion, and sought in the great white world such a place as their talents and their virtues merited, it is not for this chronicle to relate. They deserved to be happy; but we do not all get our deserts [*sic*], as many a lucky rogue may congratulate himself, and as many an ill-used honest man can testify. (112)

The narrator, apparently a racial subjectivist, grants the newlyweds their freedom to elect their own racial identities. Note, however, that he prudently withholds any promises about the consequences of their choice. Tom and Mandy, if they choose to live as white, will do so together and, presumably, with Mandy's mother, who had participated in Mandy's earlier crossing of the color line. The narrative in this way removes one of the most important barriers in other literary treatments of the passing theme. Frequently, as in Mandy's first effort, passing forces the mulatto to abandon family and friends from her or his previous existence. However, at the end of this novel we are assured that, whether Mandy lives as white or black, the emotional nucleus of her life will remain constant. This is also true in "Her Virginia Mammy," in which Clara Hohlfelder's mother and lover combine to effect her racial transition. The treatment of passing in *Mandy Oxendine* is, in comparison with Clara's story, both more radical and more conservative. Clara Hohlfelder does not herself choose to cross the color line, and thus she cannot be seen as the scheming mulatta of Southern myth. The choice is made for her by her mother and her future husband; that is, the crucial decision on racial identity is entrusted, not to the mulatto woman, but to her black mother and her white lover. In contrast, Mandy has already deliberately passed once, and if she chooses to live as white, she will do so of her own conscious volition. The novel, in the autonomy it grants its heroine, is clearly more radical than the story. But let us look more closely at what Mandy will be choosing. She is already married to a mulatto man, and, if she and Tom live as a white couple, their assimilation does not threaten the "purity" of white blood. I call attention to these facts to point out the way that novel's optimistic ending subtly undercuts itself. The freedom it grants its couple is managed by rather implausibly removing from their future two of the most important complications in the classic passing narrative: the need to break links to an earlier black life and white resistance to miscegenation.

There is, however, another, disturbing shadow that lies over Mandy's future. Her story has already dramatized, in the tragedies of Elder Gadson and Bob Utley, the deep and urgent stirrings aroused in the white unconscious by the merest suspicion of dark blood. Given the way race is constructed in the minds of their white neighbors, will the mulatto couple ever really be granted the freedom to elect their own identity in the way the narrator implies? Further, Mandy and Tom's ambivalent attitudes toward darker African Americans indicate the presence of these white constructions in their own consciousnesses. What freedom is possible within cultural binaries that encourage the mulatto couple to judge part of the population—and part of themselves—as "black, an' ugly an' pore" (23)? These constructions remain within the white, mulatto, and black characters in *The House behind the Cedars.* In addition, this novel also contains the complications of family ties and miscegenation, which are absent from Mandy's story. The result, discussed in the next chapter, is an even more complex and ambivalent demonstration of conflicting racial loyalties.

8

———⫸⫷———

The House behind the Cedars
"Creatures of Our Creation"

> Language—that fundamental act of organizing the mind's encounter
> with an experienced world—is propelled by a rhythm of naming: it is
> the means by which the mind takes possession of the named, at once
> fixing the named as irrevocably Other and representing in crystallized
> isolation from all conditions of externality. —KIMBERLY M. BEN-
> STON, "I Yam What I Yam: The Topos of (Un)naming in African-
> American Literature"

The House behind the Cedars, like *Mandy Oxendine*, begins with a young
man's arrival in a rural North Carolina town. The visitor is, despite appearances, an African American, and he has come to retrieve a light-colored
mulatto female. Despite these echoes of the earlier narrative, *The House
behind the Cedars* is, thematically and technically, a significantly different
novel. We are made aware of this fact as early as the novel's first paragraph.
The paragraph presents these musings on time in the quiet community:

> Time touches all things with destroying hand. . . . And yet there are places
> where Time seems to linger lovingly long after youth has departed, and to
> which he seems loath to bring the evil day. Who has not known some even-
> tempered old man or woman who seemed to have drunk of the fountain of
> youth? Who has not seen somewhere an old town that, having long since
> ceased to grow, yet held its own without perceptible decline?[1]

These reflections seem to come from the narrator, and they prepare us to enter a timeless world outside of history and social necessity. The next sentence, however, brings us up short: "Some such trite reflection—as apposite to the subject as most random reflections are—passed through the mind of a young man" (1). The thoughts belong not to the narrator but to the recently arrived young man, from whom the narrator carefully distances himself. The narrator and the complex relationship he establishes with his characters will be discussed later on, but for the moment the focus will remain on the newly arrived visitor. His name is John Warwick, and he is, it seems, a singularly unreliable observer. Charred buildings, Jewish names on storefronts, and even a black policeman prove that the town has not escaped the historical transformations occasioned by war, immigration, and Reconstruction. Although Warwick notes these details, he ignores their significance. He prefers to linger nostalgically in an earlier time.

The discrepancy between things as they are and things as they are perceived—dramatized in Warwick's encounter with the town—takes us to this novel's thematic heart. The woman Warwick seeks is Rena Walden. Rena is, in literary terms, Mandy Oxendine's sister—or at least her near cousin. Both are fictional protagonists conceived by Chesnutt during the 1890s, and both are light-colored black women who cross the color line and live as whites. In *The House behind the Cedars,* Chesnutt explores once again the consequences of his heroine's decision to change her racial identity. But these consequences are imagined differently in the two novels. The consequences that flow from Mandy's choice are felt most powerfully in the lives around her, in the convulsive sexual passions her presence arouses in two white males and in the vindictive jealousy it elicits from a black girl. Tragedy in *Mandy Oxendine* occurs around the central couple, in the deaths of Bob Utley and Rose Amelia, but Mandy Oxendine and Tom Lowrey themselves escape and begin a new life elsewhere. We do not know where or how Mandy and Tom will live their lives, but we are told that they will freely elect their social affiliation in terms of their own interests. The narrative thus defends the mulatto couple's right to choose their own racial identity.

Rena Walden's story casts doubt on this assertion of the mulatto's sovereign independence. In *The House behind the Cedars,* emotional confusion occurs not only around Rena, but within her. She cannot escape this confusion because not only does she live in a racist society, but that society also lives within her. She is not exempt from the contradictory pressures of her culture: they blind her, they frustrate her hopes, and finally they destroy her life. John Warwick's entry into Patesville at the beginning of the novel initiates the chain of events that leads to Rena's death at its end. Warwick comes, he believes, to rescue his sister from life as a Negro, but he brings instead another form of imprisonment—entrapment within white Southern ideology. John and Rena are the illegitimate children of a white man and his mulatto mistress, and thus they are, under North Carolina law, black, and they bear their mother's family name, Walden. Ten years earlier, John left home and became a white man in South Carolina. He married into the white social elite, and he acquired property. More important, he embraced the privileges and the values of his new class. He was, his white peers judged, "sound on the subject of negroes, Yankees, and the righteousness of the lost cause" (42). It is this ideological "soundness" that locks Warwick in the distorting historical nostalgia noted in the opening paragraph. He has affirmed his new identity by changing his family name from Walden to Warwick. He has read avidly in the library left by his white father, and he has chosen his new name from Bulwer-Lytton's historical novel *The Last of the Barons* (1843). Unfortunately, Warwick reads literature as poorly as he did the townscape he surveyed in the novel's opening paragraph. The mulatto parvenu is obviously infatuated with Bulwer-Lytton's protagonist, Warwick, the kingmaker who deposed Edward IV and placed Henry VI on the throne. Warwick does not care to notice, however, that his namesake's career ended, in history as in fiction, with defeat, disgrace, and death. Similarly, Warwick renames his sister Rowena, after the blond princess in Scott's *Ivanhoe*. A friend suggests, however, that Warwick's dusky sister might better bear the name of Rebecca, Rowena's tragic, Jewish rival.

Warwick is not alone in venerating Walter Scott; the Scottish novelist was a revered figure in the South before and after the Civil War. In the Clarence Social Club's tournament, Southern planters and businessmen solemnly imitate Scott's medieval warriors by donning cardboard armor, poking poles through iron rings, and swinging swords at wooden balls.[2] The South's Scott cult, which Mark Twain also mocked, reflected a central tenet of Southern myth: the specious claim that the South's governing elite descended from England's cavaliers and embodied its aristocratic ethos. Warwick's commitment to his new white identity is the primary force driving his behavior. For it he abandoned his mother and sister, and for it he embraced the culture that placed an uncrossable gulf between him and his former life. John Walden was denied his father's name and forced to bear the name of his Negro mother. He attempts to name himself and to author his own identity. J. Lee Greene's description of Warwick—"a New World Ishmael who metamorphoses into a New World Adam"—suggests the conflicting narratives implicit in his project.[3] John would trump the racist biblical account of black servitude with the American myth of self-invention. In pursuing this project, he makes several fundamental miscalculations.

The first has to do with time. Warwick assumes a naive, overly simple opposition of past and future. At different moments, he will value one or the other of these seemingly opposed terms, without properly appreciating the way they interpenetrate one another. In the reflections that begin the novel, John overvalues the past, but it is a specious view of the antebellum South, the pastoral of plantation legend. At the same time, rather contradictorily, he undervalues the connection between past and future. He believes that, in crossing the state line, he leaves his past behind. This leads us to his second miscalculation, a reliance on another reductive binary: the opposition between subjective, psychological identity versus public, social identity. Warwick leaves home believing that *what* he is depends on *where* he is. Legally, he is correct on this point: in North Carolina he was a Negro, and in South Carolina he is a white man. But law is the least of it. He is still—regardless of space, time, and legislative fiat—Rena's brother and Molly's son. These powerful personal bonds pull him back in space and time, convulsing his life and the life of his family. John, anticipating none of this, moves ahead in his project of self-authoring. What he accomplishes, however, is not invention, but replication. He inscribes himself within the dominant cultural narrative, the racist ideology that consigns his mother to inferior status. His fabrication is a lie within a lie, for the myth of a white Southern chivalry was itself a fiction, a cover for a brutal social order based on slavery and exploitation. Chesnutt's novel calls into question the viability of fabrications that blatantly ignore the past.

The House behind the Cedars also reminds us of the consequences of fictions that ignore our ties to others. The novel's first chapter introduces connections that seriously threaten the identity Walden/Warwick has constructed. Warwick left home ten years earlier at the age of eighteen, and he has not seen his family during the war or after. Now he returns to the house behind the cedars where he was raised and where his blood kin still live. Warwick knows that this journey into the past can put his new identity at risk, but he feels compelled to make it. His wife has died, and his son is without a mother; the child "needs some woman of its own blood to love it and look after it intelligently" (23). The natural solution, reinforced by Molly's "tearful yearning" (24), would be to place the child in his grand-mother's care, but Molly bears the "mark of the Ethiopian" (184), and her presence would threaten John's white identity. He will instead take his sister with him, leaving his mother alone. Warwick speaks of his son's need, not of his own, and in fact, he seems to have no strong feelings for his blood relations, although there is a disturbing hint of a sexual attraction for Rena. For the most part, Warwick is less concerned for the family he left than for the one he will found. His son, Albert, first of the Warwick line, needs care; so the boy's aunt will become his surrogate mother, his "mammy." Here again Warwick fatally miscalculates, ignoring the connection of future and past. Rena cannot so easily cut her ties to her mother; they draw her fatally back to her past life and explode her and her brother's new identities.

The pull between natural feelings and social identity provides the emo-tional armature for the novel's three tragedies: the death of Rena Walden and the ruined hopes of George Tryon and Frank Fowler. In all three lives flow the forces of affection, love, and desire; in all three this natural flow is frustrated by the ideologies of race and class. Judge Straight, a jurist who spent his life in the South and who has tried to mitigate some of its worst features, comments on the general problem that Chesnutt's narratives illus-trate. Humans band together, tell stories, and create systems of belief, which help them to organize reality. But at some point these systems become more powerful than the people who created them, and they crush the lives they were meant to enrich: "We make our customs lightly; once made, like our sins, they grip us in bands of steel; we become the creatures of our cre-ation" (35). One of its victims, George Tryon recognizes the destructive power of ideology and the greater value of human feeling: "Custom was tyranny," he concludes, too late. "Love was the only law" (292). George Tryon meets Rena as "Rowena Warwick," sister of the prominent South Car-olina attorney and planter John Warwick. He falls in love immediately and as "Sir George," victor of the Clarence tournament, crowns Rena "Queen of

Love and Beauty." However, when he learns of her African ancestry, he sees her through an ideological lens: the same woman becomes, in his fevered dream, "a hideous black hag" (147). Tryon's natural feelings for Rena gradually reassert themselves, and he sets out in search of her, determined, against all social odds, to "make her white" (208).

He finds her at her mother's home in Patesville, dancing with blacks. As Tryon peers through a window into the brightly lit room, his socially conditioned responses are triggered once again, and he reacts with revulsion:

> To-night his eyes had been opened—he had seen her with the mask thrown off, a true daughter of a race in which the sensuous enjoyment of the moment took precedence of taste or sentiment or any of the higher emotions. Her few months of boarding-school, her brief association with white people, had evidently been a mere veneer over the underlying negro, and their effects had slipped away as soon as the intercourse had ceased. With the monkey-like imitativeness of the negro she had copied the manners of white people while she lived among them, and had dropped them with equal facility when they ceased to serve a purpose. (223)

When Tryon observes her, Rena is dancing to the same air played at her coronation as Queen of (White) Love and Beauty. Her "sensuousness" is no greater at this dance than at the preceding one. And the "imitativeness" of which Tryon accuses the black folk is surely less grotesque than his own society's bizarre charade of English knights and ladies. George, in this moment of reaction, is seeing things not as they are but as racist ideology would have them. Natural feeling will reassert itself and lead Tryon to the rueful recognition quoted above. It will be too late; when he returns penitently to the house behind the cedars, Rena will lie dead within.

Rena is also loved by the black man Frank Fowler. Frank and his father, Peter, had been Molly Walden's retainers under slavery. Molly Walden, a free colored woman before the war, embraces her own variant of white Southern ideology: she holds herself proudly aloof from the darker, recently emancipated blacks around her. For Molly, a match between her daughter and the worthy Frank Fowler would be totally unacceptable. After the failure of Rena's marriage to Tryon, Molly promotes the suit of the unscrupulous but light-colored Jeff Wain. Sadly, Frank Fowler's perceptions are also clouded by ideology. He unconsciously clothes Rena "with the attributes of the superior race" (129) and declares his love only when it is too late. Peter Fowler resents Molly Walden's superior airs and rebukes his son's love-struck servility to Rena and her mother. But Peter's perceptions are not always accurate. He praises John Warwick's gift of a mule and cart to Frank in contrast to the stingy pretensions of the mulatto Molly Walden. Warwick's generosity, according to Peter, is "somethin' lack rale w'ite folks" (188). Peter does not recognize that "Warwick" is actually John Walden, Molly's mulatto son. His remark, although legally and biologically inaccurate, does capture John's moral core. John has made the gift, not in the spirit of genuine friendships but in the hope of buying Frank's silence about his and his sister's racial secret.

Rena Walden is more sensitive than her mother or brother, but she shares their color bias. Her attitudes are revealed in this description of black workers from her point of view: "she watched the boat hands send the yellow turpentine barrels down the steep bank. . . . The excited negroes, their white teeth and eyeballs glistening in the surrounding darkness to which their faces formed no relief" (42). Dark-skinned Negroes for Rena, as for her brother and her white suitor, are exotic, bestial inferiors. Although she is grateful to the ever-faithful Frank, there is never a possibility during her years in the house behind the cedars that she could reciprocate his love for her. These prejudices are intensified by her life as a white woman. However, matters change after her past is discovered by Tryon and she resumes life as a Negro. Rena overcomes some of this class difference when she finds herself living among those she had been taught to despise, but gradually she overcomes some of these attitudes and commits herself to service to those whom she now sees as "her inalienable race" (194). During these final months of her life, Rena also sees Frank differently. Robert Sedlack, who has studied the novel's genesis, reports that Chesnutt's criticism of Rena Walden's colorism was stronger and more explicit in the earliest, 1891, version of *House*. The narrative's primary focus at that point "was an attempt to awaken the conscience of America by showing that color consciousness *within* the Negro community destroys Rena."[4] In the version of the novel we have, Rena gradually softens her prejudice. Before she leaves Patesville, Rena thanks Frank, who once saved her life, as "a true friend" (39). But after her return, she acknowledges him as "our very good friend" (185), and when her brother tells Frank how much he appreciates his kindness, Rena interjects warmly, "How much we all appreciate" (185). Frank's own self-esteem grows during this period. He is able to observe Rena's mulatto suitor, Jeff Wain, at close range, and he can see that, despite differences in skin color, he is clearly Jeff's superior. He expresses his estimation simply but eloquently in his native dialect: "I knows 'im, an' don' know no good of 'im. One er dese yer biggity, braggin' niggers . . . jes' a big bladder wid a handful er shot rattlin' roun' in it" (284).

In the novel's last pages, Rena, pursued by Wain and torn by contradictory feelings for Tryon, finally collapses in the forest. Frank finds her, and his initial reaction is that she is a white woman. He then recognizes the woman he has loved for so many years. He first addresses her as "Miss Rena," the customary address of a servant to his mistress. But he immediately follows with the more intimate "Rena." He then declares his love, "Oh, my honey, my darlin' . . . Frank loves you better 'n all de worl'" (289). Even at this moment, however, Frank cannot quite put himself on the same level as Rena. When he declares his love, he hides in the third person, and, as a result, sounds more like a consoling nurse than an ardent lover. Rena, for her part, is moved to the following avowal: "Frank . . . my good friend— my best friend—you loved me best of them all" (293). Rena feels genuine esteem for Frank, but he remains a friend, not a lover; she acknowledges his love for her, but she is silent about her own deepest feelings. At Rena's death, Rena and Frank approach, but do not quite manage to cross, the fissure dividing the dark-skinned from the light. Thus in the tragic stories of Frank, Rena, and George, prejudices of race and class conspire to frustrate the deepest feelings of black, mulatto, and white.

The novel illustrates in several of the lesser characters the informational loop that reinforces these social attitudes. Dr. Green, Patesville's racially prejudiced physician, complains that his black assistant, Dave, is entirely too forgetful. Not surprisingly, a little later we find Dave striking precisely this theme as he plays the darky for Tryon: "Dis yer recommenb'ance er mine is gwine ter git me inter trouble ef I don' look out, an' dat's a fac', sho'" (139). In this way the racist doctor encourages the behavior that will confirm his prejudices. A more complex and consequential illustration of the way whites create and reinforce black stereotypes is seen in the interactions of George Tryon and Plato, a black boy once owned by Tryon's family. Tryon meets Plato while walking with Blanche Leary, Rena's successor in his affections, and Plato entertains them with his singing and clowning. Tryon tosses a coin to the boy, who is profusely grateful. Unfortunately, while Tryon is absorbed by this spontaneous performance, Rena, now a teacher in the area, passes by. Blanche sees Rena, but Tryon does not. Later, when Tryon learns of Rena's presence he tries to arrange a face-to-face meeting, but he never succeeds. Had Tryon been less absorbed in watching and rewarding Plato's minstrel capers he might have had the meeting he wanted and averted Rena's tragic death.

Also, had Tryon been less amused by Plato's playing the comic darky, he might have noted the import of his song. Here is its second verse:

> De oak grows tall,
> De pine grows slim,
> So rise you up, my true love,
> An' let me come in. (236)

The poem calls attention to the forces governing nature and urges lovers to forget differences and unite. This is, of course, the lesson Tryon ought to have heeded in his relations with Rena. The quatrain also advocates and achieves union of different cultures on a formal level. The first, second, and fourth lines are in black dialect; their simple rhythms are those of popular poetry, perhaps a children's rhyme. The third line, however, has literate diction, more complex meter, and a sophisticated syntax that echo the English art lyric.

Tryon employs Plato in his attempt to meet Rena alone, but his effort turns out tragically. Plato leaves her alone in the forest, where she is pursued by the treacherous Jeff Wain. Plato is rebuked by a black person for pandering to his former owner, but Plato has been conditioned from birth to respect "Mars Geo'ge" with almost religious reverence. He has also been conditioned to denigrate his own abilities. Plato, a semiliterate schoolboy, has been deliberately "mocked with the name of a great philosopher" (270). By such ironic naming, slave owners deride the pretensions of their black property to fully human status. The same derisive humor is found in George's question to Plato at one of their meetings: "why are you absent from the classic shades of the academy to-day?" The question, of course, alludes ironically to Plato's illustrious namesake. It is deliberately phrased in a stilted diction that Plato cannot understand. The boy can only respond in dialect, "W'at wuz dat you say?" (278)

In these two encounters between George Tryon and Plato we see how Tryon and other whites perpetuate a cognitive loop that reinforces their racist assumptions. Tryon rewards Plato for a performance that confirms his stereotypical assumptions of the black's "sensuous enjoyment" (223). Tryon also referred, while spying on Rena, to the Negro's "monkey-like imitativeness," and we now understand that phrase in a different light. Blacks are rewarded for comic behavior: Plato walks on his hands and hangs from a tree. In serious areas of cultural activity, black efforts are mocked by ironic comparison to inappropriate European models. The black boy does not imitate the Greek philosopher—he would be content to read and write. It is Tryon who initiates the ludicrous comparison so that he and his peers may mock the black boy's educational ambitions.

The House behind the Cedars provides a more thorough examination of the ideological and emotional forces controlling black-white relations than does *Mandy Oxendine*. It is also more technically complex than its predecessor, particularly in handling point of view. Charles Hackenberry notes the lack of distance between the narrator and his male protagonist in *Mandy Oxendine*: "Quite simply, the narrator of *Mandy Oxendine* speaks with the too-studied correctness of the hero" (xx). The narrator of *The House behind the Cedars* immediately sets himself at some distance from his character, as seen in the discussion of the first paragraph. The narrator, in fact, employs varying degrees of distance for different effects. The narrator can stand well above the characters and speak in his own voice, editorializing in the manner of the traditional omniscient narrator. From this perspective he sermonizes in defense of the mulatto (128) and the carpetbagger (244). At other moments, he limits himself to an ironic aside, as in this comment on a local landmark "known as Liberty Point,—perhaps because slave auctions were sometimes held there in the good old days" (7).

The narrator also deploys irony more subtly, not in direct commentary, but in stylistic inflation. Here is an example:

But no Southerner who loved his poor, downtrodden country, or his race, the proud Anglo-Saxon race which traced the clear stream of its blood to the cavaliers of England, could tolerate the idea that even in distant generations that unsullied current could be polluted by the blood of slaves. The very thought was an insult to the white people of the South. (143–44)

The narrator feels no need to comment. The elevated diction and elaborate syntax—including the eighteen word appositive to "race"—the trite metaphor of "clear stream," and the indignantly terse restatement in the second sentence say all that needs to be said about the racist Southerner's fatuous pomposity. Elsewhere the narrator focuses through the consciousness of a character or characters and then brings us up short with comments that identify the source of the thoughts and their ideological coloring. This is evident in the first paragraph's presentation of Warwick's musings, and this is also what happens when the narrator characterizes Patesville's values and then identifies the view as the citizens' own self-satisfied estimate: "Kindness, hospitality, loyalty, a chivalrous deference to women,—all these might be found in large measure by those who saw Patesville with the eyes of its best citizens, and accepted their standards of politics, religion, manners, and morals" (134).

Another, quite subtle, technique is to present the character's perspective without comment and allow us to judge its ideological source. This is what occurs in the description of Negro deckhands through Rena's perspective, quoted above. It is also what happens when Frank Fowler, a spectator at the Clarence tournament, is struck by a broken piece of lance. Frank is subject to the chaffing of white spectators who "made witty and original remarks about the advantage of being black upon occasions where one's skull was exposed to danger" (49). Frank ties a red bandanna around his wound and in that moment becomes the dark double of the red-sashed George Tryon. The reader is left to judge who is the more worthy suitor—George, who twice renounces Rena, or Frank, who never falters—and to see the obtuse cruelty of the white spectators' humor.

The discussion of the novel's complex narrative strategies call attention to the difficulties they pose in sorting through its conflicting meanings. Trudier Harris writes that "blackness is a source of entertainment and the butt of jokes—from Chesnutt as well as from the characters he creates."[5] The derisive attitude Harris describes is certainly present in several characters. The evidence she cites in support of her assertion is Rena's perception of the black deckhands and the white spectators' jokes at Frank Fowler's expense. Both passages come, not from an omniscient narrator outside the narrative, but from the dramatized consciousnesses of characters within the narrative. If we are to consider Harris's charge, we must make some distinctions about the "Chesnutt" to whom she refers. If "Chesnutt" is taken to mean an omniscient narrator, speaking from outside the narrative frame, Harris is mistaken, for the comments to which she refers come from characters within the narrative frame. If, on the other hand, "Chesnutt" denotes the implied author of the narrative, the matter is more complex, and Harris touches a sensitive and relevant issue. An implied author is present, not only in the thoughts of his characters or in the opinions of a narrator, but also in what happens to these thoughts and opinions in the working out of the narrative. A narrative is more than a set of attitudes; it is the testing of those attitudes by a sequence of experiences. The events of *The House behind the Cedars* prove that both Rena and the prejudiced white spectators are wrong. The narrator records Rena's stereotypical reaction to the stevedores without comment. The critique of Rena's colorism is not as strong as in the novel's first draft; nonetheless, in the final version, Rena changes her attitude toward darker blacks when she resumes her life in the black community. Subsequent events also prove that Frank Fowler is superior to the ignorant whites who mocked him. Nonetheless, Harris's criticism is apposite, for it asks if the narrative's challenge and refutation of these distasteful attitudes are sufficiently strong. The implied author uses his omniscient narrator to attack negative images of the mulatto directly and forcefully (128), while he challenges white and mulatto attitudes to dark blacks through the less forceful indirect method. The question is not so much where the implied author stands on these issues as it is the firmness and consistency of his stance. "Chesnutt"—understood as the implied author—is as complex and conflicted as any of his characters. He clearly opposes America's invidious racial binaries, but it is less clear that he is entirely innocent of them himself.

These reflections on authorial ambivalence are relevant to the narrative's climax. Rena, fleeing Jeff Wain, becomes lost in a dark, rain-lashed swamp. We are here in the portentous setting of the fictional sketch "Lost in the Swamp" recorded in Chesnutt's journal. Rena, panicked by "a huge black snake,—harmless enough, in fact, but to her excited imagination frightful in appearance" (273), rushes on and then collapses. She is discovered in the forest by Frank Fowler. The formerly menacing woods are described differently in this scene: pine trees provide "the stately arch of a cathedral aisle" (285), jessamine flowers scent the air, a silver-throated mockingbird pours out his song. Frank and Rena exchange the declarations discussed previously, and Frank fashions a bed for Rena of forest bows and flowers. It is both a funeral pyre and a chaste nuptial couch. As Frank bears Rena up, the narrator comments that "The grand triumphal sweep of nature's onward march recked nothing of life's little tragedies" (289). At Rena's death, he assures us that "the red and golden glory of the setting sun, triumphantly ending his daily course, flooded the narrow room with light" (294).

The scene is contradictory and confusing in several ways. First, there is the exultant tone that colors this scene. Where is the triumph to which the narrator twice refers? Is it in the fact that Rena has escaped the "huge black snake," the mulatto Wain's sexual predations? Near death, she has also escaped the danger of sexual contact with dark-skinned Frank. Their marriage will be a purely symbolic, spiritual union. The narrator has the advantage of a cosmological perspective, but readers may not wish to share it. Frank Fowler loved Rena faithfully and has served her until her death, yet he is not granted so much as a kiss. There is something dishonest in the narrator's sublime indifference, in his refusal to enter the black man's consciousness at this key moment, his unwillingness to confront the deep tragedy that white and mulatto prejudice has created for Frank.

Equally problematic is the narrator's gesture toward religious consolation. He acknowledges nature's indifference, but his descriptions of the forest's "cathedral aisles" and the sun's "golden glory" suggest a benevolent deity beyond human reckoning. This clashes with an earlier moment when the Christian account of human suffering was debated and seriously challenged. "God made us all," Rena tells her brother, "and for some good purpose, though we may not always see it. He made some people white, and strong, and masterful, and—heartless. He made others black and homely, and poor and weak" (181). Rena's Christian faith subtly encourages her color prejudice. Distinctions between and within the races, she reasons, are all part of God's inscrutable plan. Her brother, John, tartly refuses any religious justification of social injustice: "God has nothing to do with it. . . . God is too often a convenient stalking-horse for human selfishness" (181). John is not a particularly sympathetic character; nonetheless, his cold rationalism better captures the spirit of this bleakly secular narrative than does his sister's religious resignation or the narrator's romantic effusions. Trudier Harris quite rightly observes that this "overly sentimentalized and rather melodramatic conclusion obscures" (224) critical points made elsewhere in the novel. Events portrayed earlier in the narrative make possible—and seem to call for—a more forthright confrontation with the causes of Rena Walden's tragedy.

Mandy Oxendine and The House behind the Cedars cover many of the same themes, but they differ significantly in tone and degree of complexity. Their different titles tell us something of their different foci. The former names a person, the latter a dwelling. Mandy tells the story of an individual who, theoretically at least, is granted the freedom to choose her own racial identity. House speaks of the shadowy space between two communities where a sister and brother were raised. Viewed from within, the home is comforting, warmed by a mother's love. Seen through the window of social prejudice, however, the dwelling is a place of shame claimed by neither the white nor black community. Anomalous and contradictory, the house stands as a synecdoche for the complex society in which Chesnutt's mulattoes dwell and that dwells within them. The House behind the Cedars tells two stories. A sister and a brother leave their home to live as whites. The young woman, bound by ties of love to her mother, fails and dies, a "cullud 'oman" (294). The young man, cool and self-seeking, succeeds for a decade. His identity is exposed and his life is shattered, but he vows to try again. He disappears well before the climax and is not present at his sister's death. Will he succeed? Will his son, Albert, be the "Future American," the colored man who disappears into the white crowd? The novel does not tell us, but it does suggest that such a transition is not without cost. The boy has already lost his grandmother and his aunt; there may be other prices to pay as well.

9

―――(()―――

The Marrow of Tradition
"The Very Breath of His Nostrils"

The differences *between* entities . . . are shown to be based on repression of differences *within* entities, ways in which an entity differs from itself. —BARBARA JOHNSON, *A World of Difference*

The railroad is a potent American symbol, so readers should not be surprised to find that Chesnutt begins three of his novels with his protagonists aboard or descending from a train. But Chesnutt's trains bear a different thematic weight than do other, more familiar appearances of the iron horse. This is not the machine whose shrill whistle disturbs Thoreau's pastoral garden, nor is it the continent-spanning engine of progress celebrated in western romance. These more familiar trains follow America's most famous trajectory, which runs—for good or for ill—from east to west, from civilization to wilderness. But other routes are possible. The train that bears Dreiser's protagonist at the beginning of *Sister Carrie* carries her from rural Indiana to Chicago, from the plains to the metropolis. More important, Dreiser's train projects Carrie out of a stable world of comfortable certainties into a dynamic world of moral and social ambiguity. Like Dreiser, Chesnutt is interested in ambiguity; more specifically, in this novel he uses the train journey to introduce his key theme: the confounding problems of differences and similarities between and within the races.

Chesnutt's railroads in *Mandy Oxendine* and *The Marrow of Tradition* run north-south, from relatively broad racial tolerance to narrowly enforced Jim

Crow. The train from which John Walden descends in *The House behind the Cedars* might seem an exception from this pattern, because it has come up from South Carolina. But Walden's voyage is essentially the same as that of Tom Lowrey and Dr. Miller. The racial definitions under South Carolina law were more liberal than those of North Carolina; thus Walden boards the train legally a white man and descends, if he is discovered, a Negro.

For Chesnutt, the value of the railroad as symbol—and, more specifically, the value of the north-south road—resides in the tension between seeming clarity and deep ambiguity in racial meanings. Nothing seems more straightforward than a train's carefully timed, linear progress. And yet, at the point where the iron rails cross another line, a state boundary, the identities and rights of those who ride the road dramatically change. Even in the South, each state had its own definition of "Negro," definitions that Chesnutt described and mocked in his essay "What Is a White Man?" The conflict that Chesnutt's train journeys dramatize is, to use a linguistic metaphor, the tension between horizontal syntactical progress and the vertical proliferation of semantic meanings. It was on a train traveling through Louisiana in 1892 that Homer Plessy sought to challenge the constitutionality of Southern "separate but equal" legislation. However, independent of this recent and important historical echo, there are other features of railroad travel that recommended it for Chesnutt's deconstructive purposes. The velocity of steam-powered travel, the rapid movement of people across political and cultural boundaries, intensified the violent collision of conflicting ideologies. The new mobility brought into contact, and thus called into question, assumptions that, left in isolation, seemed natural and immutable.

Dr. Miller's journey southward, the event that precipitates his entry into this novel, began in New York. Beyond this, however, his travels have a longer itinerary, for Miller, an American Negro, studied in Paris and Vienna. We are then, initially on this journey, in contact with broad and cosmopolitan values, which will be strained and constricted as the train moves south. The narrative takes up its protagonist when he meets his former professor Dr. Burns, a white man who boards the train in Philadelphia. The meanings associated with Pennsylvania's city of brotherly love, our constitutional cradle, are, of course, immediately to the novel's ironic purpose, as is the city's proximity to the Mason-Dixon line. It is the train's transgression of that line soon after Burns's boarding that produces the novel's first ideological collision.

Before that collision, however, the narrator gives us two readings of the scene created by the chance meeting of two professional colleagues. The first is from the perspective of a "celebrated traveler," whose broad experience in the world's remote corners causes him to assert that "among all varieties of mankind the similarities are vastly more important and fundamental than the differences."[1] The traveler to whom the narrator refers is not named, but his perspective anticipates that of Franz Boas.[2] Boas, the founder of modern anthropology, was born in Germany, did research in many remote societies, and taught in the United States. His observations and research led him to argue that variations within a given race were much greater than the variations between one race and other races. Racial definitions, thus, are arbitrary distortions of a greater, shared human identity. Viewing the two physicians from the point of view of the "celebrated traveler," the narrator remarks the obvious similarities in their dress, bearing, and culture.

However, the narrator also gives us this scene from another perspective, that of an "American eye" (49). From this viewpoint, the racial differences between the men take precedence over any similarities. Dr. Miller's curly hair and swarthy complexion proclaim "what has been described in the laws of some of our states as 'a visible admixture' of African blood" (49). "Visible" must be read against "*American* eye," where the seemingly neutral organ of perception is revealed as the biased vehicle of cultural assumptions. However, as the narrator's quotation marks indicate, these assumptions have been enshrined in law, as if they were natural. The narrator extends his visual trope when he identifies the eye in question as that of the monocular Captain McBane. We have met the "Captain"—the captaincy is his self-aggrandizing fiction—in the preceding chapter, where he has been introduced as one who willingly handles the uglier tasks for the racist elite. In the pursuit of his professional activities he lost an eye to a resisting black person. The Cyclops, for Chesnutt as for Homer and Joyce, symbolizes cultural myopia. The loss of binocular vision entails the loss of depth of field, a literal flattening of significant detail and meaningful nuance.

The scandal of Dr. Miller's proximity to his former professor in the railroad car has presumably escaped the attention of the conductor and other passengers until McBane insists on Miller's removal to the Negro car. Miller complies under protest, and McBane adds to his insult by following the doctor into the Jim Crow car, flagrantly violating the law upon whose enforcement he has insisted. Miller controls his anger by burying himself in his reading. When he looks up he notices "a huge negro, covered thickly with dust" (58), crawling from underneath one of the railroad cars. This angry figure, later identified as Josh Green, is the return of the society's repressed, a dark double for both McBane and Miller. Green's appearance here in near proximity to McBane intimates the complex connections between black and white racial enmity. McBane's father was a plantation slave driver, and McBane himself has been a contractor of black convict labor. Both McBanes are scorned by well-born white planters, although, in fact, they do the elite's bidding. Rather than resenting the white aristocrats, however, McBane releases his hatred on the Negro. Two victims of McBane's brutal negrophobia were Green's father and mother. Now their son obsessively stalks McBane, planning revenge. McBane's hatred has fatally shaped that of Josh Green, and Green is, in this sense, McBane's creation and double. But the introduction of Green at this key moment also suggests that he is the embodiment of the urbane Miller's suppressed rage. The educated mulatto continually swallows his indignation at racial injustice, clinging to his hopes for racial progress. His anger and Josh Green emerge together in this scene, and they will emerge together more overtly in the novel's climactic race war.

McBane eventually leaves the Negro car, and Miller directs his attention to black farm workers who are traveling with him. His reaction to his dark companions is ambivalent. He feels an expansive warmth toward the "noisy, loquacious, happy, dirty, and malodorous" (60) lot at the same time that he resents the law that identifies him with them. He confesses that he finds their presence as offensive as do the whites whose company he was forced to leave. Miller's reflections echo the educated traveler's observations about diversity within the races and similarities across racial lines; the mulatto doctor feels he has much more in common with his fellow physician than with these rough menials. Miller gradually gains his composure by reflecting on the boisterous spirits of the black farmhands. Their "cheerfulness of spirit" (61) seems to him a wise, divine provision, equipping the working blacks for lives of servitude and humiliation. "'Blessed are the meek,'" quotes Miller at the end of these consoling reflections, "'for they shall inherit the earth? If this be true, the negro may yet come into his estate, for meekness seems to be set apart as his portion" (62). The Negro physician, preoccupied by his New Testament meditation as he descends from the train, seems not to notice the "great black figure" (62) surfacing once again to shadow McBane with murderous intent. Earlier we considered some of the railroad's meanings in American culture, but it has other reverberations in the African American imagination. There are, of course, the echoes of the train's mournful call in the blues, but there are also the larger-than-life folk heroes who helped build or who traveled the iron road. In the present instance, it is the voice of murderous Railroad Bill—"Buy me a pistol just as long as my arm / Kill everybody done me harm"—which we hear in Josh Green's ominous grumbling. Green emerges here at the end of this chapter to vividly contradict Miller's condescending generalization about the black laborers' meekness, just as he will later refute Miller's optimism about future racial harmony.

This early chapter provides an entry point on a theme and a technique that are central to the novel's meaning. The theme is difference between and within the races. Difference is central to our efforts in making sense of the world, and it is also the greatest danger to these efforts. If we cannot make distinctions, we cannot organize the stream of sense data that confronts us. At the same time, these differences can obscure continuities and distort ambiguities. Early in this narrative, two ways of organizing the scene are offered. One of these is that of McBane, a racial essentialist who insists on the priority of race over all other distinctions. McBane believes that the man with African blood is radically different from his former professor and that the two must be separated, by force if necessary. The other way of organizing the scene is represented by the two doctors. These two hotly contest McBane's reading. They deny the significance of racial difference between them, and their obvious similarities in education, profession, and bearing seem to confirm this position.

Drs. Miller and Burns do not eschew differences, but they prefer to distinguish on the basis of class rather than race. Burns is introduced twice as a "gentleman," and, when Major Carteret appeals to Burns's racial loyalty, the white doctor indignantly answers, "I am a gentleman, sir, before I am a white man" (73). Burns clearly accepts Miller as his social equal, and this class affinity is more important for Burns than any other distinction. Miller, for his part, resents being seated with the farm workers, not because they are black, but because they lack the manners of the middle class. Two points need to be made about the designation "gentleman" in this context. First, Burns and Miller both understand this term to imply more than economic status: for them it also connotes qualities of sensitivity and moral discernment. Social groups have historically defended their class privileges with moral claims—consider the different meanings associated with the word "noble" for an obvious instance—and such claims have often been specious. Nonetheless, the contrast between the two physicians on the one hand and Captain McBane on the other makes clear that the former have moral qualities that the latter, despite his economic and political power, will never attain. Second, "gentleman" must be read in its early-twentieth-century American context. This was the moment of Horatio Alger and of the self-made man. Gentility was open to such men, and the term "gentleman" could connote membership in an aristocracy, not of birth, but of merit. Dr. Miller is the third generation of black men who committed themselves to America's success narrative:

> Miller's father, Adam Miller, had been a thrifty colored man, the son of a slave, who, in the olden time, had bought himself with money which he had earned and saved, over and above what he had paid his master for his time. Adam Miller had inherited his father's thrift, as well as his trade, which was that of a stevedore, or contractor for the loading and unloading of vessels at the port of Wellington. . . . His savings, shrewdly invested, had by constant accessions become a competence. He had brought up his eldest son to the trade; the other he had given a professional education, in the proud hope that his children or his grandchildren might be gentlemen in the town where their ancestors had once been slaves. (50)

Dr. Miller's acceptance by his white colleagues in the North and in Europe causes him to believe that he is on the way to realizing his father's ambition. He also believes that his progress can be a model for the race as a whole; he is confident that black economic and social progress can eventually erase racial difference.

Sadly, Miller's subsequent experience refutes his hopes. Racial distinctions are not, as McBane believes, essential differences in nature, but they are no less intractable for that. The emphasis on race above all other dif-

ferences grows from the powerful sense of superiority it bestows on the
one who stands on the privileged side of the racial line. Dr. Price, Miller's
Southern colleague and friend, understands this truth about himself and
other whites: "His claim of superiority to the colored doctor rested fundamentally upon the fact that he was white and Miller was not; and yet this
superiority, for which he could claim no credit, since he had not made himself, was the very breath of his nostrils" (75). Price's metaphor of the lungs'
constant, unconscious action suggests the deep level at which our racial constructions feed us. To pursue this idea further, let us shift to the metaphor
of Chesnutt's title. Tradition, the solid accretion of our experience in time,
is figured as bone marrow. The human skeleton is hard and coruscated, and
it may seem dead, but at its center is the blood-carrying tissue that nour-
ishes it. The marrow of tradition is the deep-flowing ideological juice that
perpetuates social custom.[3] Chesnutt's book aims to crack tradition's hard
shell and expose the soft, vital tissue within. Dr. Price accedes to tradition
and Carteret's wish to bar Miller from his home. So, rather guiltily, does
Dr. Burns. This early scene is a prelude to the apocalyptic massacre near its
conclusion. In that scene, Miller will find himself abandoned by his white
colleagues and ranked with the black roughneck Josh Green. The novel,
then, demonstrates the power of racial constructs to distort and corrupt all
other social and moral affinities.

The discussion of the episode on the train has also given an opportunity to observe the structural device that is crucial to the novel's exploration
of racial difference: the doubling and ironic juxtapositioning of the novel's
black and white characters. This technique dramatizes the play of difference
and similarity, and it helps to organize the novel's many characters and its
numerous plots. Among the novel's intraracial contrasts, the most important are formed by the symmetry of the Miller and Carteret families. Each
family is a leader in its respective racial community. Major Philip Carteret
and his wife, Olivia Markel Carteret, descend from two of Wellington's
most prominent white families. The major, after distinguishing himself in
the Civil War, now edits the area's leading newspaper. Dr. Miller and his
wife, for their part, are among Clarendon's most successful and cultured
black citizens. Nonetheless, the Carterets and other white aristocrats resent
what they take to be the Millers' pretensions to gentility: William and Janet
Miller are, after all, the grandson and the daughter of former slaves. The

Millers' gentility, like that of other members of the emerging black middle class, seems to the Carterets and other whites the Negro's insolent aping of their moral and social superiors. And yet, one might argue, the Millers have a greater claim to membership in an elite, understood in its modern, American acceptance, than do the Carterets. Dr. Miller's wealth comes from his own and his father's industry and thrift. Adam Miller, the doctor's father, became a person of means through hard work and thrift; he was, then, a true member of America's self-made aristocracy of merit, and his son follows in this tradition. Carteret's situation, on the other hand, is founded on his wife's inherited wealth, which he hopes to improve by risky financial speculation. The doctor's son is bursting with health, while the Carteret baby is constantly ill. We are meant to recognize how these dispiriting facts reflect on the major's masculinity, for a vigorous virility was central to the redeemed South's self-image. Viewed in the light of these contrasts, the Carterets are—quite literally—pale imitations of the more authentic natural aristocrats, the Millers.

The Carterets are aware of these contrasts, which are exacerbated by two additional factors. The Millers own and inhabit the former Carteret family home. More wounding still, the families are bound by an intimate but unacknowledged connection: Janet Miller is Olivia Markel Carteret's half-sister, a fact all too evident in their nearly identical appearance. It is precisely the anxious recognition of this kinship that drives the Carterets' hysterical insistence on distance between the races. The paradox that this novel reveals is the complex relation between similarity and difference in Southern racial relations. The claim of white racial superiority justified the white right to hold blacks as property; this in turn made possible white male exploitation of black women. The consequences of that exploitation were abundantly evident in the South's mixed-blood population. The fact of sexual contact between whites and blacks—whether in lust or in love—asserts not only a family relation between individual whites and blacks but also a deeper connection between individuals of all colors within the human family.

Claims of white superiority required redeemed Southerners to strenuously deny the obvious: not only were whites and blacks not members of the same families, they were not even of the same species. It is precisely the recognition of similarity that produces the exaggerated insistence on difference. In the Carteret-Markel family, this insistence has an economic basis, the fear that Samuel Merkel's mulatto daughter might claim her share of her father's property. Elsewhere in the South, even where no specific family inheritance was at issue, the economic motive for exaggerating racial difference existed. Acknowledging the human kinship between blacks and whites would require recognition of black claims on the wealth blacks and whites had jointly created in the plantation South.

The Marrow of Tradition is, at one level, a family narrative. The story of the separated family—one of the oldest in the history of the novel—had special relevance for African Americans. The reunification of parents, children, and brothers and sisters scattered by slavery and its aftermath is one of the most important structural devices of abolitionist and post–Civil War narratives. Harriet Beecher Stowe's *Uncle Tom's Cabin,* Frances E. W. Harper's *Iola Leroy,* and Paul Laurence Dunbar's *The Sport of the Gods* are all instances of this urgent theme. The latter novels, however, tell of the dispersal and recovery of black families. What makes Chesnutt's novel distinctive and audacious in this tradition is that the family in question consists of two parallel black and white lines. The narrative's central complication begins with Major Carteret's refusing to admit Dr. Miller to his home, and it concludes with Carteret's wife imploring her half-sister to allow the doctor to heal her child. The fact to which Chesnutt returns is the one that utterly confounds racial separatists: the American people, particularly in the South, are already a mixed race, and this mixing was introduced by white males. *The Marrow of Tradition* ends without any firm assurances about authentic family unity emerging from the Carterets' urgent pleading. The novel is, however, categorical about the fact that without white acceptance of a broad human family embracing blacks, whites, and people of mixed race there can be no lasting civil peace and prosperity.

The novel's family plot and political plot can be understood as a contest between opposed strategies for mapping the cognitive field of a biracial society. The family plot is driven by the Millers' wish to overturn the assumption of significant differences between the races. Janet wants to be united in one family with her white sister, Olivia Carteret, and William hopes to be accepted as his white colleagues' equal. The political theme, on the other hand, grows from an opposite cognitive strategy. Major Carteret has launched a political campaign that strenuously insists on radical differences between the races and the necessity of rigid racial segregation. The

Miller map is overdetermined socially, emphasizing class affinities across racial groups; the Carteret map, on the other hand, is overdetermined racially, insisting on white solidarity against any concessions to even the most educated and successful African Americans.

The Carteret-Miller contrast is the most important in the novel, but these couples have or develop significant connections within their respective communities. These connections unite the family plot and the political plot, and they open a broader system of comparisons between and within the races. The following schema represents the Miller and Carteret families with other characters from the novel's family and political plots. The schema will help us to explore similarities and differences within the novel.

Major Carteret	Dr. Miller
Olivia Carteret	Janet Miller
General Belmont	
Mr. Delamere	Sandy
	Mammy Jane
	Jerry Letlow
Captain McBane	Josh Green

The schema has two coordinates. The horizontal coordinate focuses on race, juxtaposing the white and black groups. The political plot denies any continuity along this plane. It insists that there is a radical break between the two columns on the schema—that whites are inherently different and superior to blacks—and that movement on this axis must be stringently controlled. This insistence on difference explains Carteret's refusal to admit Dr. Miller to his home. The vertical coordinate organizes each racial group socially. Members of the higher social class are at the top and those of lower social rank are below them, with a significant break between the social classes in each column. This coordinate reveals the social tensions within each group. Although Major Carteret and Dr. Miller disagree on the importance of racial difference, they share surprisingly similar views on social difference. Both men, members of their respective racial elite, are wary of movement on this vertical axis. They accept assimilation with some members of their race—those within their social class—but resist being associated with others. We have already noted Miller's discomfiture at being place with black laborers on the train. Assimilation of the doctor with less-cultured members of his race threatens links he wishes to emphasize, such as his class affinities with Dr. Burns. Similarly, Carteret accepts McBane's political assistance, but he bitterly resents the parvenu's assumption of social equality, as do other members of Clarendon aristocracy. McBane's heavy-handed attempt to gain admission to Clarendon's inner social circle is a significant subplot in the novel.

The novel's family and political plots can then be understood in terms of explosive tensions: an insistence on discontinuity and immobility on both axes, social as well as racial. But society and history are continuous and dynamic, creating new communities and forcing changes. The results of these conflicting pressures are convulsive and tragic. Similarities and ironic echoes among the novel's characters confound these coordinates from the novel's beginning. Already discussed is the direct challenge to claims of racial difference represented by the half-sisters and their families. This schema reveals the real affinities that the competing cognitive strategies obscure. One of these is a resistance to racial accommodation found in both ethnic communities. Thus Captain McBane stands to other whites as Josh Green does to other blacks.

Similarly, despite significant differences in race and class, Mr. Delamere and his servant Sandy mirror each other as common products of plantation culture's racial paternalism. Their loyalty to one another, an authentic moral bond, is as strong or stronger than the ties binding them to their respective racial groups. The title to chapter 24, "Two Southern Gentlemen," calls attention to this anomalous pair. It also focuses our attention on "gentlemen" and on "gentility," the problematic notion at the heart of Miller's hope for social elevation. Delamere is the only white man who still honors the ethos of aristocratic honor. He is the last remnant of the antebellum landed aristocracy, the only character to still live on, and presumably gain his living from, his plantation. These facts, his age, and his spotless honor ought to make him the community's respected elder, but they do not. His real power in Clarendon politics is less than that of Carteret, Belmont, and even McBane. This trio of conspirators control local politics without consulting Delamere. The following exchange occurs when Delamere tries to save Sandy from the lyncher's rope. In it, Carteret treats Delamere with insulting condescension.

"This man is innocent of this offense, I solemnly affirm, and I want your aid to secure his safety until a fair trial can be had."

"On your bare word, sir?" asked Carteret, not at all moved by this out-
burst. . . .

"Time was, sir, when the word of a Delamere was held as good as his bond,
and those who questioned it were forced to maintain their skepticism upon
the field of honor." (211)

The key terms in the exchange are *name* and *word*. Delamere remains,
anachronistically, committed to the mythos of the ancien régime. In the old
order, the king and his retainers stood outside the system of exchange. Their
names were the names of the lands they ruled, and their authority was as
solid as their forests and fields. These names gave them the power to signify
by the force of their word alone. Todd McGowan, in his reading of the
novel, explains: "The power of the master (the monarch) is present in the
very name; thus, because the name always realizes itself as the social reality,
there is, for the master, no disjunction between his/her will and the social
reality."[4] The post-Reconstruction South was a capitalist economy, and its
leaders were pragmatic business and professional people who appropriated
the aristocratic rhetoric of "honor" and "gentility" for their political and
economic purposes. The hollowness of this language is demonstrated by
the pathetic situation of Delamere, who is forced to *lie*—that is, to invoke
his family name falsely—to save Sandy. Equally mistaken is Dr. Miller, who
naively counts on the honor of the white middle class for his own social
recognition.

The schema shows that the vertical social organization represents a continuum and not the sequence of radically discrete units some characters
choose to see. Delamere would never shake McBane's hand, and Carteret
regards the "Captain" as a vulgar upstart. Nonetheless, McBane bodies
forth, in crude but candid form, the ugly hatred that animates Carteret
and his racist allies. Even Delamere finally accedes to the conspiracy that
McBane, Carteret, and Belmont have hatched. Similarly, Dr. Miller would
surely resist comparison of himself with the black vagrant he sees from the
train window. But the staging of the scene on the train suggests the connection between Miller's repressed anger and that of Josh Green. Miller is
forced to explore this affinity when he treats Green for an arm broken while
punishing a white mariner's racial insult. Miller fears that Green's violent
behavior will cause whites who do not distinguish between Negroes to see

all members of the race in a negative light. At the same time, the doctor admires Green's defiant racial pride, and he realizes that Green's courage reflects badly on his own prudent caution. Note, as Miller tries to calm Green's anger, the shift in personal pronouns; they hint at the middle-class physician's complex identification with his dark double: *"you're* feverish, and don't know what *you're* talking about. *I* shouldn't let my mind dwell on such things" (114, my emphasis).

Another similarity, which Miller—and readers who idealize him—would resist, occurs at the lower end of the black continuum. Jerry Letlow, Carteret's menial, tries to bleach his face with cosmetics and at the time of troubles wants "ter git in de ark wid de w'ite folks" (39). He is the ultimate accommodationist, or, as the title to chapter 9 has it, "A White Man's 'Nigger.'" Jerry, like Josh Green, also embodies qualities in Miller, in this case, the doctor's wish to be accepted by his white colleagues, whose culture and manners he has adopted. Miller is a political moderate, in General Belmont's judgment, a "good sort of negro," one who "doesn't meddle with politics" (251–52). Dr. Miller is, to be sure, significantly different from Jerry, but both men—in different ways and to different degrees—look for white acceptance. The question that the comparison of Miller and Jerry raises is: when does "a good sort of Negro" become "a white man's nigger"?

This discussion of Jerry leads to consideration of his position and that of his grandmother, Mammy Jane, on the schema. They are placed in the second column with the blacks and at the bottom with the working class, in effect, among the lowest of the low. And yet if we look at Jerry and Jane's deepest loyalties, we see that they go against race and class; they are firmly directed toward the white aristocrats in the upper, opposite corner. These black servants believe that loyalty to their masters protects them from the worst aspects of class and race. To understand this self-deception, we should reflect further on the phrase "white man's nigger," surely one of the most pregnant locutions in this novel. This phrase, a crude vernacular noun preceded by a possessive, is first of all, a redundancy. There are no "niggers" that are not "white man's niggers": niggerhood is a white fiction, a set of behaviors invented by whites and kept in place by white incentives and punishments.

Nonetheless, it is well to retain the possessive in this formulation to underscore the fact that Jerry and Jane are owned. I do not mean simply that they are former slaves or that Major Carteret purchases their labor and loyalty with the meager wages he pays them. In a deeper and more important sense, they are owned from within. Their consciousnesses are possessed by their white employers. The white construction of Jerry's identity is *his* sense of identity, the breath of his nostrils. It is also the source of his desperate need, by any expedient—cream, pomade, or betrayal—to be white. In Jerry and his grandmother, the novel presents two staples of nineteenth-century racial stereotyping: the shiftless darky and the dutiful mammy. Chesnutt's treatment of these figures here is essentially the same as the treatment of Plato, the youthful black performer in *The House behind the Cedars*. Chesnutt does not contest the existence of such types; rather, he indicates their origins in white social programming. And he also indicates the consequences for those who accede to this programming. Jerry and Jane's loyalty to the Carterets gains them nothing: they are swallowed in the racial violence fomented by their protector.

The novel's family and political plots draw blacks and whites together in a complex pattern of relationships. The relations mapped schematically illustrate how, in the binaries by which we signify, differences are created by the repression of similarities. Racist ideology distorts perceptions, denying kinships of blood and class. McBane crudely but accurately asserts the essentializing principle that guides his thinking: "All niggers are alike" (181). This logic, which groups all members of a race as a single, undifferentiated Other, leads to a fundamental rule of the lynch mob, enunciated, once again, by McBane: if a Negro is suspected of a crime, and the guilty party cannot be readily identified, "burn *a* nigger" (182); any Negro will do; they are all the same. Miller understands the brutal implications of this logic, and this helps to explain his political caution. Any violent act by a black, no matter how justly provoked, puts at risk innocent black lives and property. What makes the situation particularly tragic is that some characters seem prisoners of their own ideology, trapped in a self-reinforcing cognitive loop. Major Carteret loudly proclaims Caucasian superiority, and when he finds that his servant has accepted this idea and is trying to bleach his skin, he finds in this a further sign of black inferiority.

As suggestive as the connections are within the family and political plots, the narrative achieves another level of complexity and richness near its midpoint when it introduces a third plot, Polly Ochiltree's robbery and murder.

This story thrusts previously minor characters to center stage, introducing an additional, even more problematic set of connections. Central to the crime plot is Tom Delamere's impersonation of his grandfather's black servant, Sandy. Tom blackens his face with cork and puts on Sandy's clothes to kill Polly Ochiltree and steal her hidden wealth. Earlier, in a kind of rehearsal, Tom performed a similar masquerade, entering a cakewalk contest wearing Sandy's clothes. The "twinning" of Tom and Sandy is surprising, first of all, because nothing in the family and political plots prepares us for it. Tom is only distantly related to the Carterets, and he is indifferent to the major's political machinations. His name was omitted from the schema for this reason and because Tom, along with Lee Ellis, required extended, separate discussion. Tom's grandfather, John Delamere, is, of course, closely related to Sandy, as we have seen, but this deeply moral aristocrat is very different from his dissolute grandson. Tom's imitation is also astonishing because of its perfection: Tom copies Sandy's bearing and speech so perfectly that even Sandy is confounded. The black servant, who has glimpsed the impersonation without understanding it, asks Tom "ef I wuz in yo' place, an' you wuz in my place, an' we wuz bofe in de same place, whar would I be?" (168). Sandy's question seems to come directly from the comic sketch—the "perplexed nigger" scratching his head and asking a comic question in dialect. But once again Chesnutt's narrative signifies on a stereotype, and the dialect speaker says more than at first is understood.

Eric J. Sundquist provides a key for understanding the Tom and Sandy subplot in his discussion of the cakewalk.[5] This dance, performed first by slaves and later by white and black minstrels, derived ultimately from African cultural practices. On the antebellum plantation, when presented by slaves for their white masters, the dance often included subversive satirical elements. Blacks donned white hand-me-downs and offered exaggerated versions of their masters' European dances. The owners, oblivious or indifferent to the satire, enjoyed these spectacles as confirmation of the Negro's stereotypical gaiety. It was in the latter spirit that white minstrel performers included their own versions of the dance as the climactic moment for their "coon shows." When blacks joined the minstrel circuit, they also incorporated the dance, sometimes adding another level of mocking signification on their white competitors. The cakewalk of the late-nineteenth-century music hall was, like many popular representations of the African American, a confusing series of reflecting and distorting mirrors. A black person gazing at the image of his race created by white performers might well wonder, as Sandy does watching Tom, "whar would I be?" Sandy sees an image of himself, in some ways accurate, but appropriated, distorted, and deployed for purposes hostile to his interests. Tom, in fact, creates two images of the black man: the fun-loving darky who wins the cakewalk and the black brute who ravishes and murders the white widow. These two, seemingly contradictory stereotypes were both crucial to racist ideology. Even more boldly than with the stereotypes considered earlier, the novel dramatizes the source of these images in the white imagination and in white representations.

An additional key for understanding the pairing of Tom and Sandy is John Delamere. Delamere, Tom's grandfather and Sandy's master, is the third term that joins these two seemingly dissimilar individuals. As we observed earlier, John Delamere and Sandy are both products of pre–Civil War Southern society. So also is Tom, but with a difference. Old Delamere and his servant represent the high moral sense that, Southern apologists tell us, animated plantation society at its best moments. They live by the code of responsibility and service that bound aristocrat and retainer under the old order. Tom Delamere, on the other hand, represents the decay of this moral sense. Tom lives by no other principle than his personal pleasure, and in this he resembles Chesnutt's other fallen aristocrats, Malcolm Murchison and Bob Utley. Although Tom matches and perhaps surpasses the latter characters in dissolute behavior, he differs in one important way.

Tom Delamere embodies a cynical lucidity about what he is doing; this enables to him to skillfully manipulate and exploit others. When he is reproached by his fiancée for drinking and gambling, he selects exactly the right clichés from popular romance to soften her: "My home life is not ideal,—grandfather is an old, weak man, and the house needs the refining and softening influence of a lady's presence. . . . With you by my side, dearest, I should be preserved from every influence except the purest and the best" (101–2). Tom's instinct about American narratives of gender and race is unerring, and his handling of their expectations is masterful. He understands immediately that in Wellington the first suspect in any robbery and assault, especially on a white woman, will be a black man. He plans his crime in a way that skillfully plays upon these cultural expectations. Tom is intimately familiar with Sandy's speech and behavior, and this explains why his imitation is so perfect—too perfect. The first suspicion about Sandy's victory in the cakewalk occurs to Lee Ellis, who notes an unreality, an exaggeration of real elements, in the performance. As established in chapter 4, there is a distinction between the vernacular spoken among rural blacks and "minstrel speech"; the latter is a skillfully stylized version of the former, fashioned by whites for white entertainment. Exaggeration is the key to the psychological power of this stereotypical representation and a tip-off to its falsity. The culturally sanctioned cliché simplifies reality, obscuring troublesome nuance and complexity. Of course, this simplicity also announces a deformation of the real world's ambiguous play of similarity and difference.

Lee Ellis is paired with Tom Delamere in the novel's fourth plot, the rivalry for Clara Pemberton's hand in marriage. This rivalry is important in the novel's political implications, for Clara will inherit wealth and social position. The man who shares her wealth and status will be able to decisively shape Wellington's future for good or for ill. Clara's choice of Lee Ellis is one of the novel's few rays of hope. Ellis matches Tom's mental acuity, but he is not cynical, and he is not tied to plantation ideology. Ellis is a Southerner, but his family was not among the landowning class and did not defend slavocracy. Others—Carteret and McBane, Jane and Jerry—are so contaminated by the ideological air they breathe that they seem incapable of any perspective on their situations. Although the novel shows the way we are possessed by our forms of thought, it also shows that we can glimpse ideology's power in our lives. Both Tom and Lee understand the assumptions that control Southern perceptions; Tom chooses to exploit these assumptions, but Lee rejects them and has the power to help change them. Lee Ellis discovers the truth about Tom's murder and theft, and he discovers the facts that save Sandy's life. He also triumphs in the novel's marriage plot, winning the hand of Clara Pemberton, daughter of an important planter family.

The joining of Clara and Lee is, then, a union of old and new, the fusion of the old planters with a new generation of professionals and business people. Chesnutt once again echoes the late-nineteenth-century "New South" narrative. Henry W. Grady, in his 1886 address of this title, stressed to his New York audience that a new leadership had emerged in the former Confederacy and that they embodied a new spirit: "We have found out that in the general summary the free Negro counts more than he did as a slave. . . . We have sowed towns and cities in the place of theories and put business above politics."[6] Lee Ellis, the best of Clarendon's white citizens, might fairly be taken as an instance of the New Southerner. Nonetheless, we might look closely at Ellis and ask how much has been gained in the transition from old to new in the South. Lee, with Mr. Delamere, saves Sandy's life, but neither publicly accuses Tom. As a result, a murderer and a thief, a man who deliberately prepared the lynching of his innocent servant, goes unpunished. In the "New South," as in the old, racial loyalty is still more important than justice. Lee works for Carteret's newspaper, the noisy mouthpiece of white supremacy. He disapproves of Carteret's editorial policy, but he does not risk his position by trying to change that policy. In the "New South," as in the North, racial loyalty and economic interests prevail over moral principle.

Thus far this discussion has traced Chesnutt's analysis of Southern society through the novel's subplots. It is time now to return to the central narrative, the family story, to see how this struggle is resolved. The tumultuous riot that climaxes the political plot creates a crisis for the half-sisters, Janet Miller and Olivia Carteret. The Millers' son is killed by a rioter's stray bullet, and the Carteret child, struck by a respiratory illness, can be rescued only by Dr. Miller's surgical skill. The Carterets hasten to the home of the man they earlier had shunned. Dr. Miller finds Olivia Carteret at his door: "A lady stood there, so near the image of his own wife, whom he had just left, that for a moment he was well-nigh startled. A little older, perhaps, a little fairer of complexion, but with the same form, the same features, marked by the same wild grief" (323). Olivia pleads for Miller's compassion: "You know what it is to lose a child! . . . You will come to mine!" (324).

Where earlier the Carterets had insisted on an uncrossable differences, they now appeal to the similarities joining them to the black parents. The doctor leaves to his wife the decision as to whether he should aid the white couple, and the plot seems to have come full circle, for Janet Miller has within her grasp the family recognition she has sought. Olivia acknowledges Janet as her father's legitimate daughter, her sister, and heir to the family name and fortune. But now, at her moment of seeming triumph, it is Janet who insists on difference. "I throw back your father's name, your father's wealth, your sisterly recognition. I want none of them,—they are bought too dear! . . . But that you may know that a woman may be foully wronged, and yet may have a heart to feel, even for one who has injured her, you may have your child's life, if my husband can save it!" (329). The difference that Janet claims for herself—and for her race—is ethical. She and her husband can legitimately claim a moral superiority based on patient and proud triumph over injustice. She grants Olivia's plea not as a sister but as noblewoman to supplicant. This is both the triumph of the Millers' social project—the trumping of race with class—and its ironic deconstruction. In the moment of gaining the acceptance to which she and her husband aspired, Janet realizes its emptiness. The name that she hoped to claim is an empty signifier; the innate fairness that the Millers had hoped to find in the best white citizens is a myth; the white aristocrats know only physical necessity. Janet demonstrates the generous gesture of which the Carterets are incapable, and in so doing asserts a moral gulf between them, deeper than the divisions of race or class.

The Marrow of Tradition is, from its beginning, anxious about the future. The precarious birth of Major Carteret's son, before the novel opens, rescued his family from extinction, and, at the end of the novel, the child is at risk again. If Dr. Miller's intervention is successful and the child survives, he will have two male parents: a white father who gave him life and a black uncle who saved it. The doctor who lost a black son will gain a white nephew. Will these tenuous bonds suffice to overcome the differences and affirm the similarities observed in this Southern community? The novel makes no promises; it says only that the cause is urgent.

10

The Colonel's Dream
"Sho Would 'a' Be'n a 'Ristocrat"

In the past year the work of the Negro hater has flourished in the land. Step by step the defenders of the rights of American citizens have retreated. —W. E. B. DU BOIS, "The Niagara Movement" (1906)

The Colonel's Dream, the last novel that Chesnutt saw into print, is by critical consensus the least successful of the long fictions published during his lifetime. It is also judged to be the most overtly didactic work. The novel, it is true, does strain toward a moral lesson, and yet, at the same time, the actual nature of that lesson remains obscure or contradictory. For Ernestine Pickens the novel shows that the "loss of aristocratic values is a loss of moral force in southern communities."[1] The protagonist, Colonel Henry French, represents the best values of the Old South, and he has also had a successful business career in the North. The colonel's return to the region where he was raised echoes two late-nineteenth-century narratives, the narrative of the "New South" and the novel of North-South reconciliation. French's success in Northern commerce and in his return home figures two regional elites coming together to create a new society below the Mason-Dixon line. The colonel's engagement to Laura Treadwell, a daughter of the local aristocracy, prepares us for a marriage that will unite North and South.[2] However, unlike *The Conjure Woman,* which invokes these narratives seriously and optimistically, *The Colonel's Dream* deliberately frustrates the expectations they evoke. The colonel fails as a reformer, and he abruptly breaks off his engagement with Laura Treadwell and returns North. It is true that French is morally superior to the novel's other white characters, and the narrative is structured in such a way as to cause readers to identify with him. Thus the novel can be taken as an elegy to the South's vanished moral elite. But this novel also offers another, contradictory interpretation. In this reading, French is not simply victim but also nemesis. The tragedies recounted here result not so much from the *disappearance* of aristocratic values but from their *survival* in Southern communities. The colonel's dream turns into a nightmare not merely because of the situation he confronts but because of the contradictions he embodies.

Henry French is a Southern aristocrat, a designation that, for French, denotes more than simple class affiliation. He descends from a family that has rendered distinguished service over many generations, and he himself served in the Confederate Army, rising to the rank of colonel. Membership in the Southern aristocracy, then, for French, has both social and moral implications. He learned early the responsibilities imposed on members of his class. His father impressed upon him that "to whom much is given, much will be required," and French believes, "he had made the performance of duty his criterion of conduct. To him the line of least resistance had always seemed the refuge of the coward and the weakling."[3] French is indeed a remarkable individual, and he gives proof of his moral fiber at the novel's beginning. The manufacturing firm he built in the North after the war is under heavy pressure from a powerful trust; French resists the pressure until the final hour and then sells out at a very large profit. He believes that in this transaction he has "won a notable victory against greed and craft and highly trained intelligence" (10). This victory later gives him the confidence to confront the reactionary forces he meets in the South. He fails completely in this Southern confrontation, and in light of this failure, it is worth considering the moral assumptions he brought to the struggle.

The Northern "victory" against big business is important in this respect, for it is the prelude to his Southern test. French believes he has triumphed over the trust's greed and guile by forcing them to pay a higher price than they wanted to pay. But for whom is this a victory? The narrator gives us French's reflections on the consequences of his bargain:

The firm . . . would receive liberal compensation; the clerks, for their skill, experience, and prospects of advancement, would receive their discharge. What else could be expected? The principal reason for the trust's existence was economy of administration; this was stated, most convincingly, in the prospectus. There was no suggestion, in that model document, that competition would be crushed, or that, monopoly once established, labour must sweat and the public groan in order that a few captains, or chevaliers of industry, might double their dividends. Mr. French may have known it, or guessed it, but he was between the devil and the deep sea—a victim rather than an accessory—he must take what he could get, or lose what he had. (5)

The sale of French and Company, Limited, is certainly a victory for its former owners; they are paid double the firm's book value. But they profit at the cost of the firm's employees and the general public. French understands these consequences, and his rationale is a pragmatic acquiescence to a superior force: "What else could be expected? . . . he must take what he could get, or lose what he had." French has no illusions about the jungle of turn-of-the-century capitalism, and my point is not to fault his realism, but simply to call attention to the way it conflicts with his aristocratic code. That code requires that he eschew "the line of least resistance . . . the refuge of the coward and the weakling." But in this key test, the knight does not fall on his shield; he gathers his booty and abandons the field. In this pursuit of self-interest it is hard to find any difference between the Southern cavalier and the Northern "chevaliers of industry."

In all fairness, it should be pointed out that French does not act for himself alone, for he also chivalrously protects the financial interests of Mrs. Jerviss, the widow of his former partner. But she is a member of his caste, and French's "aristocratic" values emphasize class solidarity. Southern honor derived from two sources and had two components: pre-Christian primal honor, which emphasized obligations to blood kin, and Christian gentility, which asserted obligations to all humans, especially the weak. As a practical matter, "primal honor"—the ties of family, clan, and caste— dominated in key tests between the two components.[4] The maintenance of slavery is the most obvious instance of class economic interest prevailing over Christian compassion for the less fortunate. French's own class loyalties assert themselves at a key moment in his Southern test—the lynching of Bud Johnson. Johnson is the most flagrant victim of the cruel convict labor system that the novel exposes. French is unable to persuade Bill Fetters, the local political boss, to release Bud Johnson, so he secures Johnson's freedom by bribery. Once at large, Johnson retaliates for his cruel mistreatment by attacking Fetters's son and overseer. Ben Dudley, a member of the local aristocracy, is guilty of an earlier assault on Barclay Fetters, and because of this, he is accused and jailed for Johnson's crimes. To free Dudley, French discloses Johnson's responsibility for the attacks and reveals his hiding place. This proves a fatal mistake, for shortly after his arrest, Johnson is taken from his cell by a mob and murdered.

French mistakenly believes that he can guarantee Johnson's safety in jail. French is plagued here, as he is throughout his Southern test, by fatally underestimating the evil he faces. But there is also another crucial fault in his moral calculations. Even had French been able to provide Johnson with a trial, he must surely have known that Southern justice would have dealt very harshly with a black man who had assaulted powerful whites. Had "justice" prevailed, Johnson would have been returned to a chain gang or to a prison where Fetters would have dealt him a slower, more painful death than the one provided by the lynchers. It is true that Johnson was legally guilty of assault, but it is also true that he was driven to this crime by the cruelty of white men and the impossibility of legal redress. Why then surrender a black man to gain the release of a white man, particularly when the white man would surely have had a much better chance than the black man for a fair trial and acquittal? French apparently never considers these different possibilities and their implications. Ben Dudley is, in French's mind, "a gentleman by instinct" (129). The Dudley and French families have been linked by friendship over several generations. Moreover, the two men are, by their engagements with the Treadwell sisters, prospective brothers-in-law. It is not surprising, then, that Dudley's situation is more present in French's consciousness at this key moment, influencing his fatal miscalculation. Despite his sincere interest in democracy, French's instincts and behavior are strongly determined by aristocratic class loyalty.

With this thought in mind, it is worthwhile interrogating the idea of aristocracy more thoroughly. The aristocratic code has several limitations as a moral compass. First of all, it is based on blood, and therefore inherently racialist. According to aristocratic ideology, certain individuals are, by birth, superior to other individuals, and this innate superiority imposes moral obligations. Noblesse oblige, whatever its good effects in any particular instance, is an act of condescension; it defends as a general principle an unjust and unequal relationship at the same time that it permits individual exceptions to it. Moreover, the Manichaean binaries of this system obscure the world's true moral complexity. Biological essentialism leads to an equally procrustean moral essentialism: a binary that contrasts a noble class endowed by birth with a broad and generous moral perspective and a base-born, narrowly egoistic majority. Moreover, the linkage between "blood" and behavior implies a connection between physical being and moral character. This logic encourages efforts to discover a person's ethical predisposition in his or her physical appearance: in an individual's bearing, facial features, and indeed, in a person's color. But humans are rarely one thing, simply noble and altruistic or base and self-serving. Moreover, these qualities cannot be discovered on our faces or in our bodies. Human behavior is simply too ambiguous and various to be encompassed by the reductive categories of aristocratic ideology. The self-consciously aristocratic French is, as a consequence, continually surprised and undone by the complex reality he confronts.

French returns to a South that, in many ways, seems unchanged. He is addressed as "Colonel," his former military rank, and accorded the deference traditionally reserved for the local aristocracy. This deference and his recent triumph in the North lull French into a complacent self-confidence, and he seriously underestimates the forces that he faces. Surveying the community's economic and moral torpor, he resolves "to shake up this lethargic community; to put its people to work, and to teach them habits of industry, efficiency and thrift. This, he imagined, would be pleasant occupation for his vacation" (106). He is, of course, grievously mistaken in these calculations. The obstacles he faces are much greater, and his own moral and intellectual resources are much less than he imagines. These limitations are dramatized in three crucial encounters, each of which turns on the theme of the Southern aristocracy, old and new.

One of the most important encounters is French's meeting with the man who becomes his enemy, Bill Fetters. Fetters's father was a slave trader and slave catcher; he did the brutal dirty work for slave-owning planters, such as the Frenches, who held him in contempt. Here, as in Carteret's relation with McBane in *The Marrow of Tradition,* we see the aristocracy's dishonest attempt to distance itself from a group upon which their social and economic system depended. French shares this class prejudice: as a child, he kicked young Bill down the streets of Clarendon in punishment for a youthful act of treachery, and he now recalls him as a poor white boy "who could not have named with certainty his own grandfather" (77). In this utterance, as elsewhere in Southern ideology, there is a faith in the family name as an infallible moral signifier. There is also an assumed biological determinism, a connection between one's genetic inheritance and one's moral disposition. The narrator, reporting what is clearly French's own opinion, informs us that French's son, Phil, "had inherited the characteristics attributed to good blood. Features, expression, bearing, were marked by the signs of race" (16–17). French boasts that the boy is a "born gentleman," and when a friend adds that Phil descends from "a race of gentlemen" (32), French does not demur.

These assumptions of a biologically grounded superiority shape French's attitude toward his opponent, encouraging a false sense of security. He is a "born aristocrat"; Fetters, an "upstart" (36). French's condescension becomes contempt when he learns of Fetters's unscrupulous and exploitative business practices. He arranges a meeting with Fetters, expecting to meet, if not Simon Legree, at least the vulgar Captain McBane—in short, "the typical Southerner of melodrama." But stage narrative is poor preparation for the real world, and French finds instead "a keen-eyed, hard-faced, small man, slightly gray, clean-shaven, wearing a well-fitting city-made business suit of light tweed. Except for a few little indications, such as the lack of crease in his trousers, Fetters looked like any one of a hundred business men whom the colonel might have met on Broadway in any given fifteen minutes during business hours" (223). External indications are not the sure moral guide French expects. French finds that, at least physically, the New South aristocrat and commoner are surprisingly similar. French's discovery of changes in Southern society highlights the tensions and contradictions in his attitudes toward aristocracy and democracy. The discovery of Fetters's fortunes earlier had prompted French to muse about these themes. On one hand, he denies believing "that blood alone entitled him to any special privileges." He mentally congratulates Fetters for his realization of the democratic dream. At the same time, other aspects of Fetters's behavior make him wonder:

But, these, perhaps, were points where blood *did* tell. There was something in blood, after all, Nature might make a great man from any sort of material: hence the virtue of democracy, for the world needs great men, and suffers from their lack, and welcomes them from any source. But fine types were a matter of breeding and were perhaps worth the trouble of preserving, if their existence were compatible with the larger good. (37)

These conflicts in French's values are also seen in another encounter: his interaction with William Nichols, a mulatto barber. French enters Nichols's shop for a shave, and, after he is seated, learns that the barber owns the French family's ancestral home. The black man comments on his residence: "we've b'en mighty comfo'table in it, suh. They is a spaciousness, an' a air of elegant sufficiency about the environs and the equipments of the ed'fice, suh, that does credit to the tas'e of the old aristocracy an' of you-all's family, an' teches me in a sof' spot." The colonel, we may imagine, is surprised by the barber's mixture of literate diction and vernacular pronunciations. More disturbing to his aristocratic sensibilities is the familiarity implied in the black man's compliment to his family's "tas'e." None of this, however, prepares French for the avowal that comes next from the barber: "For I loves the aristocracy; an' I've often tol' my ol' lady, 'Liza,' says I, 'ef I'd be'n bawn white I sho' would 'a' be'n a 'ristocrat. I feels it in my bones'" (80). Before the black barber can apply the bay rum, French offers to pay literally any price to reclaim his family property. French is flooded during these minutes by nostalgia for the home in which he was raised. The suddenness and excessive generosity of his offer, however, suggest that more is involved than sentimental memories. Here, as in the meeting with Fetters, there is pull of conflicting values within the colonel:

> In principle the colonel was an ardent democrat. . . . But in feeling he was an equally pronounced aristocrat. A servant's rights he would have defended to the last ditch; familiarity he would have resented with equal positiveness. Something of this ancestral feeling stirred within him now. While Nichols's position in reference to the house was, in principle, equally as correct as the colonel's own, and superior in point of time . . . the barber's display of sentiment only jarred the colonel's sensibilities and strengthened his desire. (81)

We are inclined to judge Colonel French more favorably than Major Carteret and are correct in doing so. Nonetheless, like that other survivor of the Southern aristocracy, French is shocked when he discovers blacks living, not as servants but as masters, in his ancestral home, and unlike Carteret, he is able to remove them. For French, the thought of the former slave as a "'ristocrat"—in his family seat, no less—is too unsettling to bear, and he immediately offers to pay any price to remove him.

The first two encounters discussed were with the new "aristocracy"; a third is with a member of the old planter class. French journeys to the decaying mansion of Malcolm Dudley, a friend of his father and grandfather. Here again, physical indications prove to be an ambiguous guide to moral character. Malcolm Dudley has the face "of a highbred and strongly marked type," which seems to identify him as an aristocrat. But he also has "the hawk-like contour, that is supposed to betoken extreme acquisitiveness" (138). This acquisitiveness—Dudley is obsessed with buried treasure—links him morally to the parvenu Bill Fetters. The Malcolm Dudley plot is actually a revision of "The Dumb Witness," Chesnutt's unpublished short story, inserted with changes into the novel. In both versions Malcolm (Murchison in the story, Dudley in the novel) abuses his slave mistress, Viney, after she speaks to her master's white fiancée. Malcolm's savage abuse of Viney causes her to lose the power of speech, a fatal mistake because Viney alone knows the location of the family treasure and, without speech, she cannot reveal it. Here, as in the earlier unpublished story, Viney's situation allegorizes the consequences of the white aristocrat's abuse of the black female and the brutal taboo against admitting this crime. These crimes rebound on the white elite, blocking recovery of the South's former wealth.

In the novel as in the story, Viney's experience explodes the myth of a benevolent slave-owning aristocracy. The novel drives home this moral point with two changes in the original short story. In the first version, Malcolm himself cuts Viney's tongue; in the novel he gives her to his overseer, who nearly beats her to death. Malcolm, of course, is no less guilty of the atrocity for delegating it to another, but the novel makes clear his mechanism for evading that guilt. This subplot reiterates a theme from the Fetters encounter. The aristocratic slave owners profess contempt for the men who managed their human chattel. Nonetheless, the Fetterses, the McBanes, and their kind, were "a necessary adjunct of an evil system" (35). In a second change from the short-story version, the white doctor who attends Viney after her beating makes clear the divine malediction on the Southern aristocracy: "If we are whipped in this war and the slaves are freed, as Lincoln threatens, it will be God's judgment" (172), he tells Dudley.

Malcolm Dudley's story is linked to the main plot by his nephew Ben Dudley. Ben aspires to the hand of Graciella Treadwell, sister to Laura Treadwell. The Dudley family decay threatens the present generation, for Ben is also under the spell of an imagined family treasure, and this obsession with the past blocks his adaptation to the present. Ben's attendance at the Assembly Ball produces an event that thematically links the carnivalization of social categories seen in the encounters with Fetters, Nichols, and Ben's uncle. The Assembly Ball, a survival of antebellum society, is the key social event for Clarendon's white elite. Ben is by birth a member of this elite, and thus his attendance is expected, all the more so in that Graciella will be present. But the Dudley family's fallen fortunes will not allow him to arrive at the ball properly attired and in a carriage. He shows up on foot wearing ill-fitting hand-me-downs at the moment Barclay Fetters, Bill's son, descends handsomely dressed from his carriage. "You boy there, by the curb, open this door," Fetters orders Ben. Then when Ben steps into the light, Fetters carelessly remarks, "Oh, I beg pardon . . . I took you for a nigger" (203). The twinning of Tom and Sandy Delamere, white and black, is replayed with a difference. In *The Marrow of Tradition,* white Tom *means* to be mistaken for black Sandy, but here the mistake is *unintentional,* and all the more galling for that. French's meetings with Bill Fetters, William Nichols, and Malcolm Dudley have already confounded familiar and overly facile distinctions between aristocrats and upstarts, as well as between whites and blacks, in the New South. Ben's experience at the Assembly Ball takes this confusion one step further, for this member of the old elite finds himself demoted to the status of "nigger" by the descendent of a man his ancestors regarded as white trash. Dudley retaliates for his humiliation by drunkenly assaulting Fetters. This behavior, stereotypically associated with working-class whites and blacks, further disgraces Ben among his peers.

These encounters might have alerted Colonel French that the world to which he has returned is more complex than he had imagined, but they do not. Here is his vision for a reformed South expressed after the episodes we have discussed:

> His aim was to bring about, by better laws and more liberal ideas, peace, harmony, and universal good will. . . . The very standards of right and wrong had been confused by the race issue, and must be set right by the patient appeal to reason and humanity. Primitive passions and private vengeance must be subordinated to law and order and the higher good. A new body of thought must be built up, in which stress must be laid upon the eternal verities, in the light of which difficulties which now seemed unsurmountable would be gradually overcome. (247)

The intellectual underpinnings of the colonel's vision are those of the eighteenth-century French and British Enlightenment. The colonel assumes, as "eternal verities," a natural moral order based on a common human nature. He also assumes that this moral order is discoverable by reason, and, once demonstrated, will be understood and embraced by men and women of goodwill, who will see their own self-interest in promoting a common good. There is no mention in this passage of a personal God, but implicit in it is an almost religious faith in human reason and in an ultimately rational natural order. On the matter of race, French seems to adopt the subjectivist position, that is, he assumes that racial distinctions are simply a logical error that can be set right "by patient appeal to reason." We should note that this subjectivism is in fundamental contradiction with the racial essentialism implicit in the aristocratic ideology discussed earlier.

The brutal lynching of Bud Johnson and the whipping of local blacks are, of course, a rude shock to French, but rather than weakening him, they seem to strengthen his resolve. He knows that victory will not be easily or quickly won; nonetheless, he is confident that it must eventually come. He prepares a letter to his Northern associates that will mean a definitive break with them and a lifelong commitment to his Southern project. Serene in his resolution, the colonel retires for the night. He is briefly awakened by a noise, then falls into a deep, dreaming sleep.

> As the colonel slept this second time, he dreamed of a regenerated South, filled with thriving industries, and thronged with a prosperous and happy people, where every man, having enough for his needs, was willing that every other

man should have the same; where law and order should prevail unquestioned, and where every man could enter, through the golden gate of hope, the field of opportunity, where lay the prizes of life, which all might have an equal chance to win or lose. (280)

This literal dream crystallizes the metaphorical dream to which the novel's title alludes. It is given to us in a single long sentence. The parallelisms, the regular rhythm, and the repetitions create a pleasing sense of harmony. The eight subordinate clauses that follow the main clause postpone closure, suggesting a progressive, swelling movement toward a glorious future. As the colonel continues his dream, he prospectively reviews what he expects will be a long and useful life. Imagining himself at life's end resting beside his son and his father, he selects as his memorial a line borrowed from Leigh Hunt's "Abou Ben Adhem": "Here lies one who loved his fellow-men . . . and tried to make them happy" (281).

A little later, French, who recently buried Peter, his black servant, in his family's plot, is awakened to find Peter's casket on the piazza. Nailed to the casket is a message that brutally repudiates the epitaph French has just composed.

> *Kurnell French:* Take notis. Berry yore ole nigger somewhar else. He can't stay in Oak Semitury. The majority of the white people of this town, who dident tend yore nigger funarl, woant have him there. Niggers by there selves, white peepul by there selves, and them that lives in our town must bide by our rules. By order of
>
> CUMMITY. (281)

The eighty-three word sentence presenting French's climactic dream is rejected by seven short sentences as staccato as the hammer blows that attached them to the casket. The brutal simplicity of these three imperatives and four declaratives contrasts with French's elegantly cumulative syntax. The peremptory "Niggers by there selves, white peepul by there selves" cancels French's central metaphor, the "golden gate of hope," where all may enter together. We are, in this screed, as far as we can travel in the American language from the colonel's literate period. In this message's first word, the colonel's title, symbol of his aristocratic status, is mocked by a grotesque misspelling. "Committee" is obscenely defaced as "CUMMITY."

The misspellings actually worsen as the message progresses: "people," initially spelled correctly, becomes "peepul" in the last sentence. It is as if racist venom, corroding civilization's thin veneer, finally poisons orthography.

There is another burial in American literature that echoes ironically in this scene: George Shelby's reverent internment of Uncle Tom in Harriet Beecher Stowe's famous novel. Shelby buries the martyred body of his family's former bondsman and uses the occasion to free the family's remaining slaves. Shelby represented for Stowe a moral core, within at least a portion of the Southern population, that might be mobilized on the slaves' behalf. But Chesnutt's restaging of the black retainer's burial bitterly refutes the romantic hope of the North's greatest literary liberal.

Colonel French goes from his home to the cemetery, where he discovers the open grave, and from the cemetery to the telegraph office, where he sends a message announcing his return to the North and the death of his dream. We might wonder at the suddenness and finality of this decision. During the previous night, the deaths of his son and of his servant, the lynching of Bud Johnson, and the beating of innocent blacks have strengthened his resolve and produced the climactic dream we examined. Now, hours later, the rejection of his black servant from his burial place definitively cancels that dream. What has happened? The grotesque extraction of Peter's body from a white cemetery symbolizes the South's utter intransigence towards black equality. The silence of the "best people," the former aristocrats and the educated members of the middle class on whom French had counted, signals their complicity in this resistance to change. But more is involved. The trampled graves of his son and father, the muddy boots on the porch of his ancestral home are the ultimate desecration of his aristocratic ideal. The brutality of these gestures and the ugliness of its accompanying message finally awaken the colonel from his illusions. They explode the enlightenment assumptions upon which his dream was based, assumptions about human decency, reason, and rational human interest.

It is hardly in the white Southerner's economic interest to reject French's reforms. These reforms promise economic growth and greater democracy for everyone, whites as well as blacks. And yet the whites refuse. Their blind refusal refutes the assumption upon which the new order envisaged in *The Conjure Woman* was based. In the Julius and John stories, the two men cooperate because each sees that it is to his own benefit to do so.

This kind of benefit analysis requires a dispassionate lucidity rarely achieved in racial discourse. To see why this is so, consider the important differences between this novel and the collection of tales. *The Conjure Woman* is about *interracial* dialogue, the complex understanding achieved by a white couple and a black man. *The Colonel's Dream* is about *intraracial* negotiation: an enlightened Southerner's attempts to persuade his fellow whites to adopt different attitudes. Surprisingly, it is the latter that proves more difficult. *The Colonel's Dream* starts out as a reconciliation novel—the Northern Southerner returns home and prepares to marry a daughter of the local elite—but this match and sectional healing are brutally aborted. Albion Tourgée, who was unsparingly critical of the South, at least manages the marriage gesture, pairing Lilly Servosse, daughter of his Northern protagonist, and Melville Gurney, son of the Southern antagonist, at the end of *A Fool's Errand*. But Chesnutt raises the possibility of North-South marriage only to scotch it. When French's white neighbors dump Peter's casket in his drawing room, French abruptly decamps for the North, breaking his engagement to Laura Treadwell and marrying the Northern widow Mrs. Jerviss instead. The suddenness of this reversal testifies to French's deep frustration, but it does not suggest any reflection on the causes for his failure. Whites cannot understand blacks and dialogue with them until they understand and dialogue among themselves. The lack of such understanding is French's greatest tragedy.

A starting point for such understanding might have been a more serious consideration of Bill Fetters's motives. French approaches Fetters about releasing Bud Johnson, and he deals with him according to a simple binary. He first acts as if Fetters is an aristocrat, appealing to his chivalry, asking Fetters to free Bud to please a woman. When Fetters declines, French treats him as a base-born parvenu whose only goals are monetary. When Fetters turns down the colonel's offer of a virtually blank check, French is confounded. It does not occur to the aristocrat that the son of poor whites has his own form of pride, more valuable than any amount of cash. French is blinded by class prejudice as well as by psychological and philosophical naïveté. Dostoevsky's underground man could have explained to him that there is always an interest deeper than any motive supplied by reason. It is the wounded ego's need to wound in turn. Nietzsche called this the "politics of resentment." It is difficult to imagine thinkers more distant from French's

Enlightenment masters than Dostoevsky and Nietzsche, but it is their world in which French finds himself when he confronts Bill Fetters. Fetters coolly reminds French of how he humiliated the slave-catcher's son in Clarendon's main street years earlier. Decades have past, but Fetters remembers, and he refuses French's request.

Chesnutt's narrator, as in Chesnutt's other novels, tries to draw the narrative to an optimistic close. He surveys the colonel's noble but fruitless effort and asks, "But was not his, after all, the only way?"

> For no more now than when the Man of Sorrows looked out over the Mount of Olives, can men gather grapes of thorns or figs of thistles. The seed which the colonel sowed seemed to fall by the wayside, it is true; but other eyes have seen with the same light, and while Fetters and his kind still dominate their section, other hands have taken up the fight which the colonel dropped. (293)

The narrator, despite the colonel's failures, manages to find hope in his story. Note, however, that the narrator has shifted the grounds for this hope. This is not the eighteenth-century confidence in reason and progress, but rather the Christian's tragic vision of regeneration through suffering. This Christian consolation is unconvincing, as we can see if we compare it with Stowe's more consistent Christian allegory, which we mentioned earlier. Uncle Tom is brutally murdered, but his agony is efficacious, moving his former master to free his slaves. In Chesnutt's novel no such liberation seems imminent: Bill Fetters—Simon Legree's moral kin—is in firm control.[5]

The narrator claims as justification for optimism Theodore Roosevelt's recent efforts at suppressing the abuses of convict labor: "The strong arm of the Government, guided by a wise and just executive, has been reached out to crush the poisonous growth of peonage, and men hitherto silent have raised their voices to commend" (293). These efforts were, to be sure, laudable and important, but in terms of the story under discussion they were relatively inconsequential. Convict-labor reform made it more difficult for Bill Fetters to enslave men like Bud Johnson, but it did nothing about the novel's deepest evil—the venomous racism that lynched Johnson, expelled Peter French from the cemetery, and frustrated the colonel's dream of social renewal. Interestingly enough, it was racism that provided impetus for the convict-labor reform to which the narrator refers. Richard Berry, writing in 1907, described the motives for reform: "The

monumental error made by the employers of Florida was in going beyond
the black man with their slavery. Had they stuck to the racial division they
might have escaped castigation, as they have for a decade. But, insatiate,
and not finding enough blacks to satisfy their ambitious wants, they reached
out and took in white men." The *Cosmopolitan* editor who prefaced Berry's
article indignantly described the white person's "galvanic shock . . . to find
that this new form of slavery places white and black on a plane of perfect
equality, and enslaves them both with generous disregard of ancestry or
complexion."[6] The narrator's comments at the end of *The Colonel's Dream*
are unconvincing; it is hard to descry the presence of either "the Man of
Sorrows" or a "wise and just executive" in the America he describes. The
narrator's strained optimism, like that attempted at the end of *Mandy Oxendine* and *The House behind the Cedars,* achieves an effect opposite to the one
intended. These remarks announce, by their inappropriateness to the narrative they conclude, the real bleakness of the moral landscape that has been
portrayed.

The Colonel's Dream, as I have said, is Chesnutt's least esteemed novel,
and there are legitimate literary reasons for this. Nonetheless, its neglect is
unfortunate, for this novel dramatizes the complex and conflicting racial attitudes that exist in even the best-intentioned individuals. Chesnutt's
novel recounts the failure of a liberal white American. Joseph McElrath and
Robert Leitz find in the novel's protagonist a reference to Albion Tourgée,
author of *A Fool's Errand,* the reforming best-seller that inspired Chesnutt
in his diaries: "That Chesnutt named his *idéaliste manqué* hero French seems
his testimony to the recently deceased Tourgée, whose alter ego in the autobiographical *Errand* was a 'fool' with a Gallic surname, Servosse" (Intro.
to Chesnutt, *"To Be an Author,"* 20). These comments are perceptive and
useful, and I would like to pursue them. However, I would like also to
consider two other literary figures who can be glimpsed in the outlines of
Chesnutt's colonel. These are George Washington Cable and Walter Hines
Page, both of whom aided and advised Chesnutt. Tourgée's social impact
was the greatest of the writers I have mentioned, for in addition to
unmasking Southern "redemption" in his popular novel, Tourgée argued
Homer Plessy's case before the United States Supreme Court. That suit
failed, however, and it resulted in the disastrous decision of *Plessy v. Ferguson.*
In *A Fool's Errand,* Tourgée acknowledged that most of the freed slaves were

not prepared for citizenship and that they would have to remain for some time under white political tutelage. As a result, as Matthew Wilson points out, "Tourgée's nuanced analysis of the failure of Reconstruction was . . . misread and translated into its political opposite: evidence for the foolishness of the whole Reconstruction project of equal political rights for blacks."[7]

George Washington Cable encouraged Chesnutt early in his career; he read the novice writer's manuscripts with care and commented on them candidly. Walter Hines Page, as an editor at *Atlantic Monthly*, Houghton Mifflin, and later at his own firm, Doubleday Page, helped shape several of Chesnutt's publications. McElrath and Leitz recognize these two writers' importance for Chesnutt in the titles of the first and third parts of their edition of Chesnutt's letters, "Cable's Protégé 1889–1891" and "Page's Protégé 1897–1902." Unlike Tourgée, but like French, Cable and Page were Southerners who lived in the North. Both men were concerned about the South and supported the Negro cause. Cable disappointed Chesnutt, however, when he turned more conservative, as evidenced by the stereotyped portrait of a grafting mulatto in *John March, Southerner* (1894).[8] Page, like Chesnutt and French, was a North Carolinian. He returned frequently to his home state to lecture, observe, and report. His most important contribution to the national racial debate was "Rebuilding the Old Commonwealth," which appeared in the *Atlantic Monthly* in May 1902. In this essay, Page "notes the persistence of reactionary ideas about race and class." Despite these observations, Page remained optimistic and "predicted inexorable progress through education."[9] In the same year that he brought out *The Colonel's Dream,* Page also published Thomas Dixon's virulently racist *The Clansman,* and he apparently sent Chesnutt a presentation copy of Dixon's novel.[10] Tourgée, Cable, and Page were exceptional among white men of their time for their dedication to improving the black person's material condition. Nonetheless, all three opposed full and immediate political rights for black citizens. At their best, they favored an enlightened white paternalism, such as that of Colonel French. The colonel's focus, like that of Booker T. Washington and the white reformers mentioned here, was on preparing blacks for economic self-sufficiency, not for political and legal equality.[11] But the colonel's defeat at the hands of Bill Fetters shows that economic progress would always be fragile and uncertain without effective political rights and legal protection for blacks.

There is one more figure behind this novel's chastened idealist, another liberal Southerner gone North: Chesnutt himself. Chesnutt was not an aristocrat, although his white antecedents were probably from the planter class. Nonetheless, the idealist we meet in Chesnutt's journals cherished many of the same values as the colonel: dedication to service, confidence in reason, and, most important, faith in a basic human decency, which could be mobilized on the behalf of the less fortunate. In marking the colonel's passing, Chesnutt was mourning part of himself. The mourning would last nearly two decades, for Chesnutt would not attempt another major fictional project on a racial theme until 1921.

II

———◦◦◦———

Paul Marchand, F.M.C.

"F.M.C." and "C.W.C."

It is in the name of the father that we must recognize the support of the Symbolic function which, from the dawn of history, has identified his person with the figure of the law. —JACQUES LACAN, *The Language of the Self: The Function of Language in Psychoanalysis*

Paul Marchand, F.M.C., the novel with which Chesnutt sought to break a sixteen-year literary silence, is a geographic, historical, and generic anomaly in Chesnutt's canon.[1] Chesnutt's previous novels and many of his stories are set in North Carolina during the 1880s through the first years of the twentieth century. With *Paul Marchand, F.M.C.,* however, Chesnutt moved his attention to Louisiana in the 1820s. His two previous novels, *The Marrow of Tradition* and *The Colonel's Dream,* were executed in the style of muckraking realism popular at the time of their composition, but with *Paul Marchand, F.M.C.* Chesnutt seems to offer a local-color romance, a literary form more than twenty years out of fashion. And yet, despite these gestures toward an earlier movement and an earlier style, *Paul Marchand, F.M.C.* is, in many ways, Chesnutt's most modern work. It is so in virtue of the strikingly modern, even postmodern, meditation that it offers on personal and authorial identity.

The theme of identity will be the guiding focus of this chapter, but, before pursuing it, more must be said about the novel's setting. J. Noel Heermance, one of the few critics to comment on the novel, views the shift away from the present as an effort to accommodate readers unwilling "to face real-istic, contemporary racial material."[2] However, the novel's foreword contra-dicts this escapist thesis, for it promises "interesting parallels between social conditions in that earlier generation and those in our own."[3] Indeed, while 1920s Cleveland—the time and place of the novel's composition—might seem very different from Louisiana in the years following its accession to the United States, the sad truth was that, for black Americans, conditions in many ways remained the same. By rolling back the clock exactly one hun-dred years, Chesnutt's narrative mocks white assumptions of a century of social progress.

Antebellum Louisiana offered special circumstances with which to rein-force this point. The former French colony already had, before the Civil War, a significant number of blacks who were not slaves. Members of this special caste had cultural and economic opportunities that many of Chesnutt's black contemporaries might well have envied. Many Louisiana quadroons were educated in France, and they often controlled significant economic interests, including large plantations. Quadroon males, however, were required by law to signal their difference by signing "f.m.c." after their names. These initials undid the sense of autonomy implied in the name that they followed. The free men of color, despite their freedom from slavery and their cultural and economic attainments, had few legal rights that whites were bound to respect. As Chesnutt's novel shows, free men of color could be publicly humiliated, imprisoned, even enslaved by white Americans on the flimsiest pretexts. Chesnutt, who saw systematic discrim-ination, brutal lynching, and peonage—slavery by another name—in early-twentieth-century America, could appreciate, fully as much as his protago-nist, the bitter irony embedded in the initials that follow the protagonist's name. F.M.C., *Free* Man of *Color:* the final word in the designation canceled the first. In 1920s America, as in the 1820s, a man's rights as a free citizen were significantly conditioned by the color ascribed to his skin.

Early-nineteenth-century New Orleans provided fertile ground on which Chesnutt could continue his reflections on the language and the constructs we use to describe ourselves. The city was, following its accession to the United States, perhaps more than at any time in its history, the capital of carnival, a city of dynamically shifting identities. In a little over forty years, at the end of the eighteenth and the beginning of the nineteenth cen-tury, Louisiana was successively French, Spanish, French again, and then

American. Following admission to the Union, the population exploded, swollen by immigrants from all parts of the republic and from elsewhere. The quadroon class was an important component of this polyglot, hybrid population. Slave mistresses and their half-white children were, of course, common elsewhere in the American slave states, but they were kept "behind the cedars," shrouded by white hypocrisy and denial. In Louisiana, however, the *gens de couleur* occupied an acknowledged place in the social order. Their world, with its activities and hierarchies, in many ways mirrored that of the whites. The strange coexistence of these parallel universes—the accepted world and its shadow—becomes evident when in Chesnutt's novel a French nobleman visits the Louisiana capital. He attends on successive nights a white ball and a colored one. The quadroon ball becomes a key juncture in this narrative, a kind of looking glass through which the protagonist steps, successively, to three radically different identities: he is first an accepted businessman, then a black prisoner, and finally a white aristocrat—all with dizzying celerity.

Paul Marchand, F. M. C. introduces in its title the ambiguities and tensions within this paradoxical society. There are, first of all, the contradictions in the initials and in the class they designate. Moreover, this class designation, as applied to the novel's protagonist, is not accurate. He is, he learns in the course of the narrative, of pure white ancestry. And the name Paul Marchand is not his true name. He briefly rejects this name and class status for those that his ancestry provides, only to renounce these and reclaim the name and designation in the novel's title. In so doing, he dramatizes a complex and strikingly contemporary set of themes, which include appearance and reality, personal and social identity, and the power of language to create all of these.

Quadroons were proud of their status, and they often aggressively separated themselves from others of African ancestry. But even among this group, Marchand snobbishly holds himself aloof. A number of dramatic events, however, force him to reconsider his personal and social identity. Marchand had protected his proud isolation by swallowing his anger at indignities and carefully respecting the narrow boundaries laid down for members of his caste. A crisis is posed, however, by the presence of his sister-in-law, Lizette, at the Quadroon Ball. Attracted by its seeming romance, the naive girl attends this social event against her sister and her brother-in-law's wishes and without understanding its true meaning. The ball, essentially an

opportunity for white aristocrats to select mixed-blood mistresses, dramatizes the hypocrisy of Southern racial separation. Race mixing—for wealthy
white males and select quadroon females—was not only permitted but publicly facilitated by such events.

Quadroon males, of course, were strictly barred from attending. Marchand, seeking to protect his ward's honor, enters the ball, and this precipitates his first crisis of identity. His presence is discovered, and he is beaten
and thrown into jail. Because he has struck a white man in self-defense, he
faces the possibility of a whipping, the loss of his hand, or even death. Late
that night, he is awakened by voices from the adjoining cell. They belong
to a Negro and a mulatto, both free blacks. They have been shipwrecked,
and found without proper identification, they are going to be sold as slaves.
Marchand listens to their whispered conversation:

> "It is an outrage. . . . We have done nothing; they had no means of knowing
> that we intended to do anything. We were beaten without mercy; we were
> thrown into prison; we are to be sold into slavery, because, forsooth, we cannot
> prove that we are free men!"
>
> "We shall have revenge," returned a harsher voice, which to Marchand
> sounded vaguely familiar. "I hate them all, root and branch. I would kill the
> last one, even as our people did in San Domingo." (81)

Marchand senses something familiar in the voice, but he knows neither of
the men, who are strangers to the area. What he recognizes, without quite
knowing it, is not the voice, but what it says. The men have described his
own situation, and they have articulated his own desire for violent retri-
bution. Here, as in *The Marrow of Tradition,* Chesnutt provides his light-
skinned protagonist with a darker, more violent double. In the earlier novel,
Dr. Miller is forced into the Jim Crow car on a Southern train. The mulatto
physician looks out the train window and glimpses, crawling from under
a car even further back, Josh Green, the black giant who will take bloody
revenge during the race riot that climaxes the novel. The identification between Marchand and his alter ego, however, is worked out more consciously
and more fully than in any of the instances of doubling in Chesnutt's previous fiction.

Marchand, a property owner himself, knows that he should alert the
authorities and warn the threatened aristocrat about the conspiracy he has

overheard. But the plantation owner "was a white man, and for this night all white men were Paul Marchand's enemies; what should happen to them was no concern of his. They were all his enemies" (83). Marchand drifts off, then wakes again. He now realizes that the overheard conversation provides a solution to his own dilemma: to reveal blacks plotting against whites would gain his immediate release and other rewards as well. But he cannot act on his knowledge. "The two prisoners, like himself, were martyrs to caste; whatever their characters or their crimes, it was not for these that they were incarcerated, but for the unpardonable and unescapable crime of color" (84). This night began with Marchand acting in conformity with the highest standards of white Southern chivalry, striving gallantly to protect an innocent young woman's honor. But this act has caused him to be cast down among the lowest of the black unfortunates. The confrontation with the fate of others of his race precipitates a reversal of his previous values and class affiliation.

The ironic shifts in identity are not over—in fact, they have hardly begun—because morning brings another, even more surprising, reversal. Pierre Beaurepas, one of New Orleans's wealthiest and most powerful citizens, has died recognizing Paul Marchand—now Paul Beaurepas—as his son and heir. Paul Marchand knows this family well, for he had been publicly humiliated at different times by four of Pierre Beaurepas's five nephews. As a person of color, Marchand could not respond, but now, as a white man, he can. Paul calls his cousins together and, challenging each of the offenders to a duel, systematically avenges each insult. And yet there remains a fundamental ambiguity about the identity and motives of the man who accomplishes this vengeance. Is this the black man in the jail cell who swore vengeance against the white oppressors? In his explanations to his cousins, Paul Beaurepas argues just the opposite. White honor and family pride, he says, require that he act as he does. The Beaurepas motto is *Coup sur Coup.* Paul is now head of the family and he was insulted: he must return blow for blow. Despite his seeming logic, something in Paul's tone suggests that this rigorous implementation of white honor is also its deliberate and ironic deconstruction.

In the following days, Paul's resemblance to his father grows stronger. Like Pierre Beaurepas before him, Paul neglects his children and becomes coldly manipulative. The similarities between Paul and the white patriarch are particularly evident when Paul finds an important letter among his father's papers relating the history of his cousins. They were orphaned in the Haitian rebellion and brought to their uncle in New Orleans by the faithful family slave Zabet Philosophe. However, the letter mentions four nephews and a niece, and there are now five nephews. Paul guesses that the black woman has made a substitution and decides to question her. As we watch him force her confession, we see how completely he has become the white oppressor whom he had hated:

> "You are my slave, Zabet. . . . There is here a whip. If with it I should beat you to death, no one would have a word to say!"
>
> . . . Paul Beaurepas strode over to the trembling hag and seized her by the arm.
>
> "Down on your knees, huzzy!" he thundered. "Down on your knees and tell me the truth, or take your choice—the slave gang, the whip, the pistol, or the sword." (122–23)

Zabet admits that the young girl died and that she substituted her mulatto grandson. Paul forces her to whisper the boy's name. Paul now has the power, by disclosing this name, to change white to black, to transform the identity and status of one of his cousins. How will he act? *Who* will act: Paul Marchand or Paul Beaurepas? The issue is resolved by yet another dramatic event. Pierre Beaurepas had, before his death, made provisions to ally his family with that of another Creole patriarch, Don José Morales. Don José had agreed that Pierre Beaurepas's heir would have the right to marry his daughter, Josephine. Paul is encouraged to set aside his quadroon wife and children and to marry Josephine. While he is considering what course to take, Paul learns that the two blacks he had overheard in prison have made their escape, and he recalls that the plantation upon which they plan revenge is the Morales estate. He hurries to warn the Moraleses and arrives just as the rebels attack. They have just killed Mendoza, the overseer who captured them, and the mulatto has seized Josephine. Paul knows he must act, but he hesitates. Here is his second encounter with his dark double:

> Paul Beaurepas—for the moment Paul Marchand—saw, beyond the evil countenance of the man who had faced him, the long night of crime which had produced this fruit—the midnight foray in the forest, the slave coffle, the middle

passage, the years of toil beneath the lash, the steady process of inbrutement which the careless endowment of white blood had intensified by just so much vigor and energy as the blood of the master had brought with it. He must save the woman, but he pitied, even while he condemned, the ravisher. . . .

And this pity was very nearly his undoing. For while he paused, the second desperado, still bearing the bloody ax with which he had slain Mendoza, crept up behind him. Some instinct, or else some hidden change in the mulatto's expression, warned him in time to see the uplifted weapon, and by a quick sidewise spring, learned in fencing, to avoid the blow. Ere the Negro could recover from his frustrated effort Marchand had drawn his sword and run him through.

The mulatto, seeing his scheme foiled, hesitated, lifted his knife over Josephine's fair throat, and then with a lingering remnant of pity, threw her limp body to the ground and disappeared in the underbrush—sure, wherever he went, to be so long as he lived the bane of the society which had produced him. (159–60)

A strange recognition flashes between the white man and the mulatto, and it saves them both. Paul sees himself in the man with whom he was so recently imprisoned, and he does not attack. The mulatto, perhaps out of returned sympathy, alerts Paul to the other rebel's approach. Paul saves himself, the mulatto releases his captive, and Paul allows him to escape. Like Conrad's secret sharer on the deck of his ship, Paul watches his double slip back into the darkness.

The event dramatizes the conflicting identities and loyalties that inhabit the protagonist. Paul achieves a kind of resolution with the aid of another double: Philippe Beaurepas. Philippe is the only one of Paul's cousins who treated Paul decently before his status changed. In fact, he rescued Paul's sister-in-law when Paul was arrested at the Quadroon Ball. Philippe is also the only cousin to sincerely welcome Paul into the Beaurepas family, even though Paul's recognition has ended Philippe's own hopes of inheriting the Beaurepas fortune. Philippe, it turns out, loves and is loved by Josephine Morales, the woman to whom Paul was engaged by his father. Paul resolves his own situation by ceding the Beaurepas fortune, family leadership, and Josephine Morales to Philippe. Paul cannot accept the role planned for him by Pierre Beaurepas, for this would require him to abandon his wife and children. Such an act would violate the Beaurepas family honor: "I have spoken, as you have spoken, of the honor of the Beaurepas. Is it honor to forswear a solemn obligation, assumed with the sanction of God and man—for these our marriage had until a few weeks since? Is it honorable to abandon one's children to a nameless and hopeless future, as my parents so long abandoned me? . . . To me it would seem the depth of dishonor" (177).

Paul once again invokes his white family's name and its code of honor to defend his actions, and as in the earlier instance, he ironically signifies on both, turning them against the family. To be a Beaurepas and a white gentleman is to be bound by one's word, and Paul will honor his bond— even when it binds him to a mulatto. To be a Beaurepas he must be Marchand; to be white, in this instance, means to remain colored. Paul knows, of course, that the Beaurepas family has never been honorable, and he is casting back an identity he despises. There is another barb. It appears that Zabet Philosophe named Philippe as the mulatto child she inserted among the Beaurepas nephews. If this is so, Paul Marchand and Philippe Beaurepas's situations are opposite and yet strangely symmetrical: a white man raised as a mulatto; a mulatto man raised as white. Paul rescues Josephine, Philippe's beloved, as Philippe had earlier saved Lizette, Paul's ward. Paul now steps aside for his double, but in so doing, he forces the race-proud Beaurepas family to accept, unwittingly, a mulatto as its leader. But, in one final irony, one might argue that this action truly restores the family's honor, for Philippe Beaurepas was always its most virtuous member. In saying this, however, we must take care not to idealize Philippe; his fatuous insistence on taking his cowardly brother's place in the duel represents an unthinking commitment to the family code of honor as indiscriminating, in its own way, as the mulatto rebel's blind hatred of all whites. Philippe, we learn, proves an ineffective leader and does not stop the family's moral and economic decline. The point with both of Paul's doubles—Philippe and the mulatto rebel—is that they represent exaggerated versions of elements in Paul's own personality and situation, which Paul must recognize and surmount.

So what is learned about personal identity in the course of this novel's sudden sequence of reversals, inversions, and doublings? Who, finally, *is*

Paul Marchand/Beaurepas? What is his racial identity? The novel offers at least three approaches to the question.[4] There is, first of all, racial essentialism, which asserts fundamental biological and moral differences between whites and blacks. White aristocrats, like the Beaurepas family, use this argument to justify their absolute political and social domination of the blacks. The narrative refutes the assumption of innate moral difference by showing mulattoes and blacks—Philippe and even the black rebels—as more noble and courageous than their white "superiors." A further corollary of the white aristocrat's racial essentialism is the claim that even the slightest degree of African ancestry marks one morally, and that this mark can be read in an individual's behavior. Raoul and Hector Beaurepas claim to see this identity in Paul Marchand, whom they publicly label *"canaille"* (15), or rabble. But the falseness of their claims is mocked by the fact that Paul turns out to be white and their social superior. Paul pointedly calls the Beaurepas family's racial hypocrisy to their attention when he tells the cousins that one of them is of mixed blood and asks if they wish to know which nephew it is. They consider quickly and realize that the signs are ambiguous; each has at least one physical feature that might be interpreted as "black." Their purported certitude about racial identity and their concern for the family's racial purity give way quickly before self-interest, and they choose not to learn this family secret.

Raoul and Hector's mistakes about Paul's racial and moral identity show that the real determinants in this society are not biological essence but social assumptions. Raoul and Hector assume they are dealing with a quadroon, and that is what they perceive. In short, racial identity is socially determined. Monsieur Renard, the Beaurepas family's attorney, is remarkably candid in explaining this social definition. Identity, for Renard, is essentially linguistic and legal; it is carried in one's name, and the name is affixed by those in society who have the power to do so. The Beaurepas patriarch has announced that Paul is white and legitimate, and therefore, under Louisiana law, the person "hitherto known on the legal records of New Orleans as 'Paul Marchand, f.m.c.'" (94) has ceased to exist. Renard pushes his reasoning so far as to assert that not only has Marchand disappeared, but with him, his marriage to his quadroon wife and their children. In their place stands Paul Beaurepas, scion of Louisiana's most powerful family and fiancé of Josephine Mendoza. Renard's account, thus, is quite the opposite of biological essentialism: race does not come from within, but is imposed by society from without.

Renard's legal and linguistic casuistry may arrange things for the courts, but it cannot settle the matter for Paul or for those who must deal with him. Despite his changed legal status, the mulatto stubbornly refuses to disappear, as Paul's ambiguous actions after his inheritance suggest. Some portion of his previous history and identity remains ineradicably present. This fact is dramatized by the clumsy locutions—"Monsieur Paul Beaurepas, *ci-devant* Marchand" (97) and "Monsieur Paul Beaurepas, hitherto Marchand" (97)—Renard must invent to refer to his new client.[5] The Beaurepas nephews' embarrassment is even more painful than the lawyer's. They try to exploit Renard's legal casuistry to escape their obligation to duel Paul. Henri Beaurepas explains that "to us Paul Beaurepas did not exist; and we could not insult one who had not come into being. The acts of which you complain were directed against a certain *soi-disant* quadroon, who, in his turn, no longer exists" (133). Unfortunately for Henri and the others, a man was insulted, and he stands before them, saber in hand, demanding satisfaction.

Marchand finally resolves his identity in a manner that is both free and determined. Identity is the result of personal choice. Paul has been "colored," and he has been "white," and he can now choose to be either. Although his choice is free, he cannot make it in a vacuum; his choice takes place in the context of his life experience and the bonds he has formed. Racial labels may be arbitrary and socially imposed, but they leave psychological traces on the individual, and they establish moral bonds between those whom they have marked. "A man cannot," Paul explains, "at my age, change easily his whole outlook upon life, nor can one trained as quadroon become over night a—Beaurepas. In New Orleans, where a man must be of one caste or another, where there is no place for an individual as such, I, who have been all my life without father or mother, now find myself, in sympathy, without a race" (177–78).

Marchand is without parents and without a caste—and he is in this sense "without a race"—but he is not without wife and children, and he makes his choice in solidarity with them and with others who have suffered racial exclusion. He refuses to join a group that enslaves and humiliates others, and he emancipates those slaves whom he has the power to free. He renounces the Beaurepas name and assumes the name he bore as a mulatto. He will remain with his colored family, and they will leave America for France. The "man of color" will finally be free. Despite this liberation, the tone at the end of the novel is hardly triumphant. Expatriation to Europe was a solution seriously considered by Chesnutt in his own life and by Dr. Miller in *The Marrow of Tradition*, but both rejected it as an abandonment of blacks who could not escape the United States. Marchand may believe he is without a race, but it is difficult to imagine him entirely at ease in Europe, even in France. The narrator tells us that Marchand's son—in another return of the repressed—sails into New Orleans harbor, an observer in the French navy, to witness the city's capitulation to the Union forces.

Paul Marchand leaves New Orleans, but another mulatto who has been crucial in these racial and social reversals remains: Zabet Philosophe. Zabet opens the novel and introduces its key characters and themes. She is an effective synecdoche for this city of ambiguous and shifting identities. She has had many jobs over the years—the narrator lists a half dozen—but these are a cover for her principal service as Pierre Beaurepas's spy and agent. Zabet was once a slave, and "her immunity from slavery had lasted so long that her free papers were never asked for—no more than one would have looked for the charter of the city or the title deeds of the Cabildo" (10). The narrator's statement contains ironies that dramatize, once again, the precariousness of identity established by legal statute or linguistic label. Later in the narrative, Paul Beaurepas challenges Zabet's seemingly unshakable status, threatening her with slavery. Her free status is compared by the narrator in the passage just cited to that of the city and the Cabildo; but New Orleans had been French, Spanish, French again, and American in its short history, and its administrative center—"the Cabildo, or Hotel de Ville or City Hall, as it was successively called" (7)—had reflected these changes in its many names.

Zabet Philosophe's own name—a combination of Gumbo dialect and literate French—suggests a fusion of disparate elements and hints at her special status. She is an old mulatto market woman, but she dominates the city's most important square, drawing powerful white aristocrats in search of her occult powers. But like old Julius McAdoo, Zabet's powers are those of an artist rather than those of a witch. They derive less from sorcery than from skillful reading of character, knowledge of family secrets, and most important, her craft as a storyteller. She earns a steady living recounting her "dreams," weaving comforting prophecies for her clients. She is also the author of one of the Beaurepas family's central narratives. She has recounted the story of her escape and delivery from the Haitian slave revolt in a way that has gained her freedom and changed her grandson's identity. As a fabulist and creator of identity, she rivals Pierre Beaurepas, who imposed a false identity on Paul and then reversed it. And Zabet Philosophe remains potent at the narrative's end. Paul discovers the document that discloses Zabet's substitution. He threatens torture and slavery, and apparently—we don't hear her words, we only see Paul's reaction—she names Philippe as the mulatto nephew. The tender glance she directed toward Philippe as he passed before the cathedral suggests that he is indeed her grandson. Perhaps she intuits that she can reveal his identity without risk. Paul has said he will treat the mulatto according to his desserts, and Philippe, who has never insulted Paul, is the only nephew who need not fear being named as the interloper. Zabet names Philippe and, by this act, gives Paul the final weapon for his ironic revenge. She makes it possible for Paul to place a quadroon at the head of the Beaurepas clan. Decades earlier, before the novel's first scene, Zabet was already Pierre's collaborator in assigning identity, and in its final scene, she assists Paul in the same function. Her role underscores once again the arbitrary nature of racial and social labels. They are communicated in the stories told about our origins and imposed by those who control these narratives. Zabet Philosophe usurped a crucial portion of that power years before this novel begins, and she retains it at its conclusion. It is also important—to understand Chesnutt's own literary purposes—to recognize that it is a black storyteller who has infiltrated and helped to direct the destiny of this white dynasty.

This discussion of public narration and private identity can be extended by looking closely at Monsieur Renard's account of Paul Marchand's origins. This explanation is crucial for establishing the protagonist's identity, and thus it lies at the heart of this narrative and deserves careful attention. In regard to Renard's testimony, we will consider three related issues: the reliability of the narrator, the credibility of the facts he presents regarding Paul's birth, and the plausibility of the motives he adduces for Pierre Beaurepas's concealment of these facts. The first thing to remark in this regard is that these events are not revealed by an omniscient narrator outside the narrative; Monsieur Renard, a character within the narrative who claims to have learned them from Pierre Beaurepas shortly before Pierre's death, provides this information. Readers are then, while gathering these key narrative elements, at two removes from the actual events. Renard cannot be said to be disinterested in the story he tells or in the reputations of its principal characters. He is, quite understandably, loyal to Pierre Beaurepas, the client who retained him for many years. Renard is perhaps even more solicitous of Paul Beaurepas, Pierre's heir, whom Renard now hopes to represent and whom he shamelessly flatters throughout his story. Nor can it be said that Renard has always been entirely candid; on the contrary, he was the principal agent in the deception that hid Paul's true origins from him. Renard insists that he only recently learned the facts he narrates, but he was for more than twenty years the intermediary between Pierre and Paul. Renard knew, at the very least, that the obscure quadroon was linked to one of Louisiana's most powerful patriarchs, and he hid this fact from Paul.[6] Even as Renard narrates, he reveals his mendacity. He insists that if Paul had known the secret of his parentage, he would have willingly sacrificed his life to protect it. Paul has made no such declaration, and his icy reserve as he listens suggests something other than the filial piety that Renard ascribes to him.

Renard's account of the facts surrounding Paul's birth deserves careful scrutiny on several points. First, is Paul the son of Pierre Beaurepas? It seems very likely that he is. Philippe Beaurepas, the most reliable of the cousins, claims to see an unmistakable resemblance between Paul and the old man's portrait. Is Paul the son of Beaurepas's white wife, or might he be, as had previously been assumed, the product of an illegitimate union with a quadroon? This is less certain, for there is no physical evidence either way, only Pierre's word. Is Pierre's word trustworthy? Would a white aristocrat lie about such a matter? Would Pierre Beaurepas claim that an illegitimate mulatto is legitimate and white? The answer is that he has already done so. He has accepted into his family the quadroon male whom Zabet Philosophe inserted in the flight from Haiti. Paul discovers proof of this substitution in Pierre's papers hours after he gains access to them, and it is inconceivable that Pierre himself did not know of it. We can only speculate about the reasons for Pierre's complicity in this deception. Perhaps the patriarch feared that an able successor might not emerge among his legitimate nephews, and he wished to increase his options. In any case, Pierre's acceptance of this substitution initiates his long-term complicity with Zabet in deceit and subterfuge.

Assuming for the moment that Paul's origins are as Renard recounts, what are the reasons for Pierre Beaurepas's concealment of his only son? According to Renard, Pierre Beaurepas courted Paul's mother and was loved by her. Nonetheless, her parents married the young woman to another suitor against her wishes. Early in this marriage, it is reported that the husband has died at sea. After her husband's presumed death, Paul's mother resumes her friendship with Pierre Beaurepas, and they are secretly married. The first husband suddenly returns alive to New Orleans, only to die days later in a street brawl. Pierre and his wife marry again, this time publicly. Unfortunately, she has conceived before the second, public wedding, and to escape the embarrassment of Paul's early birth, Beaurepas's wife withdraws to a distant plantation, where she bears her child and gives it to a quadroon to raise as her own. Renard insists that the couple intended eventually to adopt Paul, but this was no longer possible after Pierre accepted responsibility for his orphaned nephews. Paul's mother's mental and physical health was weakened by the loss of her child, and, we are told, Pierre Beaurepas kept his son's existence a secret until after his own death to spare the feelings and protect the reputation of his wife, Paul's biological mother. Pierre Beaurepas, in his attorney's telling, was an impetuous romantic, a gentleman obsessed by protecting the honor of his wife and the feelings of his nephews. It is, the nephews complain sarcastically, "a pretty story" (104), but is it true?

The narrative gives grounds to doubt. Pierre claims that he thrust his only son into the mulatto caste out of chivalrous concern for Paul's mother and her honor. The whole sad sequence began when the woman's parents frustrated her love for Pierre and forced her to marry a man she had never seen. It is a piteous story, and yet Pierre is prepared to repeat it. He must know— his spies are everywhere—that Josephine Morales loves Philippe Beaurepas and that Philippe loves her. And yet he has, with deliberate cruelty, frustrated their love and arranged that Josephine should marry Paul, a former quadroon whom she has never met. Pierre's only concern, Renard insists, was "the good name of a lady" (99), and yet, what was that lady's name? We know the family names she took in her first and second marriages, but we do not know *her* name. To Renard she is simply "Madame Beaurepas"; neither her Christian name nor her own family name is ever disclosed. Moreover, the woman died many years before her husband: why couldn't Paul have been released from the quadroon caste after her death? How could she have suffered dishonor in her grave? Why is it only now—at the patriarch's passing—that the truth can be told? *Whose* name and *whose* honor, finally, are at stake: that of the nameless woman or of Pierre Beaurepas himself? And what can "honor" possibly mean to this man whose fortune was built by participating in John Law's infamous Mississippi Scheme, a man who delights in spying on his nephews and in exploiting their weaknesses. It is precisely this Creole family's specious claims to honor that Paul Marchand mercilessly exposes and explodes. Renard unintentionally does as much himself. Here is Renard praising Madame Beaurepas:

> she is a woman of fine feeling; she respects the conventionalities (100);

> her high sense of honor, her strict view of propriety, her delicate sensitiveness to public opinion. (102)

Note the equivalencies established in these utterances. Fine feeling equals respect for the conventionalities. High sense of honor means a delicate sensitiveness to public opinion. In other words, among the Creole aristocracy, the moral is the social, the internal is the external, and, as we have seen, female honor is male ego.

Renard's narrative is an elaborate romance, replete with frustrated lovers, rapacious pirates, and a dramatic return from the dead, followed quickly by a fatal stabbing. Renard announces his account as a "romantic story" (99) and initially proposes it only as hypothesis. Once he has caught his audience in his narrative spell, he claims it is true. The attorney clearly relishes its telling, giving "his forensic powers full play," unfolding his "interesting mystery in a dramatic way" (106). It is a bravura performance, and Renard almost seems poised for a bow at its end. The nephews, however, are not convinced, and it is unclear if readers should be. The skillful and highly theatrical narration cannot quite conceal its many implausibilities and contradictions. Paul's mother must be sent away during her pregnancy to hide the child conceived before her public marriage to Beaurepas. Why could she not have extended her stay at the distant plantation, and then have brought the child back as Beaurepas's son, fudging the date of birth a few months to bring it in line with their public marriage? Beaurepas and Renard insist that the separation of mother and child was necessary to protect the mother, but it is, in fact, this separation and the attendant guilt that hastens her death. The couple had planned to adopt Paul at a later date, but Pierre claimed the arrival of his nephews prevented this. He could not, he insists, bring himself to disinherit them. And yet he is now quite prepared to disinherit these same nephews after maliciously encouraging them to believe themselves his heirs.

Thus, at the center of this narrative, where we expect to find clarity and truth, we find implausibility and contradictions. This is so, not only because of the unconvincing motives adduced by Pierre Beaurepas and Renard, but because the same events can be explained by other, less flattering considerations. Assuming once again that the key events are as Renard claims, but bracketing Renard's chivalrous narrative, there are other explanations for Pierre Beaurepas's behavior. In Renard's romance, Beaurepas acts out of a courtly solicitude for feminine virtue and paternal concern for all members of the family. These are, of course, central values in antebellum Southern ideology. Other political, economic, and psychological motives more accurately explain the workings of patriarchal society, and they may apply in this instance. Viewed from a more skeptical perspective, readers note that, by refusing recognition to his son and by hiding him as a mulatto, Pierre gained protection from the threat that a patriarch most fears: a potent rival. A son who would ascend to family leadership, with the attendant power and wealth, is the only person who could gain from toppling Pierre. But that son is safely hidden, even from himself, in another caste, leaving only the nephews, who are made obsequious vassals by their uncle's refusal to name his successor. In another matter, Beaurepas's wife was previously the wife of his business partner. Beaurepas's hasty and premature marriage with his partner's widow could be explained as easily by a nervous need to consolidate his assets as by an impetuous love that brooked no delay. The choice between these two readings of Pierre's purposes—Renard's and the one hypothesized here—is between two accounts of the motives that drive patriarchy: tender regard for feminine sensibilities or cynical calculations of personal and dynastic power.

Continuing these speculations, it is relevant to note that Pierre and Paul are Oedipal rivals. Pierre has inflicted a triple privation on his son. He has, of course, cut him from his father. He has also, by his own admission, separated the boy from his biological mother; by swearing the adoptive, quadroon mother to secrecy about the boy's paternity, he has also driven a wedge between her and Paul. For Lacan, the movement of the child from the mother to the father is the transition from the Imaginary order to the Symbolic order, from an integrated sense of self to the divided consciousness that comes with language.[7] But Paul is subject to a unique castration, which cuts him from one order without ever granting the powers of the other. He finds himself trapped in a curious netherworld, without a father or the power that a father's name bestows. Instead he bears the name "Marchand," which in French suggests a salesman or a piece of merchandise. Moreover, he is required by law to append to this name "f.m.c.," initials whose ambiguity we have already discussed. His own impotence within the linguistic order—his inability to signify—is dramatized in the scenes in which one cousin can force the auctioneer literally not to hear Marchand's bid and another cousin can publicly label him *"Cochon"* (30)—a pig, less than human, unclean—without his being able to respond.

André Bleikasten's remark about Charles Bon in *Absalom, Absalom!* is also appropriate to Paul Marchand: "Fatherlessness is not so much the absence of a relationship as a relationship to absence." Bleikasten's analysis also is useful in comparing two Southern patriarchs: Thomas Sutpen and Pierre Beaurepas. Bleikasten, describing Sutpen's dynastic project, observes that "Sutpen fantasizes it as a purely masculine filiation: the son born of the father, the father reborn in the son. *Et pas de mere alors.* No earthy Eve. No 'natural' generation to compromise the design. No (m)other to obstruct the reproduction of the same."[8] Pierre Beaurepas eliminates his son's mother even more effectively than did Sutpen. Pierre's design, if it is successful, will achieve his greatest triumph over his son after his own death. He means to appropriate Paul's procreative powers and put them in service to his own dynastic ambitions. He would cut Paul from his mulatto wife and children and set in their place a wife he has personally chosen. Paul, without friends or allies in the aristocracy, will be forced to rely on the foster father, Renard, whom Pierre has placed at Paul's side. Pierre, in a gesture of patriarchal presumption equal to that of Thomas Sutpen, aspires to survive his own death in the dynasty he will create through his son and the son's appointed bride. Sutpen and Beaurepas's ambitions are both destroyed by sons who emerge from the ambiguous world of the Louisiana quadroon. Charles Bon and Paul Beaurepas rebel in opposite directions, the former by claiming filiation, the latter by refusing it. But both rebel against paternal tyranny, the patriarch's arbitrary authority to assign or withhold personal identity.

Have these lengthy speculations managed to explain what "really" happened between Pierre Beaurepas and Paul Marchand? Is this narrative more "true" than Renard's? No. However, I will suggest, rather immodestly, that this version is more interesting and more psychologically plausible than the attorney's account. But my point in offering these reflections and proposing an alternative explanation of Pierre's behavior is not to provide "the truth." The "facts" of Paul Marchand's origins cannot be settled once and for all because this narrative will never provide unequivocal answers. The purpose of providing an alternate explanation is not revisionist but deconstructive. Paul Marchand's identity—like our own identities—is grounded in a narrative of origins. But the key events in this narrative are lost in the past, and they are relayed at several removes, by sources with interests of their own who have imposed their own interpretations. Finally, it is the controlling political authority in the society that adjudicates conflicting claims and assigns identity. Beaurepas and Renard—dynastic scion and attorney—have power on their side, and they use it to enshrine their "truth." The doubting nephews may grumble, but they have no recourse but to accept. Pierre Beaurepas is a patriarch and a fabulist; Renard is a lawyer and a narrator: the conjoining of these functions in this novel is not accidental. Our identities are grounded in custom and fixed by law, but these customs and laws find their origins and their sustaining power in stories told and accepted as authoritative in society.

The discussion of Paul's origins as related by Renard has moved from ontology to narratology. I would like to conclude by exploring another level of undecidability encountered in this narrative: the problems posed by the voice in the novel's foreword, the narrator who signs himself "C.W.C." It is useful at the outset of this discussion to recall that introductory materials performed an important function in early black autobiography and fiction. White readers encountering African American narratives for the first time in the eighteenth and nineteenth centuries had to be carefully prepared before they could accept the often-shocking stories of life under slavery. Slave narratives usually were introduced by one or more prefaces by white notables testifying to the black author's character and veracity. Such reassurances remained important when blacks began to publish crusading novels. Early African American novels, such as William Wells Brown's *Clotel, or The President's Daughter* (1853) and Frances E. W. Harper's *Iola Leroy* (1892), begin with prefaces written by their authors or others establishing their narrator's reliability and high moral seriousness. Chesnutt evidently felt such material was no longer necessary when he began to publish, for his collections of stories and his first two novels have no introductions. Nonetheless, his breakthrough fictions—the stories told by Uncle Julius—are introduced by a white narrator, whom early readers were inclined to identify as the author. Such an identification was a mistake, however, for, as we have seen, John is as much a fictional creation as Julius. *The Colonel's Dream* (1905), the last novel Chesnutt published before *Paul Marchand, F.M.C.*, begins with a two paragraph dedication "to the great number of those who are seeking . . . to bring the forces of enlightenment to bear upon the vexed problems which harass the South." The high moral tone established in this novel's dedicatory paragraphs is very much in the tradition of crusading fiction by other white and black authors. [9]

These other prefatory remarks indicate the degree to which the foreword to *Paul Marchand, F.M.C.* departs from the practice of previous black narrators and from Chesnutt's own earlier practice. If the purpose of such opening materials is to reassure readers as to the accuracy and seriousness of the narrative, this foreword seems to deliberately frustrate these purposes. First, as to accuracy, consider the foreword's first paragraph.

> The visit of a French duke to New Orleans, in the early part of the last century, and the social festivities in his honor, are historical incidents. If there was not a Paul Marchand case in New Orleans, there might well have been, for all the elements of such a drama were present, as is clearly set out in the careful studies of life in the old Creole city by Miss Grace King and Mr. George W. Cable, which are available for the student or the general reader—the author has made free reference to them—as well as in the more obscure records and chronicles from which they drew their information. Had there been such a case, it is con-

ceivable that the principal character might, under the same conditions, have
acted as did the Marchand of the story. (3)

The first sentence appeals to history to establish the credibility of the fictional narrative that is to follow. It tells us of a "historical incident," the visit
of a French duke—identified in the narrative as the Duc de Nemours—to
New Orleans in the early nineteenth century. However, there is no record
that historical Duc de Nemours, the son of King Louis Philippe, ever visited
the city. Moreover, he was not born until 1814, and thus he would be a very
unlikely participant at the Quadroon Ball, staged in 1821, which the novel
describes. As further authentication, the narrator cites his sources: Grace L.
King and George Washington Cable. King, in fact, records the visit of the
German Duke of Saxe-Cobourg to New Orleans in 1825, and she describes
his attendance at a Quadroon Ball.[10] Her account is almost certainly the
inspiration for the fictional visit narrated in Chesnutt's romance. The narrator's appeal to historical sources has the paradoxical effect of revealing the
liberties he has taken with the historical record. Furthermore, Cable and
King wrote from opposite ideological perspectives. Cable's novels and stories criticized life under slavery, and he had to leave the South because of
them. King, on the other hand, began writing specifically to answer Cable,
and her books defend the antebellum social order. The narrator of this foreword blithely collapses the significant ideological differences between his
two sources and raises the issue of his own political purposes.

The reader's perplexity as to the narrator's ideological position increases
in the second paragraph:

The quadroon caste vanished with slavery, in which it had its origin. Indeed
long before the Civil War it had begun to decline. Even the memory of it
is unknown to the present generation, and it is of no interest except to the
romancer or the historian, or to the student of sociology, who may discover
some interesting parallels between social conditions in that earlier generation
and those in our own. Quadroons and octoroons there are in plenty in the New
Orleans of today, as any one with a discriminating eye, taking a walk along
Canal Street, may plainly see; but as a distinct class they no longer exist. Since
all colored people enjoy the same degree of freedom, and are subject to the
same restrictions, there are no longer any legal or social distinctions between
the descendants of the former free people of color and those of the former

slaves. Social decree has made them all Negroes, no doubt to the advancement
of democracy among themselves, perhaps to the betterment of public morals,
but certainly at the expense of accuracy and the picturesque. (3–4)

The narrator notes that, although quadroons and octoroons still exist,
they are no longer accorded separate caste status. He then comments on
this change: "Social decree has made them all Negroes, no doubt to the
advancement of democracy among themselves, perhaps to the betterment of
public morals, but certainly at the expense of accuracy and the picturesque."
The observer in these paragraphs contrasts the present situation with the
situation that existed before the Civil War, balancing gains and losses. On
the one hand, democracy and public morals achieve gains; on the other,
accuracy and the picturesque suffer losses. The argument for an increase in
democracy is understood easily enough, for with the disappearance of the
quadroon caste, all people with any portion of Negro blood are treated the
same. But how were public morals improved? Apparently, the reference is to
the racial interaction and miscegenation that the quadroon caste facilitated
under the old order. The "betterment of public morals" is then the result of
a stricter separation of the races. The democracy described here depends on
a significant limitation in social freedom. The old caste system, on the other
hand, offered "accuracy": it recognized subtle gradations of color that the
binary, black and white, categories obscure. It also offered "the picturesque."
The reference is, presumably, to the exotic, even erotic, associations of the
quadroon caste. This caste provided a social space where official racial ideology and the laws against racial mixing could be transgressed. Because of
this aura of sweet, forbidden fruit and violated taboos, the quadroon fascinated the white imagination; but this seeming glamour covered, as the
novel shows, important psychological contradictions. The quadroon had
continually to deny an important part of himself or herself, his or her Negro
heritage, and strain after that which would always be withheld, white status.
Accuracy, in short, is here based on ambiguity and contradiction.

The narrator seems, in this passage, to prepare readers for a judgment,
contrasting present and past, offering a balance sheet of the advantages of
each condition. But the advantages, on each side of the ledger, disintegrate
under the pressure of their own internal contradictions, leaving no basis for
an easy evaluation of what has been achieved. The narrator, for his part,

attempts no judgment. Instead, in the foreword's third and final paragraph, he draws back, invoking and imitating the Mississippi River's sublime indifference:

> But the Father of the Waters recks not of such trifles and still pursues his stately course beside the Crescent City. The language of Bienville and its local variants are still heard. The roses still riot in the gardens and on the latticed galleries. The old Creole families still cherish their pride of race and their family traditions, and their ladies still retain an enviable reputation for beauty and for charm—to say nothing of their chicken gumbo. (4)

How are we to read this extraordinary paragraph? What are we to make of the lofty, riverine perspective invoked in the first sentence: is it serious or ironic? The narrator has just introduced his subject, the condition of the free blacks under slavery, and readers will learn in the narrative the painful and humiliating consequences of this condition for the protagonist and others of his class. Readers have been told, moreover, that they "may discover some interesting parallels between social conditions in that earlier generation and those in our own." How, then, can they be indifferent? They hesitate in their reaction. The clichéd personification, the archaic diction, and inverted syntax of the paragraph's first sentence seem, by their very artificiality, to mock ironically the posture adopted.

The narrator reassures us that, despite changes, things go on much as before and that Creole race pride and the Southern cult of the woman still exist. But these are precisely the elements that lay at the heart of the quadroon's tragic predicament in the novel. The quadroon caste was Southern patriarchy's means of dealing with its illegitimate colored offspring while protecting its myth of family racial purity. The nexus between the shadow world of the quadroon and patriarchy's cult of (white) female purity reveals itself at two crucial points in the narrative. Paul Marchand, we are told, was cast into the quadroon class because he was conceived before his father and mother's legal marriage. Thus, as Renard explains, "to save the mother's good name, it was necessary temporarily to sacrifice the child" (96). Later, Paul is cast into prison as a consequence of his appearance at the Quadroon Ball. This social event was the occasion for white Creole males to select mistresses from among the female quadroons. Paul goes there to rescue his sister-in-law and to protect her honor, but the virtue of quadroon women—"poor hostages of the chastity of their white sisters" (65)—has no meaning in this system.

How then, in the context of the narrative that it introduces, are readers to react to the foreword's reassurances? Are they serious or ironic? The foreword's final words, a brief phrase appended with a dash, seems to mock what immediately proceeds. White Southern womanhood's "enviable reputation for beauty and for charm" is trivialized by being reduced to the same level as a chicken stew. This particular dish, moreover, is one whose name, "gumbo," is African derived and one that, in most instances, was prepared for white mistresses by black cooks. Again the appropriate response is unclear—serious or ironic? The narrator seems indifferent to the reader's reaction. He imagines various potential readers—romancers, historians, students of sociology—all of whom have different notions of accuracy and truth, and each might be expected to react differently. And yet he adds in the same sentence that these readers may find echoes in his narrative of society's current condition. Such a correspondence would seem to require accuracy in historical and social portraiture. The pattern here—introduction of the question of accuracy, an undercutting of the question, its dismissal, and then its reintroduction—is the same pattern of vacillation and ambivalence noticed earlier. All, somehow, is to be swept away in the Mississippi's stately flood.

These observations lead the discussion back to the questions of tone and moral seriousness. This is the point at which this foreword seems most different from the other prefatory material in earlier African American narratives. The narrator's posture of sublime unconcern seems particularly disconcerting in light of his subject matter and the tradition in which he is writing. Chesnutt's narrator, in his omniscience and his distance above the scene he describes, recalls Cable's narrator in *The Grandissimes,* but Cable's novel has no preface and his narrator never addresses readers as fully and directly as does Chesnutt's. An analogue for Chesnutt's practice here is a work by Cable's partner on the reading circuit, Mark Twain, specifically "A Whisper to the Reader," which begins Twain's *Pudd'nhead Wilson* (1894). Twain's preface to this novel is a masterpiece of irony and misdirection. The narrator cites the source for the narrative's legal details, his friend William Hicks, only to mock him good-naturedly. He professes, with a straight face, his respect for nobility and for ancestry, but these turn out to be among the targets of his narrative's bitter satire. These discrepancies are not troubling because the "Mark Twain" whose voice is heard in this "Whisper" and whose name is at its end is an elaborate persona, as fully a literary creation as the narrator of Twain's travel narratives or Pudd'nhead Wilson himself.

I would suggest that the "C.W.C." in this foreword should be read the same way as the "Mark Twain" in *Pudd'nhead Wilson*'s "Whisper," as a deliberately ironic literary persona. Chesnutt respected Twain and was honored to be included among those invited to his seventieth birthday dinner in 1905. More relevant in the present context, the two novels share the same central situation—reversed racial identities—and key themes—the Southern aristocracy, its code of honor, and legal definitions of identity. The novels share similar structures: both set up elaborate patterns of doubling and repetitions and then turn these patterns on their heads in startling reversals. Black becomes white, the dominated becomes the master, and established figures are revealed as corrupt. Finally, at the deepest level, these two novels share a vision of the world as elusive, dynamic, and deceptive. Tragedy derives from the refusal to accept the variety of differences and from the will to impose a definitive shape on them, to reduce them to simple binary oppositions in which one term is privileged. The voice in the foreword grows out of this sense of the world, a sense for which irony, ambivalence, and hesitation are appropriate responses.

The initials that appear at the end of these prefatory paragraphs are reminiscent of the "Chas. Chesnutt" who signed "The Future American." The latter persona vacillated between earnest editorializing and ironic sarcasm. The voice at the beginning of Paul Marchand's story also speaks in several conflicting registers. But "C.W.C." seems more aware of his ambivalences, more playfully willing to exploit them. It is not that the author of the historical romance is more optimistic or lighthearted than the editorialist— just the contrary. The first two decades of the new century seem to have deepened the skepticism hinted in the essay. The romance, it is true, is set a hundred years distant, on the other side of the Civil War and emancipation, but its last pages bring readers up to the present moment. The Beaurepas are still powerful in Louisiana politics, and they have learned nothing. In fact, they are among the strongest defenders of white racial "purity," authors of stringent legislation against miscegenation. The temporal image figured in the Beaurepas family's obtuse refusal to learn from experience and change is of a present frozen in the past. Time is a closed loop, where the same stupid mistakes are repeated generation after generation. This historical despair reminds us once again of Twain, particularly in his last years, and of his bitterly ironic amusement.

12

——◦◦◦◦——

The Quarry
"And Not the Hawk"

No one who understandingly faces the situation with its substantial accomplishment or views the new scene with its still more abundant promise can be entirely without hope. And certainly, if in our lifetime the Negro should not be able to celebrate his full initiation into American democracy, he can at least, on the warrant of these things, celebrate the attainment of a significant and satisfying new phase of group development, and with it a spiritual Coming of Age. —ALAIN LOCKE, "Enter the New Negro" (1925)

Charles Chesnutt's writings span the last quarter of the nineteenth century and the first quarter of the twentieth. We first meet him as a teenage diarist in 1874 and we find him still active in his seventies, completing *The Quarry* in 1928.[1] Surveying this half-century of activity, we are struck, first of all, by Chesnutt's determination; for it must be admitted that Chesnutt's literary efforts met more rejection than acceptance during his lifetime. If we isolate our attention on the beginning and the end of his writing career, the journals and the last novel, we are also struck by a remarkable continuity, even a certain circularity, in themes and tone. The young schoolteacher and the retired attorney are both fascinated by the American dream, and both are buoyed by its promise. There is an additional, unintended continuity in the way the optimism in both texts is undercut by unresolved tensions and contradictions in Chesnutt's thinking on America and race.

Surprisingly, the novel from which *The Quarry* seems most distant, at least in mood, is the one that immediately preceded it, the darkly ironic story of Paul Marchand. Chesnutt's last two novels share, it is true, an important plot similarity—a white man raised as black discovers his origins—but in most other ways—in focus, in tone, and in purpose—the narratives are quite different. *Paul Marchand, F.M.C.* limits itself to the brief period during which its protagonist experiences his crisis of racial identity, and it achieves a tightness of focus and a psychological intensity greater than in any other Chesnutt novel. *The Quarry* is, in contrast, much more diffuse, moving through two and a half decades in the northern and southern United States and in Europe. Its tone vacillates from realistic reportage to sentimental melodrama and romantic idealism. Chesnutt was honest enough to admit the manuscript's literary weaknesses when he responded to Harry Bloch's letter of rejection for Alfred Knopf. "I note what you say," Chesnutt wrote, "about the central idea in the story, and my failure to carry it out success-fully, and the lifelessness of the characters and the 'priggishness' of the hero. I suspect you are right about all of this, and in the light of your criticism I shall, before I submit the book elsewhere, see if I can put some flesh on and some red blood in the characters."[2]

Chesnutt refers to his failure to carry out "his central idea," but he might better have written "ideas," for *The Quarry*'s biggest structural problem is its several, divergent purposes. In telling the story of Donald Glover, an orphan raised in black America, Chesnutt tries simultaneously to offer an exemplary success story, an idealized portrait of a race leader, and a drama of racial identity. The novel fails for a number of reasons, including Ches-nutt's diminished literary skills. The weaknesses upon which I wish to focus are, however, the conflicts within and between these very heterogeneous purposes, for they dramatize conflicts within Chesnutt's—and America's—thinking on race, class, and personal identity. The literary problem here is not so much heterogeneity itself, for Chesnutt's other fictions often prof-itably juxtapose competing narratives. Rather, in *The Quarry* this hetero-geneity is not adequately understood and exploited. The individual myths are taken uncritically, and the conflicts between them are not dramatized in an interesting fashion. Gone is the corrosive skepticism and indignant irony that we find beneath the surface of *The Marrow of Tradition, The Colonel's Dream*, and *Paul Marchand, F.M.C.* Chesnutt in his seventies seems truly to have reverted to the optimism of his youth. He seems to believe, even more than the essayist of 1900, that the Future American was at hand.

The Quarry was born when Chesnutt found himself in the role occupied by Senator Brown in the novel. A white couple who had mistakenly adopted a black child sought Chesnutt's help in finding a black family to take the child in their stead. Chesnutt aided them and later imagined the child's subsequent life for his novel.[3] Chesnutt used the imagined experiences of his protagonist, Donald Glover, to fill an absence he perceived in contemporary literature. In a talk on "The Negro in Present-Day Fiction" given in the late 1920s, the time of *The Quarry*'s composition, Chesnutt regretted that he could find "no outstanding noble male character in any of the Negro novels, written by white or colored writers" (*Essays and Speeches,* 523). Chesnutt created Donald Glover, in part, to fill the lack he lamented in his talk: he sought to provide a Negro hero to inspire black youth and to convince whites who doubted black ability and determination.

The narrative of Donald's life is, first of all, a success story. As such it participates in a venerable American literary tradition that Chesnutt admired and emulated in his youthful journal. The young Chesnutt lectured publicly on "Self-Made Men,"[4] and one of his first publications was the introduction to an 1893 collection of biographical sketches of prominent black Ohioans. In his introduction, Chesnutt showed a clear understanding of the success story's purposes. The sketches should, he wrote, "be at once an example and an incentive to every young Afro-American."[5] The exemplary tale of a young man's rise from humble origins was a staple of post–Civil War popular fiction. The novels of Horatio Alger (1832–99), Josiah Gilbert Holland (1819–81), and Edward P. Roe (1838–88) exploited this formula, and they were best-sellers during the period 1860 to 1890. These fictions were heavily moralistic; at their center was "the Protestant ethic of the American heartland of the mid–nineteenth century," which "passed virtually untouched from the Lyceum lectures of Emerson's day through the Chatauquas of the early twentieth century."[6] According to the ideology of this genre, material success came to those who embodied the traditional American values of loyalty, industry, and self-improvement.

Material success was one of the principal preoccupations of the booming twenties. Conditions for many American Negroes, who benefited from the northern migration and economic prosperity, improved during these years.

This prosperity, to be sure, was not shared by all blacks, and it was considerably less than the economic boom enjoyed by whites. Nonetheless, many blacks believed, or wanted to believe, that their situation was getting better. David Levering Lewis reports that during the twenties, black publications

> overflowed with Horatio Alger successes: frugal custodians who amassed hefty savings, invested in real estate, and sent their children to Lincoln or Syracuse universities; laundresses and barbers who parlayed modest revenues into service industry empires; graduates of Howard or Harvard who won brilliant recognition in their fields, despite repeated racist rebuffs; show people and racketeers whose unorthodox careers were capped by exemplary fortune and philanthropy. Not only newspapers like *Amsterdam News* and New York *Age* but critical organs like *The Crisis* and *Opportunity* joyously catalogued every known triumph over adversity as particular manifestations of universal Afro-American progress.[7]

The Crisis annually published a record of black enrollments in higher education. By 1928, the year in which Chesnutt's novel reaches its climax, the number of Negroes enrolled in colleges and universities had more than tripled over enrollments at the beginning of the decade, and this total included doctorates awarded to blacks by prestigious white universities.[8]

Chesnutt himself had prospered economically and socially during the 1920s: his children had completed studies at prestigious universities and had begun their careers; Chesnutt had succeeded in business, and he had been honored by both the white and black communities. The shift in opinion that he attributes to Senator Brown in the novel reflects changes in his own attitudes. When Senator Brown first meets Mr. Seaton early in the novel, he bitterly regrets Seaton's refusal to raise the boy as white. However, when the two men meet again late in the novel, Brown argues that Donald should remain a Negro. Conditions for the colored people, he tells Seaton, have changed. "Their education for the past two generations, limited though it has been, is raising their level of culture. Negro wealth is increasing—we have few if any millionaires, but our combined holdings amount to many millions. . . . And men of real parts, like Donald and some of the younger men, may find it in the future no great hardship to be classed with that race."[9] The twenty-year interval between Brown and Seaton's two conversations corresponds roughly to the interval between Chesnutt's commercial failure with *The Colonel's Dream* (1905) and the composition of *The Quarry* (1926–28). Senator Brown's changed attitude mirrors Chesnutt's own shift from the disappointed hopes that caused him to interrupt his literary career to the guarded optimism voiced in his last novel. Seen from the perspective of the moment of its composition, Chesnutt's choice of the success-story formula for his last novel appears plausible, perhaps even inevitable. Seen from a later perspective, it appears very differently. The year 1928 was not a beginning but an end: the giddy high before the disastrous crash.

Although economic opportunity was part of the twenties, the Protestant moralism of the success genre was not. In the nineteenth-century versions of the formula, the protagonist proves his worthiness by adhering to Victorian moral standards. These standards were oddly anachronistic in the decade of speakeasies and short-skirted flappers. Chesnutt tried to bring his hero up to date, but the consequences are unconvincing. Donald Glover has several adulterous affairs; nonetheless, the narrator reassures us, he never speaks of his conquests: "For however far the conduct of these young men might fall below the strictest standard of morals, their speech was always clean. According to their code, a gentleman might sin, but never with his lips" (143). Donald Glover is an incongruous combination of the Victorian and the modern—a swinging prig. The anachronisms in Chesnutt's character are also evident in the way his genteel education leaves him unequipped for twentieth-century mores. Donald, still in his teens, loses his virginity to Mamie Wilson, a woman of some experience. "He went with her as the pale knight at arms with the *Belle Dame Sans Merci,* impelled by unknown or unfamiliar forces. And there, in a leafy temple, on a grassy altar, by the immemorial rite this dusky siren sacrificed him to her god, Priapus" (74). Afterward, Donald, acting "according to the best literary traditions" (78), announces to his father that he intends to marry Mamie. "The hell you are!" Dr. Glover explodes. The jarring contrast in dictions—the poetic effusion narrated through Donald's point of view and his father's profane interjection—dramatically illustrates Donald's inadaptation to the real world.

> "By the way, Don," asked his father after a pause, "when was it that you plucked this modest violet?"
>
> "Two weeks ago Thursday," replied the boy, to whom a figure of speech

never presented any difficulty. Much of his own speech was in tropes and similes. (80–81)

Donald may have no difficulty with tropes or similes, but he does not seem to understand irony. Nor, it seems, does the narrator, who is often so breathlessly admiring of Donald that it is hard to decide if the comedy in this scene is intentional or inadvertent.

Further difficulties in Chesnutt's use of the success story appear in his effort to combine it with the portrait of a race leader. Chesnutt's novel, of course, was preceded by the autobiographies of Frederick Douglass and Booker T. Washington. These men were important champions for their people, and their life writings were among the most influential narratives of their times. Douglass died in 1895 and Washington passed in 1915; in his 1928 novel, Chesnutt was trying to look over the horizon and imagine the leader for a new generation of African Americans. In addition to looking to the autobiographies of these historical figures, Chesnutt's novel follows in a tradition of fictional portraits of black leaders, which includes Frederick Douglass's *The Heroic Slave* (1853), Martin Delany's *Blake of the Huts of America* (1861), and W. E. B. Du Bois's *The Dark Princess* (1928). This genre is not unrelated to the success story, for it recounts a movement from relative obscurity to prominence, but it conceives its protagonist in fundamentally different terms. The rags-to-riches formula requires that its hero seem typical, even ordinary, in every respect except industry and persistence. For the success genre to meet its inspirational purpose, the average reader must be able to see himself or herself in the narrative, following the protagonist's steps toward the American dream. The individual who would galvanize and lead a race must be more than typical: he or she must embody a vision and an energy that lifts him or her above the masses. Such is the case with Douglass's Madison Washington, Delany's Blake, and Du Bois's Matthew Towns: these charismatic, Promethean figures risk their lives in international racial revolt. Donald Glover seems a bloodless temporizer by comparison.

The juxtaposition of Donald with these other fictional heroes underscores an antinomy at the heart of Chesnutt's concept of race leadership: a tension between being and doing, between presence and policy. Donald's adoptive mother molds him as an exemplary figure who would "prove to a skeptical world that Negroes, as Negroes, could contribute to the best things of the world; that would make of their color, hitherto a badge of inferiority, no longer something to be ashamed of but a mark of distinction and a source of pride" (64). His leaderly function would be accomplished not in concrete political action but in offering his life as proof of innate capability. She means Donald to be "an exemplary citizen," to use the phrase W. D. Howells applied to Booker T. Washington.[10] Donald Glover is surely an example, but for whom? For the black masses he would inspire or for the white elite he would persuade? The two tasks are not easily combined. The light-skinned Donald suavely puts white philanthropists at their ease because he has mastered their language and manners. Unfortunately, to the degree that he succeeds—assimilates to this white model—he weakens his credibility as a representative spokesman for ordinary blacks.

These contradictory pressures can be seen in Mrs. Glover's ambitions for her son. She wants him to be "the Moses who should lead his people, her people, out of the wilderness of poverty and ignorance and low estate" and into "a land of opportunity and achievement" (63–64). The figure of Moses is, of course, one of the most potent in African American culture, as the spirituals attest, but Mrs. Glover's reading of the Bible story has a special twist. The child who was found in the bulrushes and raised in the pharaoh's court was spared the sufferings of the oppressed Jews he came to lead. Mrs. Glover recognizes that "most Negro leaders of the past had been born in slavery, and those who had come to the front since emancipation, had almost all done some sort of menial work in their upward struggle." Nonetheless, "Mrs. Glover could see no merit in having been a servant. . . . She not only wanted Donald to be as well-educated as any white man, but wished to save him from the inferiority complex which might result from servile employment" (96–97).

Mrs. Glover shelters Donald from the worst aspects of black life in the South. As a result, Donald appears to have spent more of his youth in the company of the dead white males in his library than among living blacks of his own age group. The novel narrates only one significant interaction between Donald and another young black person during Donald's adolescence, and that is his interlude with Mamie Wilson. This encounter and its comic aftermath illustrate Donald's distance from the world inhabited by less privileged blacks. The Glovers initially send Donald to an integrated college, where he is treated with deferential awe by Henry White, a dark Negro whose humble service Donald graciously accepts. After the white college is forced to exclude blacks, Donald resumes his studies further south at a Negro university. This leads to another unintentionally comic episode. Donald is so oblivious to the realities of Jim Crow segregation that he has to be thrown in jail and hauled before a magistrate before he realizes that local racists have been scandalized by seeing an apparently white man keeping public company with a black woman.

As a student in New York, Donald's closest male friend is Jewish, and his female lovers are white. He is fascinated and energized by black Harlem, but his perspective is not that of its residents. At a performance of *The Emperor Jones,* Donald is embarrassed by the laughter of blacks in the audience. It does not occur to him that O'Neill's portrait of a black man's reversion to African primitivism might seem ludicrous to Americans of African descent. Donald is also oddly remote from, and even condescending to, black culture. He is familiar with jazz and spirituals, but these forms for Donald are "essentially primitive—a survival of the tom-tom, the war chant, and the moaning of the slave coffle. They might, at the hands of genius, like that of Dvorak or Coleridge-Taylor, furnish themes or *motifs* for finished work" (136) in the European mode. To be properly understood, Donald's attitudes need to be seen in their historical context. During the Harlem Renaissance the relationship of black intellectuals, such as W. E. B. Du Bois, Charles S. Johnson, Alain Locke, and James Weldon Johnson, to black popular music was often "beset by paradox."[11] On the one hand, these intellectuals celebrated the success of black artists, but, on the other, they worried that more raucous forms of expressions—blues, Chicago jazz—might strengthen negative stereotypes of black behavior. The deans of the New Negro movement, like Donald, had studied European civilization in the best American and European universities, and quite naturally, they were influenced by the culture they had so diligently mastered. It was a cruel paradox for this generation of black intellectuals that, to gain exposure for black culture in white society, blacks had first to prove themselves as whites. David Levering Lewis describes how this tension played itself out in the life and career of James Weldon Johnson. Johnson "was a racial chauvinist of a special kind. He wanted his complete and natural assimilation of European culture to make such an impression that whites enjoying his cosmopolitan company would inevitably draw positive generalizations about Afro-Americans."[12] The description could also be applied to other educated blacks, including Donald Glover. Donald must first establish himself in terms that white philanthropists, like Mr. Bascomb, understand and respect before he can gain access to their resources and put them to use aiding other blacks.

For a race leader, Donald has little to offer in the way of public policy recommendations. His master's thesis, it is true, is on "the race question," but the narrator is vague about its content.

> Donald's thesis presented a simple, clear, rational and humane solution of this vexed question. Of course, to make it practicable would have required the scrapping of many cherished taboos, and the frank acceptance and cooperation of the entire American public, which it was hopeless to expect from a people still intermittently addicted to witchcraft, heresy hunting, and under different names, the *Vehm-gericht* and the *auto-da-fé;* by whom war was glorified and men kept in prison for opinion's sake. (178)

All we are told, in effect, is that Donald has proposed a rational solution for a problem—and for a public—that is fundamentally irrational. The solution Donald has in mind is never given through his words, but Senator Brown presents a point of view that, I believe, is essentially that of Donald. Brown explains this position to Mr. Seaton:

> I see no ultimate future for the Negro in the Western world except in his gradual absorption by the white race. . . . It is already far advanced. . . . There is obviously much white blood among the so-called Negroes, and among the white people much black blood that is not obvious. We'll not live to see the day, but as sure as the sun rises and sets the time will come when the American people will be a homogenous race. (266)

The resolution of America's racial problem through assimilation proposed here is essentially the same solution that Chesnutt offered in his 1900 essay "The Future American." It is also the remedy argued by the Columbia University anthropologist Franz Boas, who appears in the novel, lightly fictionalized, as Donald's mentor Dr. Boaz. The assimilationist thesis assumes that the tensions between America's diverse ethnicities will only truly disappear when the physical and cultural differences between them are effaced or at least greatly softened.

However, as George Hutchinson has noted, the assimilationist position argued by Boas and others contained paradoxical and even contradictory elements.[13] Boas argued against Anglo-American cultural hegemony and in favor of black racial pride at the same time that he foresaw eventual black assimilation in a new American type. Similarly, the movement toward a homogenous race of Americans, as presented in Chesnutt's last novel, contains paradoxes of its own. This movement does not mean immediate surrender of black identity. Donald is thoroughly versed, by wide reading and by his studies in a black university, in the black race's achievements. Donald and his mother understand that these achievements must be known, celebrated, and communicated to white Americans to convince them of the black person's worthiness for full citizenship. Nor, for Chesnutt, does amalgamation mean an immediate passing over the color line by those for whom this is possible. Quite the contrary, light-skinned mulattoes must remain with other Negroes, and their achievements must be used to strengthen claims for full equality for all African Americans. The presence of the assimilationist thesis in the novel explains much about the imaginary leader it constructs. It suggests the reason for the relative indifference to policy. The real work of racial healing can only be accomplished, slowly, by demography. In the meantime, the best that can be done is to facilitate America's inevitable, biological, and cultural movement toward the "homogenous race" Senator Brown describes. The assimilative goal also explains the novel's emphasis on behavior. Donald is the advance guard in this blending process. He proves by his ability and his achievement that he and his people may properly enter this new American "race." It also sets in context Donald's coolness toward black nationalism. Marcus Garvey, whose "Back to Africa" movement prospered and then foundered in the 1920s, appears in the novel as the fictional "President of Africa." Donald attends one of the president's lectures and, not surprisingly, he disapproves. The president's nationalism would lead blacks to Africa and away from American assimilation.[14]

The novel approves of Booker T. Washington and W. E. B. Du Bois, with whom Chesnutt had personal and intellectual affinities. Washington sought to improve the Negro condition from the bottom up, building a solid base of black artisans and farmers. In his 1895 address to the Cotton States Exposition in Atlanta, Washington accepted a subservient social status for blacks, but he was able to gain significant white philanthropic support for black technical and professional training. Du Bois attacked Washington's accommodation with the political status quo and demanded civil and political equality for all blacks. He broke publicly with Washington and led the movement that climaxed in the founding of the National Association for the Advancement of Colored People in 1910. Nowhere were the differences between the two men more apparent than in their views on education and race leadership. Du Bois rejected Washington's focus on technical education for the masses and emphasized liberal, university education for a Negro elite, whom he called "The Talented Tenth." Du Bois publicly identified Chesnutt as an exemplary member of the colored leadership, and Chesnutt shared many of Du Bois's positions, as Donald Glover's education and politics make clear. But Chesnutt also admired Washington, and Chesnutt's son and one of his daughters worked for Washington at the beginning of their careers.[15] Although Chesnutt strongly criticized the Tuskegean's positions in his personal correspondence with Washington, he refused to break with him publicly. Nonetheless, the novel does include the following comment on Washington (Jefferson in the novel) by a white Southerner: "We all like Jefferson down here. He's a good nigger, knows his place, teaches the niggers how to work, and don't preach social equality" (201). The problematic *n* word returns, and it recalls an issue raised in *The Marrow of Tradition:* how far can a black person go in accommodating white expectations without surrendering personal and racial dignity?

Chesnutt uses Donald's fictional career to suggest his own synthesis of Du Bois's and Washington's approaches. Donald studies under Dr. Lebrun (Du Bois) at Athena (Atlanta) University. Like his mentor, Donald is broadly and liberally educated and wants full equality for blacks. Here again style is at least as important as substance. In personal manner Donald differs subtly from both his mentors. He is less deferential to white Southerners than Jefferson and more personable than Lebrun. Donald demonstrates his natural gift for diplomacy when he accepts a position with Dr. Jefferson at Tuscaloosa (Tuskegee) Institute. There he meets the British philanthropist Mr. Bascomb, who requests Jefferson to send Donald to assist him in planning African education. Dr. Jefferson had hoped to make the trip to London himself, and in Bascomb's preference for Donald we see a new leader, trained in Lebrun's ideas, taking over Jefferson's movement and drawing the two camps together. The new black leader—combining the intellectual gifts of Du Bois and the political skills of Washington—can now work effectively with powerful whites to improve the black condition. Chesnutt's novel ends as Donald's career is just beginning, but he means to suggest what might be accomplished by combining the best of the two styles of black political thought and action.

The biggest difficulty this novel faces, both as portrait of African America success and as a prescription for African American leadership, is that, in the final analysis, its hero is of pure European descent. This brings us to the third theme *The Quarry* pursues. Like *Paul Marchand, F.M.C.,* this is a story of personal and racial identity. Unlike Marchand, Chesnutt provides Donald Glover with a detailed and reliably substantiated genealogy. Mr. Seaton documents Donald's family history over several centuries and two continents, and this history is confirmed by Dr. Freeman's records and by a private investigator's research. The reason for this elaborate family tree becomes apparent when we examine it in the context of 1920s racial polemics. The narrator refers in passing to certain "pseudo-scientific Nordic propagandists" (107). These are identified more specifically in Chesnutt's penultimate draft of the novel as Lothrop Stoddard and Madison Grant.[16] Stoddard's *The Rising Tide of Color against White World Supremacy* (1920) and Grant's *The Passing of the Great Race, or the Racial Basis of European History* (1921) were widely read and discussed during the decade in which Chesnutt wrote *The Quarry*.[17] As the titles of their books suggest, both Stoddard and Grant were racial essentialists who argued that the "white" race, which they regarded as the historic bearer of civilization, was under siege by the "black," "brown," "yellow," and "red" races. They saw danger on the international level in the demographic competition between the peoples of Europe, decimated by world war and low birth rates, and the rapidly growing populations of Asia, Africa, and Latin America.

But the nations of Europe and North America were also at risk internally. Both Stoddard and Grant discriminated within Europe between the superior "Nordic" race and inferior "Alpine" and "Mediterranean" races. They argued that, as a result of indiscriminate emigration policies, the United States had been contaminated by "the weak, the broken and the mentally crippled of all races drawn from the lowest stratum of the Mediterranean basin" (Grant, 89). The consequences of interbreeding between Mediterranean immigrants and other groups, including "Nordics," was almost too frightening for Grant to consider: "New York is becoming a *cloaca gentium* which will produce many amazing racial hybrids and some ethnic horrors that will be beyond the powers of future anthropologists to unravel" (92). Donald Glover's birth mother, Teresina Milfiore, an indigent Sicilian who died in childbirth, was not a Negro, but she was no less objectionable to the eugenicists for that, and her son's success is no less a refutation of Stoddard and Grant's racialist assumptions. Teresina Milfiore descended from a noble Sicilian family that had gradually declined until Teresina's father gambled away its last resources. Donald's birth father, the Reverend Sinclair Marvin, descended from a distinguished line of "Nordic" American stock; here also there had been a gradual diminution of vital force, symbolized by the minister's loss of his religious faith. Donald's brilliant career restores the former vigor of both lines from which he descends.[18] Chesnutt means by Donald's story to demonstrate two theses, both of which contradict the assumptions of the racial eugenicists. First, on a biological level, the histories of Donald's European and American antecedents suggest that continual inbreeding within one group can weaken it genetically; Donald's own history argues that breeding across groups can produce new strength. Second, on a social level, environment plays a much more important role than the genetic determinists admit. The Milfiore and Marvin families were weakened by many years of easeful living. Donald's vitality is only partially a result of his mixed genetic inheritance; it also results from the distinctive social challenges he has faced and surmounted.

The latter, social fact is crucial in this novel's definition of racial identity. Mrs. Glover states an assumption at the heart of this narrative. She rejects "the doctrine of heredity" and insists on "the controlling influence of environment" (45). Donald Glover, although of pure European descent, is African American because he has been raised as an African American. Racial identity is a social construct not a biological given. Environment is only part of the story, however, for there is also choice. At some point one must choose what attitude one assumes toward one's experience and those with whom one has shared it. *The Quarry,* like *Paul Marchand, F.M.C.,* is the story of a young man, raised as colored, who discovers that he is white. The conflict the protagonist must resolve in the novel's denouement is what choice he will make regarding his racial identity. Donald's story, like Paul Marchand's, is a narrative of naming. Neither bears the names of his birth parents nor the name he could claim under the law. Both choose as their own the names they were given as infants and that mark them as Negroes, and in so doing, they accept responsibility for their identities.

Donald is, from the beginning of the novel, such a paragon of virtue that there is never any doubt but that he will remain loyal to the community in which he was raised, and this flat characterization drains the novel's climax of narrative tension. After Donald escapes Mamie Wilson's plans for marriage, the narrator comments that "Donald, all through his young manhood, was destined to be the quarry and not the hawk, the sought and not the seeker, the hunted and not the hunter" (75). The narrator has in mind the fact that Donald will continually be the prey of others, black and white, who would turn him from his high purposes. I have selected the phrase for the title of this chapter for another reason. In this narrative Donald is too much the prey of Chesnutt's "ideas," his theses about black success and leadership, for him ever to become an autonomous and credible literary creation. These ideas, moreover, are understood in a manner that is too uncritical, and this contributes to the lack of complexity in Donald's characterization. Donald's experiences are surely noble and morally commendable, but as literature, they are as inert and as anachronistic as the nineteenth-century models they emulate.

Nonetheless, the novel's denouement is interesting for its presentation of Chesnutt's concept of racial identity. Donald discovers his racial roots in essentially the same way as Paul Marchand: he feels instinctively bound to those who have shared the same condition. At the end of the novel Donald chooses to marry the American Negro Bertha Lawrence rather than the English noblewoman Blanche Merrivale. Donald loves Bertha, but the bond that joins them grows more from the racial humiliation they shared as students in Georgia than from a conventional romantic attraction. Donald's choice is also directed by his commitment to his adoptive mother and the ideal of racial service she instilled in him. Donald Glover's racial identity, like that of Paul Marchand, derives neither from biological inheritance nor from social edict; rather, it comes from a personal choice. The choice, however, is not made in a vacuum; it grows from firsthand knowledge of the black condition. The narrator explains Donald's thinking: "He was, first of all, a man. Circumstances had made him one of a certain group. He had been reared as one of them. He had been taught to see things as they saw them, he had shared their joys, their griefs, their hopes and their fears—in fact he had become psychologically and spiritually one of them" (277–78). Racial identity, for Donald, is independent of genetics and legal categories; it is a psychological and moral affinity developed through a shared social experience.

There is in *The Quarry* an element not present in *Paul Marchand, F.M.C.* Paul's choice is, in large measure, a repudiation of the corrupt white world of the Beaurepas. He affirms his solidarity with blacks by freeing the Beaurepas slaves and by remaining with his quadroon family. But Marchand will live in the cosmopolitan, racially neutral world of Paris. In Chesnutt's penultimate novel, the Future American becomes the Contemporary Frenchman. Donald Glover is also tempted by life in Europe, but he refuses it. Chesnutt wishes to underline a point that Senator Brown argues with Mr. Seaton. Being a Negro is not a cruel fate one suffers; it is, Brown insists, a proud identity a man might freely choose. Chesnutt makes this point in the strongest possible terms by having this identity assumed by a white man. Chesnutt is particularly emphatic about Donald's racial loyalty in *The Quarry*. Donald is tempted five times to renounce his Negro identity—by Mr. Seaton, by Amelia Parker, by Moe Silberstein, by Mr. Bascomb, and again by Mr. Seaton—and five times he refuses. The strength of Chesnutt's stand against passing in this novel can be seen even more clearly when it is read against James Weldon Johnson's fictional *Autobiography of an Ex-Colored Man,* first published in 1912 but reissued to a wider audience in 1927, when Chesnutt was preparing *The Quarry.* Johnson's anonymous protagonist is a light-skinned mulatto who despairs of his situation as a Negro and decides to live as a white man. Johnson, of course, did not write the novel to encourage mulattoes to quit the black race but rather to express his disappointment in an America where a talented young African American would feel driven to do so.

Chesnutt's story echoes Johnson's in several ways. Both protagonists are of ambiguous ancestry, begin life in the north, go south to study at Atlanta University, come north to Harlem, and travel to Europe with wealthy white patrons who encourage them to pass as white.

Johnson's protagonist narrates his story retrospectively, and he tells us that he has successfully passed over the line. However, he confesses sadly in the novel's last line that: "I cannot repress the thought that, after all, I have chosen the lesser part, that I have sold my birthright for a mess of pottage." Chesnutt liked and admired Johnson, but he did not share the vision presented in Johnson's novel, and he answers it in his own narrative. The last line of Chesnutt's novel, in the penultimate draft housed in the Ohio University library, is a white friend's concession to Donald: "I'm not at all sure that you haven't chosen the better part." Chesnutt changed this sentence in the final manuscript to read, "I'm not at all sure that you didn't make the wise choice," (286) but the echo of Johnson's conclusion is still audible. Johnson's biblical metaphor occurs elsewhere in Chesnutt's novel in a friend's refusal to abandon his Jewish heritage "for a mess of pottage" (137), a decision that anticipates Donald's own refusal to surrender his black identity.

The Quarry, which might well be subtitled "The Biography of an Ex-White Man," turns the novel of passing on its head by recounting the story of a white man who decides to be colored. Chesnutt makes both Paul Marchand and Donald Glover racially white to validate the freedom of their choices. The choice of a black identity, one might argue, has greater force if the individual is at liberty to escape that identity. Donald notes that Dr. Jefferson had boasted that if he could be born again he would choose to do so as a black man and then comments drily: "It was a safe bet, since it could not happen" (162). But Donald *is* born again, and he remains black. Donald's discovery of his white ancestry, although a clumsy and improbable plot device, allows Chesnutt to make his case for loyalty and pride in black identity in the strongest possible terms.

Walter White, a leader of the NAACP and an animating force in the Harlem Renaissance, was a blond and blue-eyed Negro. White had black ancestry, which his family had always acknowledged, and White's own experience during Atlanta's bloody 1906 race riot solidified his decision to live as a Negro and to devote his life to the struggle for Negro rights. It was a choice not unlike Donald's, and the Atlanta riot is evoked in *The Quarry* shortly after Donald and Bertha's defining encounter with Athena (Atlanta) racism. Chesnutt's correspondence with White reveals that the two men discussed *The Quarry*, then in its early stages, in December 1926, and that White was warmly encouraging.[19] This should not be a surprise, for White, more than any other Negro leader, would have immediately understood Chesnutt and his project. Both men were, to all external appearances, "white";

nonetheless, they had both chosen to live and assume leadership roles as blacks. Their decisions and experiences are the real-world corollaries of the imagined decision of Donald Glover.

Interestingly enough, assimilation in Chesnutt's last two novels does not mean blacks becoming white as much as it does whites becoming black. In these novels, Paul Marchand and Donald Glover, both genetic Europeans, trade white identities for colored ones. Indeed, the logic of Chesnutt's assimilationism requires that whites must first become blacks before blacks can become white. Whites must be persuaded to enter the black world, morally and spiritually, to see the black condition from inside. This spiritual metamorphosis of whites is essential. Until it happens, whites will never understand blacks, and they will never allow blacks to enter white-dominated society as equals. Whites *can* become black: this is the drama enacted in Chesnutt's last two novels, and it is the paradoxical hope that animated Chesnutt's literary career from its beginnings. Chesnutt decided very early that he wanted to write about the black condition for a white audience. A journal entry by the young Chesnutt records what was to become a key strategy in that writing: "Nothing" he wrote, "will sooner show us the folly and injustice of prejudice than being ourselves subjected to it" (96). He believed that if whites could truly understand the black situation—could live it vicariously from within—they could be moved to change it.

This is the meaning of "Mars Jeems's Nightmare" (1899), one of the Julius and John tales. A conjure woman changes a cruel slave owner, called Mars Jeems in dialect, into a black slave on his own plantation. After a short period, the spell is lifted, and the white man resumes his original identity. But his experience in a black skin has marked him, and he is thereafter a sensitive and compassionate master. Chesnutt returned to the transformation theme in his last two novels with similar results. Paul Marchand and Donald Glover remain black in their souls even after they discover their white ancestry. These narratives of literal metamorphosis make explicit the strategy behind all of Chesnutt's stories about blacks. It is important to notice in this regard that "Mars Jeems's Nightmare" has two conjurers: Aunt Peggy, who turns Mars Jeems black, and Julius, the old black man who tells the story to a contemporary white couple. The couple finds that their own attitudes have been changed as a consequence of listening to Julius's tale, and they act more considerately with a young black man who works for them. Julius, who narrates Chesnutt's conjure tales, is one of Chesnutt's most important symbols of the literary artist. Narrative, by its ability to conjure us, to project us imaginatively into lives different from our own, has the power to forge in us a sense of solidarity with others less fortunate.

Donald Glover would seem to be, if not the Future American, at least his forbearer. In his 1900 essay, Chesnutt anticipated a moment in American history when the different ethnicities would blend and create a new, raceless American. Donald appears to be a precursor, preparing by example and precept the arrival of the new, assimilated type. There are more than a few problems with this, however. Donald's own emergence is made possible by a kind of immaculate miscegenation. Donald becomes a black man, but there has been no mixing of blood, for Donald is of pure European ancestry. The greatest obstacle to racial integration—white opposition to race mixing—has been cleverly avoided. It is true that Donald himself crosses the final Jim Crow barrier, entering a white woman's bed. The shock of this transgression is dissipated, however, when we learn that Donald is really biologically white. In fact, this encounter is softened even before the discovery of Donald's origins. Amelia Parker takes Donald as her lover by *refusing* to believe that he is black. "Don't be silly, Donald," she tells him, "of course you're not a Negro in the play, any more than you are when go around with me. . . . I believe you're a white man, just passing for a Negro for some dark and sinister reason which you dare not disclose" (132). Amelia knows the truth about Donald even before he does. The brilliant young Negro who attends Columbia is as "white" in appearance and behavior as Amelia herself. And this fact weakens his story as a portent of social change. In accepting Donald Glover, Amelia and Donald's white sponsors—Mr. Seaton and Mr. Bascomb—accept only themselves. Their embrace of Donald implies no embrace of blacks in general, for few blacks resemble their putative leader. An authentic racial amalgamation would imply a blending, a surrender of distinctive differences on *both* sides. But this has not happened: the "new type" prefigured by Donald Glover is not an innovative hybrid but the replication of an existing type, the middle-class white male.

Donald's marriage to Bertha Lawrence will precipitate the narrative's first authentic biracial sexual encounter. Here, again, there are significant qualifying details. First, it will be the joining of a white man with a black woman. Such unions have a long history in America, and they were always more tolerated than the union of a black man and a white woman. The latter union, even in 1928, could still result in tragic violence. Second, the biracial nature of Donald and Bertha's marriage will be a secret, for Donald will retain his public Negro identity. The expedients necessary in this narrative to make this union possible actually undercut the novel's optimism. There is no public acknowledgment or acceptance of racial intermarriage, and the obstacles to authentic cultural blending remain in place: whites concede little, while blacks conform to white patterns of thought and behavior.

We remarked at the outset of this chapter the continuity in Chesnutt's thinking over more than fifty years. One of the themes that unifies this thought, from his earliest journals through his last novel, is faith in progress. Chesnutt knew that he lived on the historic cusp between two eras. His narratives incessantly probe the contemporary moment, seeking the entry on to a new and better society. The change he expected, however, was not a convulsive revolution, but gradual and organic. His progressive faith was challenged, it is true, in the years following *The Colonel's Dream,* as that novel and *Paul Marchand, F.M.C.* show. Nonetheless, it never disappeared, as is evident in the vigor with which it reappeared in Chesnutt's last novel. A new order, Chesnutt believed, would grow from the best of the past. It would represent the full and final realization of the frustrated potential in the great cultural narratives of success, democracy and social mobility. The audacity of Chesnutt's thought consists in its stubborn insistence that America's dream be realized in the lives of *all* of its citizens, including the racially excluded. Chesnutt's progressive faith disposed him to patience, but it also encouraged dogged tenacity.

As he entered his eighth decade, Chesnutt believed that he saw signs of the progress he had so long awaited. The vital cultural activity of black artists and intellectuals of the 1920s seemed to proclaim the "spiritual Coming of Age" that Alain Locke described in the words quoted at the head of this chapter. This creative renaissance was not itself a political achievement, but it would, Locke and Chesnutt believed, create a new image for blacks that would energize black efforts and soften white resistance to full black-American citizenship. But Chesnutt could not see the future: he did not anticipate the terrible economic depression that was gathering as he wrote, a depression that would strike blacks far more heavily than whites. And he did not accurately gauge the depth of the white racial intransigence—stubborn prejudice that three-quarters of a century after Chesnutt's death still blocks social justice. Charles Chesnutt could not know, as his career came to a close, that subsequent generations of black American literary protagonists would not wear Donald Glover's smiling face, but rather the angry visages of Bigger Thomas, the invisible man, and Beloved.

NOTES

PREFACE

1. Scott McLemee, "The Anger and the Irony: Charles Chesnutt, the First Major Black Novelist, Regains His Former Glory," *Chronicle of Higher Education,* 1 March 2002, A14.

2. Shelley Fisher Fishkin, "Interrogating Whiteness, Complicating Blackness," 251–52.

3. Andrews's *The Literary Career of Charles W. Chesnutt* (1980) is the standard critical biography; Render's *Charles W. Chesnutt* (1980) surveys Chesnutt's life, his themes, and his prose style; Pickens's *Charles Chesnutt and the Progressive Movement* (1994) studies Chesnutt in the context of late-nineteenth-century reform. Two recent books on Chesnutt focus on formal analysis. Charles Duncan's *The Absent Man: The Narrative Craft of Charles W. Chesnutt* (1998) is a narratological study, and Henry B. Wonham's *Charles W. Chesnutt: A Study of the Short Fiction* (1999) is a close reading of Chesnutt's stories. Joseph McElrath's *Critical Essays on Charles W. Chesnutt* provides a thorough survey of Chesnutt criticism, with examples from the earliest reviews to recent essays. For dissenting voices on Chesnutt's racial politics, see SallyAnn Ferguson's articles "Chesnutt's Genuine Black and Future Americans" and "Rena Walden: Chesnutt's Failed 'Future American'" and Trudier Harris's essay "Chesnutt's Frank Fowler: A Failure of Purpose?"

4. My approach has been anticipated in articles and book chapters. William L. Andrews, discussing Chesnutt, writes suggestively of "deconstructive acts" and "their emphasis on reality as a function of consciousness mediated through language" ("The Representation of Slavery and the Rise of Afro-American Literary Realism, 1865–1920," 80). I have been stimulated by the chapters on Chesnutt in Houston A. Baker, *Modernism and the Harlem Renaissance,* 37–47, and in Craig Hansen Werner, *Playing the Changes,* 3–26. Charles Duncan, in *The Absent Man,* also makes some suggestive observations.

CHAPTER 1. Chesnutt's Language / Language's Chesnutt

1. Quoted in Thomas F. Gosset, *Race: The History of an Idea in America,* 285.
2. Charles W. Mills, *Blackness Visible: Essays on Philosophy and Race,* 45–46.

3. *The Oxford W. E. B. Du Bois Reader,* 102.

4. Brook Thomas, ed., *Plessy v. Ferguson: A Brief History with Documents,* 77.

5. See Vernon J. Williams, *Rethinking Race: Franz Boas and His Contemporaries,* 22.

6. For the evolution of Du Bois's racial thinking, see Eric J. Sundquist's introduction to *The Oxford W. E. B. Du Bois Reader,* 3–36.

7. Here is K. Anthony Appiah's account of the way the racial constructs affect individual consciousnesses: "Once the racial label is applied to people, ideas about what it refers to, ideas that may be much less consensual than the application of the label, come to have their social effects. But they have not only social effects but psychological ones as well; and they shape the ways people conceive of themselves and their projects. In particular, the labels can operate to shape what I want to call 'identification': the process through which an individual intentionally shapes her projects—including her plans for her own life and her conception of the good—by reference to available labels, available identities" ("Race, Culture, and Identity," 78).

8. Henry Louis Gates Jr., *The Signifying Monkey,* 129.

9. On white ideas of black "imitativeness," see Henry Louis Gates Jr., *Figures in Black,* 5–6, 18, 43–44.

10. Frederick Douglass, *The Narrative and Selected Writings,* 161.

11. Mikhail Bakhtin, *The Dialogic Imagination,* 293–94.

12. Henry Louis Gates Jr., *Figures in Black,* 117.

13. The story first appeared in the *Atlantic Monthly,* June 1904, 823–30. It is included in *The Short Fiction of Charles W. Chesnutt,* ed. Sylvia Lyons Render. I quote from the latter publication. Subsequent page references are given in the text.

14. I am indebted to my colleague Bob Demott for noting that even Jones's recognition of the inevitability of borrowing is itself a borrowing. The insight he has just offered summarizes the central premise of Emerson's essay "Quotation and Originality": "Our knowledge is the amassed thought and experience of innumerable minds: our language, our science, our religion, our opinions, our fancies we inherited. Our country, customs, laws, our ambitions, and our notions of fit and fair,—all these we never made, we found them ready-made; we but quote them. Goethe frankly said, 'What would remain to me if this art of appropriation were derogatory to genius? Every one of my writings has been furnished to me by a thousand different persons, a thousand different things'" (*Letters and Social Aims,* vol. 8 of *Centenary Edition of the Complete Works of Ralph Waldo Emerson,* 200).

15. Chesnutt was literally blackballed. The Rowfant membership uses a system of white and black marbles to indicate affirmative and negative votes. In defense of the Rowfant, it should be pointed out that Chesnutt was admitted to the club in

1910, and he was an active participant in club activities until his death in 1932. The Rowfant Club good-humoredly published an edition of *Baxter's "Procrustes"* in 1966 in Cleveland, edited and with an introduction by John B. Nicholson Jr.

16. The reference to the knife is wincingly poignant from a Lacanian psychoanalytic perspective, for metaphorical castration is the price for entrance into the symbolic order, the world of language.

17. Joseph R. McElrath Jr., ed., *Critical Essays on Charles W. Chesnutt,* 20.

CHAPTER 2. Chesnutt in His Journals: "Nigger" under Erasure

1. *The Journals of Charles W. Chesnutt,* 82. Subsequent page references are given in the text.

2. Kimberly M. Benston, "I Yam What I Yam: The Topos of (Un)naming in African-American Literature," 156.

3. Brown's study was the first history of blacks in the Civil War as well as the first single-volume account of black participation in three wars: the American Revolution, the War of 1812, and the Civil War. Brown borrows heavily from his earlier study *The Black Man: His Antecedents, His Genius and His Achievements* (1863 and 1865), and he includes some erroneous names and dates. See William Edward Farrison's notes for his edition of *The Negro in the American Rebellion.* Nonetheless, Chesnutt's judgment on this pioneering work seems unduly harsh.

4. LeRoi Jones, *Home: Social Essays,* 107–8.

5. Chesnutt was, throughout his life, an active reader of black writers. His private library included volumes by W. E. B. Du Bois, Booker T. Washington, Paul Laurence Dunbar, Jessie Fauset, and Benjamin Brawley, among others. "Chesnutt even owned a copy of *Appointed,* a still little-noted but important 1894 novel by 'Sanda' (the pseudonym of two radical journalists in Detroit, William H. Anderson and Walter H. Stowers, who decided to make a mark in history with their fictional treatment of a lynching—hardly an overworked story convention at the time)" (Joseph R. McElrath Jr., "Charles W. Chesnutt's Library," 102).

6. G. P. Quackenbos, *Advanced Course of Composition and Rhetoric,* 177.

7. The story was originally published in the *Atlanta Constitution* and collected in *Uncle Remus and the Legends of the Old Plantation* (London: David Bogue, 1881). I quote from the text posted online at http://xroads.virginia.edu/~UG97/remus/phone.html [cited 19 June 2002].

8. See Sterling A. Brown, "Negro Characters Seen by White Authors," 179–203, and Saunders Redding, "The Negro Writer and American Literature," 5.

CHAPTER 3. "The Future American" and "Chas. Chesnutt"

1. After appearing in the *Boston Evening Transcript,* the essay was published in *Essays and Speeches,* 131–35. Quotations are taken from the latter publication. Subsequent page references are given in the text.

2. Lorne Fienberg, "Charles W. Chesnutt's 'The Wife of His Youth': The Unveiling of the Black Story Teller," 206; Charles Duncan, *The Absent Man: The Narrative Craft of Charles W. Chesnutt,* 7.

3. Edward Livingston Youmans, *Herbert Spencer on the Americans and the Americans on Herbert Spencer,* 19–20. Perhaps the best indication of the way Chesnutt's version of Spencerian evolution deliberately flaunts late-nineteenth-century scientific thought can be found in the note Edward Livingston Youmans felt compelled to append to Spencer's comments quoted above: "This passage has been misunderstood. Mr. Spencer has been supposed to mean that great advantage will result from mixture of *all* the races now on the American Continent. Nothing could be further from his meaning. It is a corollary from biological facts that mixture of widely-divergent varieties of a species, such as are the Europeans, Africans, and Asiatics, is extremely injurious; while mixture of slightly-divergent varieties of a species, such as are the divisions of the Aryan race inhabiting different parts of Europe, is extremely beneficial" (20). The Spencerian view was championed in the United States by Columbia University sociologist Professor Franklin H. Giddings. In *The Principles of Sociology* (Macmillan, 1896) Giddings described the favorable effects of race mixing, but like Spencer, he excluded African Americans, whom he judged inherently inferior, from this mixing. See John David Smith, *Black Judas: William Hannibal Thomas and "The American Negro,"* 166.

4. Chesnutt does mention Spencer in *The Conjure Woman,* 163, and *The Quarry,* 253. The editors of the *Essays and Speeches* note Spencerian echoes elsewhere, see 94, 346.

5. Arlene A. Elder, "'The Future American Race': Charles Chesnutt's Utopian Illusion," 124; Charles W. Chesnutt, *"To Be an Author,"* 150.

6. William Z. Ripley, *Races of Europe: A Sociological Study* (New York: Appleton, 1899), 570. See also 122. John David Smith indicates the way Ripley's data and interpretation were read at the time of their publication: "Racists and nativists welcomed Ripley's notion of static racial development and his dim view of racial mixing" (*Black Judas: William Hannibal Thomas,* 168).

7. Thomas Dixon's *The Leopard's Spots* appeared in 1901. The popular novel's success, and the success of *The Birth of a Nation,* the film made from it, indicates that Dixon's best-seller captured the mood of the times, articulating white American racial fears at the beginning of the century. Dixon's position on assimilation was

categorical; it would not lead to a general lightening and a disappearance of the black person, but just the reverse: "Amalgamation simply meant Africanization. The big nostrils, the flat nose, massive jaw, protruding lip and kinky hair will register their animal marks over the proudest intellect and the rarest beauty of any other race" (*The Reconstruction Trilogy: The Leopard's Spots, The Clansman, The Traitor,* 197); "One drop of Negro blood makes a Negro. It kinks the hair, flattens the nose, thickens the lips, puts out the light of intellect, and lights the fires of brutal passions. The beginning of Negro equality as a vital fact is the beginning of the end of this nation's life" (124).

8. Frederick L. Hoffman, *Race Traits and Tendencies of the American Negro* (New York: Macmillan, 1896). I quote from the selection included in Brook Thomas, ed., *Plessy v. Ferguson: A Brief History with Documents,* 83.

9. Rayford Logan, *The Betrayal of the Negro from Rutherford B. Hayes to Woodrow Wilson,* 203. See also 29, 176, 308. John Edgar Chamberlin, editor of the *Transcript,* in 1901 gave William Hannibal Thomas's *The American Negro* one of its most favorable reviews. Thomas's book was an inflammatory, racist attack on African Americans, and Chesnutt led a campaign to remove it from print. See John David Smith, *Black Judas: William Hannibal Thomas,* 212.

10. Helen Chesnutt, *Charles Waddell Chesnutt: Pioneer of the Color Line,* 211.

11. Charles W. Chesnutt, "The Future American," ed. SallyAnn Ferguson, *MELUS* 15, no. 3 (1988): 95–107.

12. SallyAnn Ferguson, "Chesnutt's Genuine Black and Future Americans," 109.

13. Here are examples where these terms are used interchangeably. In the first two examples, "colored" and "Negro" are synonymous. The last example is the initial sentences in two successive paragraphs; in both paragraphs, Chesnutt speaks of the same group. In the first paragraph he uses "colored" and in the second "black." Emphases are added. "Another obstacle to race fusion lies in the drastic and increasing proscriptive legislation by which the South attempts to keep the white and *colored* races apart in every place where their joint presence might be taken to imply equality; or, to put it more directly, the persistent effort to degrade the *Negro* to a distinctly and permanently inferior caste" (133); "The popular argument that the *Negro* ought to develop his own civilization, and has no right to share in that of the white race, unless by favor, comes with poor grace from those who are forcing their civilization upon others at the cannon's mouth; it is, moreover, uncandid and unfair. The white people of the present generation did not make their civilization; they inherited it ready-made, and much of the wealth which is so strong a factor in their power was created by the unpaid labor of the *colored* people" (133); "The principal deterrent to race admixture, however, is the low industrial and social efficiency of the *colored*

race. . . . The forces that tend to the future absorption of the *black* race are, however, vastly stronger than those arrayed against it" (133).

14. Susan Gubar, quoting Diana Fuss, articulates the need to understand race in a way that is neither essentialist nor subjectivist: "race—'a variable and flexible term'— may work 'as a political concept' even when it is known to be a 'biological fiction.' . . . Neither an illusion nor a fact, race operates in a manner similar to gender—as a complex of meanings transformed by political frameworks" (Susan Gubar, *Racechanges: White Skin Black Face in American Culture,* 42).

15. *The Oxford W. E. B. Du Bois Reader,* 107.

CHAPTER 4. Black Vernacular in Chesnutt's
Short Fiction: "A New School of Literature"

1. E. V. Smalley, "The Political Field," *Atlantic Monthly,* January 1884, quoted in Kenneth M. Price, "Charles Chesnutt, the *Atlantic Monthly,* and the Intersection of African American Fiction and the Elite Culture," 259.

2. James Kinney, *Amalgamation! Race, Sex, and Rhetoric in the Nineteenth-Century American Novel,* 20.

3. Sterling A. Brown, *The Negro in American Fiction,* 49.

4. Albion Tourgée, *A Fool's Errand* (New York: Harper and Row, 1961), 226.

5. She could also show how slaves tricked their masters by exploiting white assumptions about a dialect speaker's ignorance. In *Minnie's Sacrifice* a slave persuades his master that he is frightened of the "bobolitionists" (14), so that the master allows the slave and the slave's wife to travel in the North. The couple takes advantage of the slaver's gullibility and escapes to freedom.

6. Gary D. Engle, *The Grotesque Essence: Plays from the American Minstrel Stage,* xx.

7. "'Jim Crow' was clearly many things to many people, of all ranks, races, and genders. At the upper social end of the male coterie that supported minstrelsy, 'Jim Crow' was a song about racial inferiority. If one just reads the newspapers—written by the educated elite, if not also the social, political, and economic elite (the same ones who believed that *Othello* was a play about the dangers of miscegenation)—one finds exactly what one would expect: Jim Crow is about a deservedly unfortunate 'nigger' worthy of a novelty laugh or two. The evidence at this level of discourse is uniform and unambiguous. It is in the streets, among the powerless, that the racial features of a blackface Jim Crow are less clear, where issues of identity, representation, and race are more complicated and less unequivocal" (Dale Cockrell, *Demons of Disorder: Early Blackface Minstrels and Their World,* 82). For a discussion of minstrelsy

that emphasizes its liberating function, see W. T. Lhamon, *Raising Cain: Blackface Performance from Jim Crow to Hip Hop.*

8. "Language—a symbol of civilization and social class—was another cloak of travesty for the stage Negro. The use, or misuse, of ponderous latinate words, the stiff, formal, pompous diction of the minstrels' interlocutor (that name itself, indeed) served the pretense and exposed it all at once. The audience was asked to look at blackfaced performers (Ethiopian Delineators as they sometimes called themselves) occasionally pretending to be civilized, and they laughed because the frequent malapropisms and misunderstandings made the pretense ludicrous. The language of the minstrel was, throughout, the language of social pretense" (Nathan Irvin Huggins, *Harlem Renaissance,* 265).

9. For representations of black dress and language, especially in regard to the stump speech, see Joseph Boskin, *Sambo: The Rise and Demise of an American Jester,* 122–24. For caricatures of the black mouth, teeth, and tongue, see the sheet music illustrations reproduced in Guy C. McElroy, *Facing History: The Black Image in American Art, 1710–1940,* figs. 5, 6.

10. William J. Mahar, "Black English in Early Blackface Minstrelsy: A New Interpretation of the Sources of Minstrel Show Dialect," 261–62.

11. See Michael North, *The Dialect of Modernism: Race, Language, and Twentieth-Century Literature,* 21–22, and Rayford Logan, *The Betrayal of the Negro from Rutherford B. Hayes to Woodrow Wilson,* 242–75.

12. Wade Hall, *The Smiling Phoenix: Southern Humor from 1865 to 1914,* 91, 82.

13. In both instances, the dialect speakers pronounce the words correctly, for the final consonant of "damn" is silent and the final fricative in "of" is voiced. Paradoxically and quite unfairly, the black speakers are mocked for failing to *spell* the words correctly when they *speak,* even when that orthography is phonetically inaccurate.

14. Mary Louise Pratt, *Imperial Eyes: Travel Writing and Transculturation,* 7.

15. "Appreciation" appeared in *Punch* 21 (April 20, 1887): 128; "The Fall of Adam" appeared in *Family Fiction,* December 25, 1886; and "The Partners" appeared in the *Southern Workman* 30 (May 1901): 271–78. All three are included in *The Short Fiction of Charles W. Chesnutt,* and my quotes are from the latter publication. Subsequent page references are given in the text.

16. Mikhail Bakhtin, *The Dialogic Imagination,* 333.

17. The story was first published in *Century* 27 (April 1884): 932–42, and it was collected in *In Ole Virginia* in 1887. In an 1890 letter to George Washington Cable, Chesnutt expressed his contempt for the plantation school stereotype of "the sentimental and devoted negro who prefers kicks to half-pence" (*"To Be an Author,"* 66.

See also 167). For a discussion of the Chesnutt-Page relationship see Matthew R. Martin, "The Two-Faced New South: The Plantation Tales of Thomas Nelson Page and Charles W. Chesnutt," 17–36.

18. Frederick Douglass, *The Narrative and Selected Writings,* 21.

19. J. Lee Greene notes the story's dual-narrative structure—Gainey's sermon and the frame tale surrounding it—but he misses the structure's ironic implications: "Chesnutt's 'Fall of Adam' asserts that blacks and whites are progeny of the same original parents; at the same time it adheres to the theory of two Adamic origins, in this case a white one and a black one" (*Blacks in Eden: The African American Novel's First Century,* 171). *Gainey's sermon* adheres to the theory of two Adamic origins; *Chesnutt's story* mocks Gainey's sermon and ridicules his account of black origins.

20. Daryl Dance, "In the Beginning: A New View of Black American Etiological Tales," 62.

21. Harriet Beecher Stowe, *Uncle Tom's Cabin,* 146.

CHAPTER 5. The Julius and John Stories: "The Luscious Scuppernong"

1. *The Conjure Woman* was originally published in Boston by Houghton Mifflin in 1899. My page references are to the reprint of this edition (Ann Arbor: University of Michigan Press, 1969). The remaining Julius and John stories are included *The Short Fiction of Charles W. Chesnutt,* which gives original dates and places of publication for each story. My quotations for these stories are from Render's edition. All page references are given in the text.

2. For "conjure tales," see Richard H. Brodhead, ed., *The Conjure Woman and Other Conjure Tales,* title page, and Charles Duncan, *The Absent Man,* 77. For "dialect stories," see William L. Andrews, *The Literary Career of Charles W. Chesnutt,* 41. For "Uncle Julius tales," see Sylvia Lyons Render, *Charles W. Chesnutt,* 1, and Henry B. Wonham, *Charles W. Chesnutt,* 75. Charles Duncan also refers to the "John/Julius narratives" (87) and Charles L. Crow mentions the "'John and Julius' stories" in "Under the Upass Tree: Charles Chesnutt's Gothic," 261.

3. For discussions of Chesnutt's relation to white dialect fiction, see Richard H. Brodhead, ed., *The Conjure Woman and Other Conjure Tales,* 3–7, and William L. Andrews, *The Literary Career of Charles W. Chesnutt,* 47–50.

4. *Henry W. Grady: His Life, Writings, and Speeches,* 15–16.

5. William Perry Brown's *Sea Island Romance* (1888) "summarizes all the clichés of the reconciliation novels of the eighties" (Herbert F. Smith, *The Popular American Novel 1865–1920,* 62). In Brown's novel, a Northern industrialist resettles his family

in Georgia where he quarrels with a Southern planter. The families are eventually united by the love of their children.

6. John F. Callahan, *In the African-American Vein: The Pursuit of Voice in Twentieth-Century Black Fiction*, 31.

7. Richard H. Brodhead, ed., *The Conjure Woman and Other Conjure Tales*, 2.

8. The narrative was not published as a story in Chesnutt's lifetime, but it appears as a subplot in *The Colonel's Dream*. Sylvia Lyons Render dates the story before 1897 and includes it in *The Short Fiction*. My quotations are from this publication.

9. Under slavery, silence was frequently advised as the wisest strategy for slaves. The John and Old Master tale entitled "Talking Bones" makes this point. John discovers human remains in the forest and asks the bones the reason for their presence: "And the skeleton said, 'Tongue is the cause of my being here.' So John ran back to Old Marster and said, 'The skeleton at the edge of the woods is talking.' Old Marster didn't believe him and went to see. And a great many people came too. They said, 'Make the bones talk.' But the skeleton wouldn't talk. So they beat John to death, and left him there. And then the bones talked. They said, 'Tongue brought us here, and tongue brought you here'" (told by Beulah Tate in Richard M. Dorson, ed., *American Negro Folktales*, 147–48).

10. William L. Andrews in William Wells Brown, *From Fugitive Slave to Freeman: The Autobiographies of William Wells Brown*, 11.

11. See Eric J. Sundquist, *To Wake the Nations*, 28.

12. See Charles W. Chesnutt, *Short Fiction*, 55 n. 30.

13. "The conviction held by American Negroes that no dichotomy exists between good and evil in the realm of the supernatural, but that both are attributes of the same powers in terms of predisposition and control, is characteristically African" (Melville Herskovitz, *The Myth of the Negro Past*, 242).

14. Herbert Spencer, *First Principles*, 412. The passage quoted in the story is paragraph 149, the first paragraph of chapter 19.

15. Henry B. Wonham, *Charles W. Chesnutt: A Study of the Short Fiction*, 16.

16. Charles W. Foster's study *The Phonology of the Conjure Tales of Charles W. Chesnutt* establishes several important facts about Chesnutt's representation of rural black dialect. First, although Chesnutt knew the work of earlier dialect writers such as Joel Chandler Harris and Thomas Nelson Page, his phonological transcriptions are uniquely his own. In addition, they have a remarkable geographical accuracy. Julius's speech can, in fact, be identified as that of Cape Fear and Pee Dee River Valley of southwestern North Carolina and northeastern South Carolina. Fayetteville, Patesville of Chesnutt's stories, lies in the Cape Fear and Pee Dee River Valley.

This does not mean, however, that Chesnutt has not shaped his transcription of dialect for artistic purposes. Let us take several dialect words we have focused on above: "watermillyum," "suckumstance," and "swivel." Based on unpublished field records of the *Linguistic Atlas of the Middle and South Atlantic States,* Foster confirms that in the dialect of this area "watermelon" was frequently pronounced with a *y* and that, in words like "circumstance," the medial *r* was often dropped. What these records do not confirm is the substitutions of *um* for *on,* or *um* for *am.* Of course, the extant records cannot give us an exhaustive description of all possibilities in the region's speech during this period. Nonetheless, it was quite possible that Chesnutt occasionally distorted dialectical pronunciation to obtain the effects we have described. Thus what might more accurately have been rendered as "watermelyon" became the even more evocative "watermillyum," and "suckamstance" became "suckumstance." Similarly, Foster's study provides no evidence that would support Julius's pronunciation of "shrivel" as "swivel"; nonetheless, the movement it introduces into Julius's vivid picture more than justifies Chesnutt's linguistic license. It is worthwhile to recall here William J. Mahar's discussion of literary dialect cited in chapter 4. Chesnutt's representation of rural black speech is, like black speech of the minstrel show, a literary dialect. Both begin with an accurate transcription of many existing phonological and semantic features, but both shape these features for their very different ideological purposes.

17. On the matter of "truth" in the Julius and John stories, see Charles L. Crow 's essay on "The Dumb Witness." Crow writes suggestively of the "silence and indeterminancy" at the heart of that tale ("Under the Upass Tree: Charles Chesnutt's Gothic," 266–67).

18. John W. Roberts, *From Trickster to Badman: The Black Folk Hero in Slavery and Freedom,* 45. Roberts notes the "individual secular ethos which envisioned all encounters in terms of 'me' and 'them' among slave tricksters" (44).

19. On Chesnutt's relation to the John and Old Master stories, see Eric J. Sundquist, *To Wake the Nations,* 330–32.

20. Henry B. Wonham, *Charles W. Chesnutt: A Study of the Short Fiction,* 54, 14, 54.

CHAPTER 6. Race in Chesnutt's Short Fiction: The "Line" and the "Web"

1. Charles W. Chesnutt, *Atlantic Monthly,* August 1887, 254.

2. Charles Duncan, *The Absent Man,* 11.

3. Thomas Dixon, *The Reconstruction Trilogy,* 82

4. "The children of colored women and white men, of whatever shade of color,

are morally and physically the inferiors of the pure black . . . the mulatto is in every way the inferior of the black, and of all the races the one possessed of least vital force" (Frederick L. Hoffman, "Race Amalgamation" [August 1896] in Brook Thomas, ed., *Plessy v. Ferguson: A Brief History with Documents*, 81).

5. Werner Sollors, *Neither Black Nor White Yet Both*, 230.

6. Discussing bourgeois realists like Jessie Fauset, Brown comments, "Too often, however, instead of typical Negro middle-class experience we get the more spectacular 'passing' and exceptional Negro artists and cosmopolitans" (Sterling A. Brown, *The Negro in American Fiction*, 142, see also 149).

7. Werner Sollors, *Neither Black Nor White Yet Both*, 235; Daphne Patai and Murray Graeme MacNicoll, introduction to *Mulatto*, by Aluisio Azevedo, quoted in Werner Sollors, *Neither Black Nor White Yet Both*, 235; Henry Louis Gates Jr., *Figures in Black*, 148–49.

8. "Her Virginia Mammy," "The Wife of His Youth," "The Passing of Grandison," and "The Web of Circumstance" appeared in *The Wife of His Youth and Other Stories of the Color Line*, originally published in Boston by Houghton Mifflin in 1899. My quotations from these stories are from the reprint edition (Ann Arbor: University of Michigan Press, 1968). "White Weeds" was unpublished in Chesnutt's lifetime and is included in *The Short Fiction of Charles W. Chesnutt*. My quotations from this story are from this publication. Page references are given in the text.

9. The story is undated, but its first sentence suggests that it was written in the twentieth century: "Students of Danforth University during the late Nineties may remember the remarkable events following the death of Professor John Carson of that institution" (391).

10. A striking instance of this myth is Lydia Brown, the mulatto mistress of a Radical Republican senator, who contrives to advance the designs of the even more dangerous mulatto Simon Lynch in Thomas Dixon's *The Clansman* (1905).

11. *Classic Baritone and Bass Songs* (Boston: O. Ditson, 1888), 38–41.

12. In discussing the story with Max Bennett Thrasher in a 1901 *Boston Transcript* interview, Chesnutt refers to Mr. Ryder as Liza Jane's "prosperous and cultured husband" ("Mr. Chesnutt at Work," 108).

13. William Andrews, *The Literary Career of Charles W. Chesnutt*, 153. Andrews discusses as instances of this pattern Rebecca Harding Davis's *Waiting for the Verdict* (1867) and Frances E. W. Harper's *Iola Leroy* (1892).

14. See Werner Sollors, *Neither Black Nor White Yet Both*, 255.

15. See Sterling A. Brown, *The Negro in American Fiction*, 21–29. William Gilmore Simms's *Woodcraft* (1854) provides an example of the myth propagated by these fictions. In this novel, a slave tells his master, "maussa, don't you bodder me wid dis

nonsense t'ing 'bout free paper any more. I's well off whar' I is I tell you." Quoted in Alan Henry Rose, "The Image of the Negro in the Pre–Civil War Novels of John Pendleton Kennedy and William Gilmore Simms," 225.

16. Charles Duncan, *The Absent Man*, 163.

17. Slavoj Zizek, *The Sublime Object of Ideology*, 49.

CHAPTER 7. *Mandy Oxendine:* "Is You a *Rale* Black Man?"

1. Charles Hackenberry, in his introduction to *Mandy Oxendine*, records that the manuscript was submitted unsuccessfully to the *Atlantic Monthly* and Houghton Mifflin in February 1897. Hackenberry also speculates that the novel may have been begun as early as 1889 (xv). The edition edited by Hackenberry (Urbana: University of Illinois Press, 1997) is the first publication of the novel. Page references are given in the text.

2. James Kinney, *Amalgamation! Race, Sex, and Rhetoric in the Nineteenth-Century American Novel*, 42.

3. Sterling A. Brown, "Negro Characters Seen by White Authors," quoted by Werner Sollors, *Neither Black Nor White Yet Both*, 225.

4. J. T. Trowbridge, *Neighbor Jackwood*, quoted by Sterling A. Brown, *The Negro in American Fiction*, 43. Pauline Hopkins, in *Contending Forces: A Romance Illustrative of Negro Life North and South* (New York: Oxford University Press, 1988), which was originally published in 1899, illustrates a significant feature of the tragic mulatta narrative: the uncanny ability of white males to discover—or imagine—the faintest trace of black ancestry in a woman. Grace Monfort has barely arrived in South Carolina when a white male decides that "thar's too much cream color in the face and too little blud seen under the skin fer a genooine white 'ooman" (41). Anson Pollock, "maddened by her beauty" (50), plots to possess Grace. He murders her husband, beats her cruelly, but is thwarted by Grace's suicide.

5. Quoted by Werner Sollors, " 'Never Was Born': The Mulatto, American Tragedy?" 302.

6. Harriet Beecher Stowe, *Uncle Tom's Cabin*, 236–37, 279.

CHAPTER 8. *The House behind the Cedars:* "Creatures of Our Creation"

1. Charles W. Chesnutt, *The House behind the Cedars* (Athens: University of Georgia Press, 2000), 1. Subsequent page references are given in the text. *The House behind the Cedars* was first published by Houghton Mifflin in Boston in 1900.

2. For a discussion of such a tournament, see Donald A. Petesch, *A Spy in the Enemy's Company: The Emergence of Modern Black Literature*, 139, 253.

3. J. Lee Greene, *Blacks in Eden: The African American Novel's First Century*, 85.

4. Robert Sedlack, "The Evolution of Charles Chesnutt's *The House behind the Cedars*," 184.

5. Trudier Harris, "Chesnutt's Frank Fowler: A Failure of Purpose?" 227.

CHAPTER 9. *The Marrow of Tradition:* "The Very Breath of His Nostrils"

1. Charles W. Chesnutt, *The Marrow of Tradition* (New York: Penguin, 1993), 49. Subsequent page references are given in the text. *The Marrow of Tradition* was originally published in Boston by Houghton Mifflin in 1901.

2. Boas was doing important ethnographic research as early as the 1880s, but his work on race difference did not become widely influential until after the publication of *The Mind of Primitive Man* in 1911.

3. Chesnutt quotes as an epigraph beneath the title of his manuscript the first three lines of Charles Lamb's "To the Editor of the Everyday Book," first published in the *London Magazine* in July 1825. Here are the first three verses of Lamb's poem, with the lines Chesnutt cites set in italics. These verses suggest an additional reason for Chesnutt's interest in the poem. Lamb praises Hone's ability to communicate a critical message in a manner that is literate and disarming. This was the purpose Chesnutt had set for his own literary career in his journals.

> *I like you, and your book, ingenuous Hone!*
> *In whose capacious all-embracing leaves*
> *The very marrow of tradition's shown;*
> And all that history—much that fiction—weaves.
> By every sort of taste your work is graced.
> Vast stores of modern anecdote we find,
> With good old story quaintly interlaced—
> The theme as various as the reader's mind.
> Rome's lie-fraught legends you so truly paint—
> Yet kindly,—that the half turn'd Catholic
> Scarcely forbears to smile at his own saint,
> And cannot curse the candid heretic.

4. Todd McGowan, "Acting without the Father: Charles Chesnutt's New Aristocrat," 61–62.

5. See Eric J. Sundquist, *To Wake the Nations*, 276–94.

6. *Henry W. Grady: His Life, Writings, and Speeches*, 15–16.

CHAPTER 10. *The Colonel's Dream:* "Sho Would 'a' Be'n a 'Ristocrat"

1. Ernestine Pickens, *Charles W. Chesnutt and the Progressive Movement,* 99.

2. Laura Treadwell is clearly one of the most enlightened members of her community. Nonetheless, like French, she is not untainted by race and class prejudice. She is appalled when French tells her he plans to inhabit a house in which blacks have lived, and as librarian, she opposes allowing blacks to use the same library as whites. She is, as Gary Scharnhorst observes, "a remarkably ambiguous heroine, the incarnation of both the best and worst attributes of the Old South" ("'The Growth of a Dozen Tendrils,'" 278).

3. Charles W. Chesnutt, *The Colonel's Dream* (Upper Sadle River, N.J.: Gregg Press, 1968), 26. Subsequent references are given in the text. *The Colonel's Dream* was originally published in New York by Doubleday Page in 1905.

4. Bertram Wyatt-Brown, *Southern Honor: Ethics and Behavior in the Old South,* 34.

5. William L. Andrews comments: "This hopeful rhetoric notwithstanding, however, the real message of *The Colonel's Dream* remains one of disillusionment and failure. As in the conclusion to 'The Web of Circumstance,' one can see in the attempt to dilute the defeatism of French's story Chesnutt's philosophy at odds with his facts" (*The Literary Career of Charles W. Chesnutt,* 255).

6. "Slavery in the South Today," *Cosmopolitan,* quoted in Harvey Swados, ed., *Years of Conscience: The Muckrakers,* 346, 344.

7. Matthew Wilson, "Who Has the Right to Say? Charles W. Chesnutt, Whiteness, and the Public Sphere," 28. For a discussion of the Chesnutt-Tourgée relationship, see Peter Caccavari, "A Trick of Mediation: Charles Chesnutt's Conflicted Literary Relationship with Albion Tourgée," 129–53.

8. See Charles W. Chesnutt, *Essays and Speeches,* 433.

9. John Milton Cooper Jr., *Walter Hines Page,* 149.

10. See Joseph R. McElrath Jr., "Charles W. Chesnutt's Library," 107.

11. See Susan L. Blake, "A Better Mousetrap: Washington's Program and *The Colonel's Dream,*" 49–59.

CHAPTER 11. *Paul Marchand, F.M.C.:* "F.M.C." and "C.W.C."

1. Chesnutt submitted the manuscript unsuccessfully to at least three publishers in 1921. See the following letters in the Charles Waddell Chesnutt Collection of Fisk University Library: Chesnutt to Houghton Mifflin Company, 8 October 1921; Chesnutt to Harcourt Brace and Company, 12 November 1921; Chesnutt to Alfred A. Knopf, Esq., 20 December 1921.

2. J. Noel Heermance, *Charles W. Chesnutt: America's First Great Black Novelist,* 178.

3. Charles W. Chesnutt, *Paul Marchand, F.M.C.* (Princeton: Princeton University Press, 1999), 3. Subsequent page references are given in the text.

4. The narrator himself has difficulty deciding among these approaches. In his comments, he vacillates between biological and social accounts of race, as in the following: "Whether or not the Creole quadroons were a philosophic race was not really important, since the pleasure-loving French temperament, superimposed upon the easygoing African, produced a usually placid acceptance of the situation which had all the effect of philosophy. In this respect, however, Paul Marchand differed from the average quadroon. Whether it was the fiery spirit of some adventurous European ancestor, or the blood of some African chief who had exercised the power of life and death before being broken to the hoe, or whether the free air of revolutionary France had wrought upon him—whatever the reason, he had chafed more than most under the restriction of his caste" (79). The characterization of the "easygoing African" invokes a familiar stereotype and implies a biological inheritance of a racial temperament. But the reference to the African chief before slavery immediately contradicts this stereotype. It shows that Africans, before being enslaved, had produced energetic and decisive leaders, and it argues that Paul's supposed black ancestry could as easily be the source of his proud behavior as could his white ancestry. The reference to Paul's student years in Paris shifts direction once again, suggesting that environmental rather biological influences were decisive.

5. The narrator echoes this confusion. He follows Renard's lead, referring to his problematic protagonist with a series of clumsy locutions: "Paul Beaurepas, late Marchand, f.m.c." (103, 105); "the quadroon of yesterday—today the heir of Beaurepas" (106); "Paul Beaurepas, hitherto Marchand" (107); and "Paul Beaurepas, late Marchand" (134). The narrator also follows the attorney's use of "Marchand" to refer to Paul when discussing his situation before his father's death and "Beaurepas" when referring to the protagonist in his new condition. Nonetheless, during the scene in which Paul is presented as new head of the Beaurepas family, the narrator trips up, three times referring to Paul as "Marchand" (105, 108). The narrator's linguistic vacillations in subsequent chapters reflect Paul's own confusion about his identity. When Paul threatens Zabet and when he duels with his cousins, the narrator refers to him as "Paul Beaurepas" or simply "Beaurepas" (121, 122, 123, 125, 130, 141, 143, 144, 148). However, when Paul confronts his double, the rebellious mulatto, he becomes "Paul Marchand" or "Marchand" (159, 160, 161). In the novel's last two chapters, as Paul seeks to resolve his identity, the narrator wavers between his two family names. Once the protagonist renounces the Beaurepas inheritance and names Philippe head

of the family, he becomes simply "Paul" (181, 182, 183), and in the narrator's last reference to his protagonist we learn that "Paul Marchand" (183) settled in France and had a successful business career there. The narrator's vacillations in naming his main character illustrate the relativity of racial and personal identity and its dependence on context. It also helps to dramatize a conflict that remains in doubt until the novel's final pages.

6. Ironically, Paul imagined in his youth that Renard, the mysterious attorney who materialized periodically in his life, was his father.

7. Daniel R. Schwartz summarizes the connection, in Lacan's thinking, between paternal identity and language. "A child has little doubt about who its mother is, but who is its father, and how would one know? The father's claim rests on the mother's *word* that he is in fact the father; the father's relationship to the child is thus established through language and a system of marriage and kinship—names— that in turn is basic to rules of everything from property to law. The name of the father (*nom du pere,* which in French sounds like *non du pere*) involves, in a sense, nothing of the father—nothing, that is, except his word or name" ("Psychoanalytic Criticism and 'The Dead,' " 94).

8. André Bleikasten, "Fathers in Faulkner," 117, 140.

9. Harriet Beecher Stowe's *Uncle Tom's Cabin* (1852) and Albion Tourgée's *A Fool's Errand* (1879) both contain prefatory material explaining their polemical purposes.

10. See Grace L. King, *New Orleans: The Place and the People,* 343.

CHAPTER 12. *The Quarry:* "And Not the Hawk"

1. Chesnutt unsuccessfully submitted the novel to at least two publishers: Alfred Knopf, Inc., in 1928 and Houghton Mifflin in 1930.

2. Quoted in Helen Chesnutt, *Charles Waddell Chesnutt: Pioneer of the Color Line,* 307.

3. See Helen Chesnutt, *Charles Waddell Chesnutt: Pioneer of the Color Line,* 285–87, 301.

4. Included in Charles W. Chesnutt, *Essays and Speeches,* 33–39.

5. Charles W. Chesnutt, introduction to *Senator John P. Green and Sketches of Prominent Men of Ohio,* by William Rogers, 6.

6. Herbert F. Smith, *The Popular American Novel, 1865–1920,* 1.

7. David Levering Lewis, *When Harlem Was in Vogue,* 109.

8. See *Crisis* 32, no. 4 (August 1926): 167.

9. Charles W. Chesnutt, *The Quarry* (Princeton: Princeton University Press, 1999), 264–65. Subsequent page references are given in the text.

10. W. D. Howells, "An Exemplary Citizen," *North American Review* 173 (August 1901): 282. Howells acknowledged, however, that he could see Washington as exemplary to the degree that he could see in him the white mentor, General S. A. Armstrong, who had trained Washington.

11. David Levering Lewis, *The Portable Harlem Renaissance Reader,* xv; see also David Levering Lewis, *When Harlem Was in Vogue,* 137.

12. David Levering Lewis, *When Harlem Was in Vogue,* 146.

13. For a discussion of Boas's position on race, see George Hutchinson, *The Harlem Renaissance in Black and White,* 62–77.

14. Chesnutt's own vacillation on the question of racial nationalism can be seen in changes in the manuscripts of *The Quarry.* In the penultimate draft Donald identifies himself as a "Negro American," but in the final draft he describes himself as an "American Negro" (140).

15. For a discussion of Chesnutt and his family's relations with Washington, see Helen Chesnutt, *Charles Waddell Chesnutt: Pioneer of the Color Line,* 191–208.

16. The penultimate draft is in the Special Collections of Ohio University. The manuscript pages are not consecutively numbered; this reference occurs in chapter 14.

17. Both books were published in New York by Scribners.

18. Chesnutt emphasizes this point by having Lady Merrivale courted by Donald's relative Count Milfiore. The British noblewoman refuses the decadent European but falls in love with Donald.

19. See Chesnutt to Walter White, 28 December 1926 and 5 January 1927, Charles Waddell Chesnutt Collection, Fisk University Library. For a discussion of Chesnutt's relationship to Negro writers of the twenties, see Dean McWilliams, "Charles Chesnutt and the Harlem Renaissance."

BIBLIOGRAPHY

WORKS BY CHARLES W. CHESNUTT

Baxter's Procrustes. Edited by John B. Nicholson Jr. Cleveland: Rowfant Club, 1966.

Charles Waddell Chesnutt Collection. Papers. Fisk University Library.

Collected Stories of Charles W. Chesnutt. Edited by William L. Andrews. New York: Mentor, 1992.

The Colonel's Dream. Upper Saddle River, N.J.: Gregg Press, 1968.

The Conjure Woman. Intro. Robert W. Farnsworth. Ann Arbor: University Michigan Press, 1969.

Essays and Speeches. Edited by Joseph R. McElrath Jr., Robert C. Leitz III, and Jesse S. Crisler. Stanford: Stanford University Press, 1999.

An Exemplary Citizen: Letters of Charles W. Chesnutt, 1906–1932. Edited by Jesse S. Crisler, Robert C. Leitz III, and Joseph R. McElrath Jr. Stanford: Stanford University Press, 2002.

Frederick Douglass. Edited by Ernestine W. Pickens. Intro. William L. Andrews. Atlanta: Clark Atlanta University Press, 2002.

The House behind the Cedars. Intro. William L. Andrews. Athens: University of Georgia Press, 2000.

Introduction. *Senator John P. Green and Sketches of Prominent Men of Ohio,* by William Rogers. Washington and Cleveland: Arena Publishing Co., 1893.

The Journals of Charles W. Chesnutt. Edited by Richard Brodhead. Durham: Duke University Press, 1993.

Mandy Oxendine. Edited by Charles Hackenberry. With a foreword by William L. Andrews. Urbana: University of Illinois Press, 1997.

The Marrow of Tradition. Edited by Eric J. Sundquist. New York: Penguin, 1993.

Paul Marchand, F.M.C. Edited by Dean McWilliams. Princeton: Princeton University Press, 1999.

The Quarry. Edited by Dean McWilliams. Princeton: Princeton University Press, 1999.

The Short Fiction of Charles W. Chesnutt. Edited by Sylvia Lyons Render. Washington, D.C.: Howard University Press, 1981.

Stories, Novels, and Essays. Edited by Werner Sollors. New York: Library of America, 2002.

"To Be an Author": Letters of Charles W. Chesnutt, 1889–1905. Edited by Joseph R. McElrath Jr. and Robert C. Leitz III. Princeton: Princeton University Press, 1997.

The Wife of His Youth and Other Stories of the Color Line. Intro. Earl Schenck Miers. Ann Arbor: University of Michigan Press, 1968.

SECONDARY SOURCES

Andrews, William L. Introduction. *Collected Stories of Charles W. Chesnutt*. Edited by William L. Andrews. New York: Mentor, 1992.

———. Introduction. *The House behind the Cedars*, by Charles W. Chesnutt. Athens: University of Georgia Press, 2000.

———. *The Literary Career of Charles W. Chesnutt*. Baton Rouge: Louisiana State University Press, 1980.

———. "The Representation of Slavery and the Rise of Afro-American Literary Realism, 1865–1920." *Slavery and the Literary Imagination*. Edited by Deborah McDowell and Arnold Rampersad. Baltimore: Johns Hopkins University Press, 1989. 62–80.

———. "William Dean Howells and Charles W. Chesnutt: Criticism and Race Fiction in the Age of Booker T. Washington." *American Literature* 48 (1976): 327–39.

Appiah, K. Anthony, "Race, Culture, and Identity: Misunderstood Connections." *Color Conscious: The Political Morality of Race*, by Anthony K. Appiah and Amy Gutmann. Princeton: Princeton University Press, 1996. 30–105.

Baker, Houston A. *Afro-American Poetics: Revisions of Harlem and the Black Aesthetic*. Madison: University of Wisconsin Press, 1988.

———. *Modernism and the Harlem Renaissance*. Chicago: University of Chicago Press, 1987.

Bakhtin, Mikhail. *The Dialogic Imagination: Four Essays*. Translated by Michael Holquist and Caryl Emerson. Edited by Michael Holquist. Austin: University of Texas Press, 1981.

Benston, Kimberly M. "I Yam What I Yam: The Topos of (Un)naming in African-American Literature." *Black Literature and Literary Theory*. Edited by Henry Louis Gates Jr. New York: Metheun, 1984. 151–72.

Bhabha, Homi K. *The Location of Culture*. New York: Routledge, 1994.

Blake, Susan L. "A Better Mousetrap: Washington's Program and *The Colonel's Dream*." *Critical Essays on Charles W. Chesnutt*. Edited by Joseph R. McElrath Jr. New York: G. K. Hall, 1999. 189–97.

Bleikasten, André. "Fathers in Faulkner." *The Fictional Father*. Edited by Robert Con Davis. Amherst: University of Massachusetts Press, 1981. 115–46.

Boas, Franz. *Race and Democratic Society.* New York: JJ Augustin, 1945.

Boskin, Joseph. *Sambo: The Rise and Demise of an American Jester.* New York: Oxford University Press, 1986.

Brodhead, Richard H. Introduction. *The Conjure Woman and Other Conjure Tales.* Edited by Richard H. Brodhead. Durham, N.C.: Duke University Press, 1993.

Brown, Sterling A. "Negro Characters Seen by White Authors." *Journal of Negro Education* 2 (1933): 179–203.

———. *The Negro in American Fiction* and *Negro Poetry and Drama.* New York: Arno Press, 1969.

Brown, William Wells. *From Fugitive Slave to Freeman: The Autobiographies of William Wells Brown.* Edited by William L. Andrews. New York: Mentor, 1993.

———. *The Negro in the American Rebellion.* Edited by William Edward Farrison. New York: Citadel, 1971.

Caccavari, Peter. "A Trick of Mediation: Charles Chesnutt's Conflicted Literary Relationship with Albion Tourgée." *Literary Influence and African-American Writers: Collected Essays.* Edited by Tracy Mishkin. New York: Garland, 1996. 129–53.

Callahan, John F. *In the African-American Vein: The Pursuit of Voice in Twentieth-Century Black Fiction.* Urbana: University of Illinois Press, 1988.

Chesnutt, Helen. *Charles Waddell Chesnutt: Pioneer of the Color Line.* Chapel Hill: University of North Carolina Press, 1952.

Cockrell, Dale. *Demons of Disorder: Early Blackface Minstrels and Their World.* New York: Cambridge University Press, 1997.

Cooper, John Milton, Jr. *Walter Hines Page: The Southerner as American.* Chapel Hill: University of North Carolina Press, 1977.

Crow, Charles L. "Under the Upass Tree: Charles Chesnutt's Gothic." *Critical Essays on Charles W. Chesnutt.* Edited by Joseph R. McElrath Jr. New York: G. K. Hall, 1999. 261–70.

Dance, Daryl. "In the Beginning: A New View of Black American Etiological Tales." *Southern Folklore Quarterly* 40 (1977): 53–64.

Dixon, Thomas. *The Reconstruction Trilogy: The Leopard's Spots, The Clansman, The Traitor.* Newport Beach, Calif.: Noontide Press, 1994.

Dorson, Richard M., ed., *American Negro Folktales.* Greenwich, Conn.: Fawcett, 1967.

Douglass, Frederick. *The Narrative and Selected Writings.* New York: Random House, 1984.

Du Bois, W. E. B. *The Oxford W. E. B. Du Bois Reader.* Edited by Eric J. Sundquist. New York: Oxford University Press, 1996.

Duncan, Charles. *The Absent Man: The Narrative Craft of Charles W. Chesnutt.* Athens: Ohio University Press, 1998.

Elder, Arlene A. " 'The Future American Race': Charles W. Chesnutt's Utopian Illusion." *MELUS* 15, no. 3 (1988): 121–29.

Ellison, Curtis W., and E. W. Metcalf Jr. *Charles W. Chesnutt: A Reference Guide.* Boston: G. K. Hall, 1977.

Ellison, Ralph. *Shadow and Act.* New York: Random House, 1995.

Emerson, Ralph Waldo. *Letters and Social Aims.* Vol. 8 of *Centenary Edition of the Complete Works of Ralph Waldo Emerson.* Edited by Edward Emerson. Boston: Houghton Mifflin, 1904.

Engle, Gary D. *The Grotesque Essence: Plays from the American Minstrel Stage.* Baton Rouge: Louisiana State University Press, 1978.

Ferguson, SallyAnn. "Chesnutt's Genuine Black and Future Americans." *MELUS* 15, no. 3 (1988): 109–19.

———. "Introduction. Charles W. Chesnutt: An American Signifier." *Charles W. Chesnutt: Selected Writings.* Boston: Houghton Mifflin, 2001.

———. "Rena Walden: Chesnutt's Failed 'Future American.' " *Critical Essays on Charles W. Chesnutt.* Edited by Joseph R. McElrath Jr. New York: G. K. Hall, 1999. 198–205.

Fienberg, Lorne. "Charles W. Chesnutt's 'The Wife of His Youth': The Unveiling of the Black Story Teller." *Critical Essays on Charles W. Chesnutt.* Edited by Joseph R. McElrath Jr. New York: G. K. Hall, 1999. 206–23.

Fishkin, Shelley Fisher. "Interrogating 'Whiteness,' Complicating 'Blackness': Remapping American Culture." *Criticism and the Color Line: Desegregating American Literary Studies.* Edited by Henry B. Wonham. Brunswick, N.J.: Rutgers University Press, 1996. 251–90.

———. *Was Huck Black?: Mark Twain and African-American Voices.* New York: Oxford University Press, 1993.

Foster, Charles W. *The Phonology of the Conjure Tales of Charles W. Chesnutt.* Publication of the American Dialect Society, no. 55. University: University of Alabama Press, 1971.

Fredrickson, George M. *The Black Image in the White Mind: The Debate on Afro-American Character and Destiny, 1817–1914.* Middletown, Conn.: Wesleyan University Press, 1987.

Gates, Henry Louis, Jr. *Figures in Black.* New York: Oxford University Press, 1987.

———. *The Signifying Monkey: A Theory of African-American Literary Criticism.* New York: Oxford University Press, 1988.

———, ed. *Black Literature and Literary Theory.* New York: Methuen, 1984.

Gibson, Donald B. Introduction. *The House behind the Cedars,* by Charles W. Chesnutt. New York: Penguin, 1993.

Gosset, Thomas F. *Race: The History of an Idea in America*. New York: Oxford University Press, 1997.

Grady, Henry W. "The New South." *Henry W. Grady: His Life, Writings, and Speeches*. Edited by Joel Chandler Harris. New York: Cassell Publishing Co., 1890. 15–16.

Greene, J. Lee. *Blacks in Eden: The African American Novel's First Century*. Charlottesville: University of Virginia Press, 1996.

Gubar, Susan. *Racechanges: White Skin Black Face in American Culture*. New York: Oxford University Press, 1997.

Hall, Wade. *The Smiling Phoenix: Southern Humor from 1865 to 1914*. Gainesville: University of Florida Press, 1965.

Harper, Frances E. W. *Minnie's Sacrifice, Sowing and Reaping, Trial and Triumph*. Edited by Frances Smith Foster. Boston: Beacon, 1994.

Harris, Trudier. "Chesnutt's Frank Fowler: A Failure of Purpose?" *College Language Association Journal* 22 (1979): 215–28.

Heermance, J. Noel. *Charles W. Chesnutt: America's First Great Black Novelist*. Hamden, Conn.: Archon, 1974.

Herskovitz, Melville. *The Myth of the Negro Past*. Boston: Beacon, 1958.

Hopkins, Pauline. *Contending Forces: A Romance Illustrative of Negro Life North and South*. New York: Oxford University Press, 1988.

Howells, William Dean. "An Exemplary Citizen." *North American Review* 173 (August 1901): 282.

Huggins, Nathan Irvin. *Harlem Renaissance*. New York: Oxford University Press, 1971.

Hutchinson, George. *The Harlem Renaissance in Black and White*. Cambridge: Harvard University Press, 1995.

Hyatt, Marshall. *Franz Boas Social Activist, the Dynamics of Ethnicity*. New York: Greenwood, 1990.

Johnson, James Weldon. *The Autobiography of an Ex-Colored Man*. New York: Penguin, 1990.

Jones, LeRoi. *Home: Social Essays*. New York: William Morrow, 1966.

———. "Philistinism and the Negro Writer." *Anger and Beyond*. Edited by Herbert Hill. New York: Harper and Row, 1966. 51–61.

Keller, Frances Richardson. *An American Crusade: The Life of Charles Waddell Chesnutt*. Provo, Utah: Brigham Young University Press, 1978.

King, Grace L. *New Orleans: The Place and the People*. New York: Macmillan, 1896.

Kinney, James. *Amalgamation! Race, Sex, and Rhetoric in the Nineteenth-Century American Novel*. Westport, Conn.: Greenwood, 1985.

Kristeva, Julia. *Strangers to Ourselves*. Translated by Leon Roudiez. New York: Columbia University Press, 1991.

Lacan, Jacques. *The Langauge of the Self: The Funciton of Language in Psychoanalyis*. Translated by Anthony Wilden. New York: Dell, 1968.

Lewis, David Levering. *The Portable Harlem Renaissance Reader*. New York: Penguin, 1994.

————. *When Harlem Was in Vogue*. New York: Oxford University Press, 1981.

Lhamon, W. T. *Raising Cain: Blackface Performance from Jim Crow to Hip Hop*. Cambridge: Harvard University Press, 1998.

Locke, Alain. "Enter the New Negro." *The Survey Graphic,* March 1925, 631–34.

Logan, Rayford. *The Betrayal of the Negro from Rutherford B. Hayes to Woodrow Wilson*. New York: Macmillan, 1970.

Mahar, William J. "Black English in Early Blackface Minstrelsy: A New Interpretation of the Sources of Minstrel Show Dialect." *American Quarterly* 37 (summer 1985): 260–85.

Martin, Matthew R. "The Two-Faced New South: The Plantation Tales of Thomas Nelson Page and Charles W. Chesnutt." *Southern Literary Journal* 30, no. 2 (1998): 17–36.

McElrath, Joseph R., Jr. "Charles W. Chesnutt's Library." *Analytical and Enumerative Bibliography* 8, no. 2 (1994): 102–21.

————. "W. D. Howells and Race: Charles W. Chesnutt's Disappointment of the Dean." *Nineteenth-Century Literature* 51, no. 4 (1997): 474–99.

————. "Why Charles W. Chesnutt Is Not a Realist." *American Literary Realism* 32, no. 2 (2000): 91–108.

————, ed. *Critical Essays on Charles W. Chesnutt*. New York: G. K. Hall, 1999.

McElroy, Guy C. *Facing History: The Black Image in American Art, 1710–1940*. San Francisco: Bedford Arts, 1990.

McGowan, Todd. "Acting without the Father: Charles Chesnutt's New Aristocrat." *American Literary Realism* 30, no. 1 (1998): 59–74.

McLemee, Scott. "The Anger and the Irony: Charles Chesnutt, the First Black Novelist, Regains His Former Glory." *Chronicle of Higher Education*, 1 March 2002, A14–16.

McWilliams, Dean. "Charles Chesnutt and the Harlem Renaissance." *Soundings* 30 (1997): 591–606.

Mills, Charles W. *Blackness Visible: Essays on Philosophy and Race*. Ithaca: Cornell University Press, 1998.

Nathan, Hans. "The Performance of the Virginia Minstrels." *Inside the Minstrel Mask: Readings in Nineteenth-Century Blackface Minstrelsy*. Edited by Annemarie

Bean, James V. Hatch, and Brooks McNamara. Hanover, N.H.: University Press of New England for Wesleyan University Press, 1996. 35–42.

North, Michael. *The Dialect of Modernism: Race, Language, and Twentieth-Century Literature*. New York: Oxford University Press, 1994.

Page, Thomas Nelson. *In Ole Virginia; or, Marse Chan, and Other Stories*. New York: C. Scribner's Sons, 1887.

Patai, Daphne, and Murray Graeme MacNicoll. Introduction. *Mulatto*, by Aluisio Azevedo. Rutherford, N.J.: Farleigh Dickinson University Press, 1990.

Petesch, Donald A. *A Spy in the Enemy's Company: The Emergence of Modern Black Literature*. Iowa City: University of Iowa Press, 1989.

Pickens, Ernestine. *Charles W. Chesnutt and the Progressive Movement*. New York: Pace University Press, 1994.

Pratt, Mary Louise. *Imperial Eyes: Travel Writing and Transculturation*. London and New York: Routledge, 1992.

Price, Kenneth M. "Charles Chesnutt, the *Atlantic Monthly*, and the Intersection of African American Fiction and Elite Culture." *Periodical Literature in Nineteenth Century America*. Edited by Kenneth M. Price and Susan Belasco Smith. Charlottesville: University of Virgina Press, 1995. 257–74.

Quackenbos, G. P. *Advanced Course of Composition and Rhetoric*. New York: D. Appleton and Co., 1875.

Redding, Saunders. "The Negro Writer and American Literature." *Anger and Beyond: The Negro Writer in the United States*. Edited by Herbert Hill. New York: Harper and Row, 1966. 1–19.

Render, Sylvia Lyons. *Charles W. Chesnutt*. Boston: G. K. Hall, 1980.

Roberts, John W. *From Trickster to Badmun: The Black Folk Hero in Slavery and Freedom*. Philadelphia: University of Pennsylvania Press, 1989.

Rose, Alan Henry. "The Image of the Negro in the Pre–Civil War Novels of John Pendleton Kennedy and William Gilmore Simms." *Journal of American Studies* 4 (1970): 217–26.

Scharnhorst, Gary. " 'The Growth of a Dozen Tendrils': The Polyglot Satire of Chesnutt's *The Colonel's Dream*." *Critical Essays on Charles W. Chesnutt*. Edited by Joseph R. McElrath Jr. New York: G. K. Hall, 1999. 271–80.

Schwartz, Daniel R. "Psychoanalytic Criticism and 'The Dead.'" In *The Dead: Complete, Authoritative Text with Biographical and Historical Context, Critical History, and Essays from Five Critical Perspectives*, by James Joyce. Boston: Bedford Books, 1994. 85–96.

Sedlack, Robert. "The Evolution of Charles Chesnutt's *The House behind the Cedars*."

Critical Essays on Charles W. Chesnutt. Edited by Joseph R. McElrath Jr. New York: G. K. Hall, 1999. 181–88.

Smith, Herbert F. *The Popular American Novel, 1865–1920.* Boston: G. K. Hall, 1980.

Smith, John David. *Black Judas: William Hannibal Thomas and "The American Negro."* Athens: University of Georgia Press, 2000.

Sollors, Werner. *Neither Black Nor White Yet Both: Thematic Explorations of Interracial Literature.* New York: Oxford University Press, 1997.

———. " 'Never Was Born': The Mulatto, American Tragedy?" *Massachusetts Review* 27 (1986): 293–316.

Spencer, Herbert. *First Principles.* New York: Appleton, 1862.

Stoddard, Lothrop. *The Rising Tide of Color against White World Supremacy.* New York: Scribners, 1920.

Stowe, Harriet Beecher. *Uncle Tom's Cabin.* New York: Bantam, 1981.

Sundquist, Eric J. *To Wake the Nations: Race in the Making of American Literature.* Cambridge: Harvard University Press, 1993.

Swados, Harvey, ed. *Years of Conscience: The Muckrakers.* Cleveland: World Publishing, 1962.

Thomas, Brook, ed. *Plessy v. Ferguson: A Brief History with Documents.* Boston: Bedford, 1997.

Thrasher, Max Bennett. "Mr. Chesnutt at Work." *Critical Essays on Charles W. Chesnutt.* Edited by Joseph R. McElrath Jr. New York: G. K. Hall, 1999. 108–11.

Walcott, Derek. *Dream on Monkey Mountain and Other Plays.* London: Mathan Cape, 1972.

Watson, Steven. *The Harlem Renaissance: Hub of African-American Culture, 1920–1930.* New York: Pantheon, 1995.

Werner, Craig Hansen. *Playing the Changes.* Urbana: University of Illinois Press, 1994.

Williams, Vernon J. *Rethinking Race: Franz Boas and His Contemporaries.* Lexington: University of Kentucky Press, 1996.

Wilson, Matthew. "Who Has the Right to Say? Charles W. Chesnutt, Whiteness, and the Public Sphere." *College Literature* 26, no. 2 (spring 1999): 18–35.

Wonham, Henry B. *Charles W. Chesnutt: A Study of the Short Fiction.* New York: Prentice Hall, 1999.

Wyatt-Brown, Bertram. *Southern Honor: Ethics and Behavior in the Old South.* New York: Oxford University Press, 1982.

Youmans, Edward Livingston. *Herbert Spencer on the Americans and the Americans on Herbert Spencer.* New York: D. Appleton, 1883.

Zizek, Slavoj. *The Sublime Object of Ideology.* London: Verso, 1989.

INDEX

Absalom, Absalom! (Faulkner), 199

"Abu Ben Adhem" (Hunt), 176

Alger, Horatio, 152, 210

Amsterdam News, 211

Andrews, William L., x, 80, 229 (n. 3, 4), 239 (n. 13), 242 (n. 5)

Appiah, K. Anthony, 23, 27, 40, 230 (n. 7)

Appointed (Sanda), 231 (n. 5)

"Appreciation," 65, 66–67, 78, 80

Aristocracy, 152, 161, 166; family name, 158, 171, 190, 220; genealogy, 108; masculine filiation, 199; Southern chivalry, 107, 136, 190, 198. *See also* Gentility

Armstrong, Gen. S. A., 245 (n. 10)

Arnold, Matthew, 14

Assimilation, 44–56, 216, 217, 224, 225, 232 (n. 7)

Atlanta Constitution, 63, 77, 231 (n. 7)

Atlanta University, 218, 222

Atlantic Monthly, 12, 240 (ch. 7, n. 1)

Authorial persona, 144, 180, 206, 213

Autobiography of an Ex-Colored Man, The (Johnson), 222

Autoethnography, 64

Baker, Houston A., x, 1, 229 (n. 3)

Bakhtin, Mikhail, 10, 65–66, 70, 75; *The Dialogic Imagination,* 57

Baraka, Amiri (Leroy Jones), 31–32

"Baxter's *Procrustes,*" 12–22

Benston, Kimberly M., 29; "I Yam What I Yam," 133

Bhabha, Homi K., vii

Binary oppositions: in culture, xi–xii, 2, 3; between empiricism and imagination, 84; in language, xi–xii, 12, 20; in literary criticism, 14–19; between oral and literate cultures, 72–75; between proprietary and predial ownership, 85; in racial thinking, 25, 42, 101, 117–18; in sexual thinking, 125; in Southern honor, 168; between white aristocracy and black middle class, 156

Birth of a Nation, The (Griffith), 232 (n. 7)

Blair, Hugh, 36

Bleikasten, André, 199

Boas, Franz, 7, 149, 216, 217, 245 (n. 3); *The Mind of Primitive Man,* 241 (n. 2)

Boston Evening Transcript, 43, 52, 233 (n. 9), 239 (n. 12)

Brawley, Benjamin, 231 (n. 5)

Brodhead, Richard H., 27, 35, 36

Brown, Sterling A., 42, 103, 231 (n. 3)

Brown, William Perry, 236 (n. 5)

Brown, William Wells, 81; *Clotel*,
    102; *The Negro in the American
    Revolution*, 31
"Bruno," 39
Bulwer-Lytton, Edward George, 135
Bunyan, John, 34
Burns, Robert, 34
Byron, Lord George Gordon, 31

Cable, George Washington, 82, 180,
    202, 235 (n. 17); *The Grandissimes*,
    205; *John March, Southerner*, 181
Cakewalk, 161
Callahan, John F., 78
Chamberlin, John Edgar, 233 (n. 9)
Chesnutt, Charles W.: abandons
    business for writing, 17; assists
    adoption of mulatto child, 210; birth
    of first child, 26; marriage to Susan
    Perry, 25, 26; at Peabody School, 23;
    relationship to community, 24–25,
    35, 211; self-instruction, 26; at State
    Colored Normal School, 29; vision
    of future, 53. *See also specific works*
Christian Union, 34
Clansman, The (Dixon), 181, 239 (n. 10)
Clotel, or The President's Daughter
    (Brown), 102
Colonel's Dream, The, vii, 53, 166–82, 183,
    201, 209, 211, 226
Colorism, 54, 102, 139
Columbia University, 216, 225, 232 (n. 3)
Conjure, 224
"Conjurer's Revenge, The," 86, 88
Conjure WomAn, The, 35, 70, 76–99, 88,
    93, 100, 166, 177
Conrad, Joseph, 189
Contending Forces (Hopkins), 240 (n. 4)

Cosmopolitan, 180
Cowper, William, 37
Crow, Charles L., 238 (n. 17)
Cultural narratives, xi, 5. *See also* Race,
    cultural fictions of

Dance, Daryl, 69
Dark Princess, The (Du Bois), 213
"Dave's Neckliss," 85
Davis, Rebecca Harding, 239 (n. 13)
Deconstruction, 2
"Deep Sleeper, A," 85
Delany, Martin, 213
Demott, Bob, 230 (n. 14)
"Der Shönste Engel" (Graben-
    Hoffman), 108
Dialect (Black English vernacular),
    xi–xii, 1, 10, 12, 36, 95, 235 (nn. 8–10,
    13, 15), 237 (n. 16); "goopher'd,"
    84; "Mammy," 105; of North
    Carolina,!23–38
Dialect humor, 63–64, 70
Dialect tales, 57–77
Dialogic Imagination, The (Bakhtin), 57
Dialogic narrative, 70, 79, 99
Dickens, Charles, 31
Dixon, Thomas, 232 (n. 7); *The
    Clansman*, 181, 239 (n. 10)
Dostoevsky, Fyodor, 178
Double-voicing, 42
Doubling, 150, 153, 160, 161, 174, 185,
    186, 188–89, 190
Douglass, Frederick, 9, 32, 69, 101; *The
    Heroic Slave*, 10, 213
Dreiser, Theodore, 147
Du Bois, W. E. B., 215, 230 (n. 6),
    231 (n. 5); political positions of, vs.
    Washington, 217–18; quoted, 56,

166; and "veil" metaphor for black identity, 6–7, 11, 30, 121. Works: *The Dark Princess,* 213; *The Souls of Black Folk,* 6, 30

Dumas, Alexandre, 33–34, 39

"Dumb Witness, The," 79, 80, 87, 173, 238 (n. 17)

Dunbar, Paul Laurence, 118, 231; *Oak and Ivy,* 32; *The Sport of the Gods,* 155

Duncan, Charles, 44, 101, 229 (nn. 3, 4)

Elder, Arlene, 50

Ellison, Ralph, 17, 79

"Eloquent Appeal, An," 80

Emerson, Ralph Waldo, 14, 230 (n. 14)

Emperor Jones, The (O'Neill), 215

Enlightenment, 175, 179

"Enter the New Negro" (Locke), 208

Etiological tales, 69

Eugenicists, 220

"Fall of Adam, The," 65, 66–67, 78

Family narrative, 155

Farrison, William Edgar, 231 (n. 3)

Faulkner, William, 86; *Absalom, Absalom!,* 199

Fauset, Jessie, 231 (n. 5), 239 (n. 6)

Ferguson, SallyAnn, 53–54

Fienberg, Lorne, 44

Figures in Black (Gates), 100

First Principles (Spencer), 91

Fishkin, Shelley Fisher, viii, x

Fisk Jubilee Singers, 34

Flipper, Henry Ossian, 41

Fool's Errand, A, (Tourgee), 69, 180

Franklin, Benjamin, 25, 27

Fuss, Diana, 234

"Future American, The," 43–56, 74, 206, 210

Garrison, William Lloyd, 9

Garvey, Marcus, 217

Gates, Henry Louis, Jr., x, 8, 11, 62–63, 103; *Figures in Black,* 100; *The Signifying Monkey,* 63

Gentility, 115, 151, 157, 158, 168, 171. *See also* Aristocracy

Gibbon, Edward, 27

Graben-Hoffman, Gustav, 108

Grady, Henry W., 77

Grandissimes, The (Cable), 205

Grant, Madison, 219

Greeley, Horace, 27

Greene, J. Lee. 136, 236 (n. 19)

"Grey Wolf's Ha'nt, The," 80

Gubar, Susan, 234 (n. 14)

Hackenberry, Charles, 142, 240 (ch. 7, n. 1)

Haeckel, Ernst Heinrich, 12

Hall, Wade, 63

Hamlet (Shakespeare), 115

Harlem Renaissance, 11, 82, 102, 245 (n. 19)

Harper, Frances E. W., 9, 81, 102; *Iola Leroy,* 32, 60, 155, 201, 239 (n. 13)

Harris, Joel Chandler, 59, 64, 82, 237 (n. 16); *Legends of the Old Plantation,* 78; Uncle Remus tales, 40, 78, 231 (n. 7)

Harris, Trudier, 143, 146, 229 (n. 3)

Heermance, J. Noel, 183

Hegelianism, 12

Heroic Slave, The (Douglass), 10, 213

"Her Virginia Mammy," 104–6, 131

Hildreth, Richard, 102
Hoffman, Frederick L., 51
Holland, Josiah Gilbert, 210
Homer, 27, 149
Hopkins, Pauline, 210; *Contending Forces,* 240 (n. 4)
"Hot-Foot Hannibal," 77, 85, 86, 90, 160, 180
Houghton Mifflin, 240 (ch. 7, n. 1), 242 (ch. 11, n. 1)
House behind the Cedars, The, 133–46
Howells, William Dean, 214, 245 (n. 10)
Hume, David, 9
Hunt, Leigh, 176
Hurston, Zora Neale, 98
Hutchinson, George, 217, 245 (n. 13)

Ideology, 66, 121, 138, 153, 163
Iola Leroy (Harper), 32, 60, 155, 201, 239 (n. 13)
"I Yam What I Yam" (Benston), 133

Jefferson, Thomas, 9, 31
"John and Old Master" tales, 77, 97, 238 (n. 19)
John March, Southerner (Cable), 181
Johnson, Barbara, 147
Johnson, Charles J., 215
Johnson, James Weldon, 215; *The Autobiography of an Ex-Colored Man,* 222
Journals of Charles W. Chesnutt, The, xi, 4, 12, 21, 23–42, 210, 224
Joyce, James, 149

Kant, Immanuel, 9
Kayyam, Omar, 13

King, Grace L., 202
Kristeva, Julia, 122

Lacan, Jacques, 231 (n. 16), 244 (ch. 11, n. 7); *The Language of Self,* 183
Lamb, Charles, 241 (ch. 9, n. 3)
Language of the Self, The (Lacan), 183
Larsen, Nella, ix
Last of the Barons, The (Bulwer-Lytton), 135
Law, John, 197
Lectures of Rhetoric and Belles Lettres (Blair), 36
Legends of the Old Plantation (Harris), 78
Leitz, Robert, 180, 181
Lewis, David Levering, 211, 215
Locke, Alain, 82, 215, 226; "Enter the New Negro," 208
Logan, Rayford, 52
Lohengrin (Wagner), 109
"Lonesome Ben," 85
"Lost in the Swamp," 38, 144

Macaulay, Thomas Babington, 27, 37
MacNicoll, Murray Graeme, 103
Mahar, William J., 62, 65, 238 (n. 16)
Mandy Oxendine, 4, 122–32, 134, 142, 146, 147, 180
"Marked Tree, The," 85
Marrow of Tradition, The, 53, 147–65, 218
"Marse Chan" (Page), 66
"Mars Jeems' Nightmare," 83, 86, 98
Marxism, 2
"Matter of Principle, A," 54
McElrath, Joseph R., Jr., x–xi, 12, 21, 180, 181, 229 (n. 3)
McGowan, Todd, 158
McKay, Claude, ix

Mills, Charles W., 5–6

Mind of Primitive Man, The, (Boas), 241 (n. 2)

Minnie's Sacrifice, 234

Minstrel show, 60–62, 65

"Morte d'Arthur" (Tennyson), 110, 112

Mulatto: in African American history, 101; as apologist for African Americans 114; as challenge to racial binaries, 101; as free men of color, 184; as Future American, 51; as inferior, 239; as tragic, 103. *See also* Passing, for white; Race, cultural fictions of

National Association for the Advancement of Colored People, 218

National reconciliation, 178

Negro in the American Revolution, The (Brown), 31

New Criticism, x

New Historicism, 2

"New Negro," 82

"New South, The," 77, 163, 164, 166

New York Age, 211

New York Times, 3

Nietzche, Friedrich, 178

Nordau, Max Simon, 12

Oak and Ivy (Dunbar), 32

Ohio University, 223, 245 (n. 16)

O'Neill, Eugene, 215

Opportunity, 211

Oral culture, 74

Our Nig (Wilson), 103

Page, Thomas Nelson, 237; "Marse Chan," 66

Page, Walter Hines, 180; *Rebuilding the Old Commonwealth,* 181

"Partners, The," 65, 70–75, 78

Passing, for white, 25, 114, 116, 118, 132, 217, 222

"Passing of Grandison, The," 104, 116–18

Patai, Daphne, 103

Paul Marchand, F.M.C., xii, 4, 183–207

"Perplexed Nigger, A," 40–42

Persona, 42

"Philly Me York," 98

Pickens, Ernestine, x, 229 (n. 3)

Plantation fiction, 59, 66

Plessy, Homer, 148, 180

Plessy v. Ferguson, 180

"Po' Sandy," 85, 86

Poststructuralism, 2, 3

Pratt, Mary Louise, 64

Progressive Movement, ix

Pudd'nhead Wilson (Twain), 205, 206

Quadroon Ball, 186, 189

Quarry, The, xii, 4, 208–28

Race, cultural fictions of: "blackness," viii, x, 191; black sexuality, 125, 154; "blood infusion," 102; essential difference, 5, 8, 55, 56, 107, 137, 151, 170, 191, 219; nationalism, 245 (n. 14); "nigger," 24, 29, 35, 119, 159, 160, 174; "tragic mulatto," 103; "whiteness," viii, x. *See also* Mulatto; Race, definitions of

Race, definitions of: constructivist, 5, 7, 55, 220; essentialist, 5, 8, 55, 56, 107, 151, 170, 191, 219; legal, 148, 149, 191; scientific discussion, 45, 51; subjectivist, 5–6, 27, 55

"Race Prejudice," 52

Races of Europe (Ripley), 51

Race Traits and Tendencies of the American Negro (Hoffman), 51

Railroad, as symbol, 122, 147

"Railroad Bill," 151

Rebuilding the Old Commonwealth (Page), 181

Reconstruction, 59, 102

Redding, Saunders, 42

Render, Sylvia Lyons, x, 52, 229 (n. 3)

Ripley, William Z., 232 (n. 6); *Races of Europe,* 51

Rising Tide of Color against White World Supremacy, The (Stoddard), 219

Roe, Edward P., 210

Rowfant Club, 17, 18, 230–31 (n. 15)

Saxe-Cobourg, Duke of, 202

Scharnhorst, Gary, 242 (n. 2)

Schopenhauer, Arthur, 12

Schwartz, Daniel R., 244 (ch. 11, n. 7)

Scott, Sir Walter, 135

Sea Island Romance (Brown), 236 (n. 5)

Shakespeare, William, 37, 113; *Hamlet,* 115

Signifying Monkey, The (Gates), 63

Simms, William Gilmore, 117; *Woodcraft,* 239 (n. 15)

"Sis' Becky's Pickaninny," 86, 88, 92

Sister Carrie (Dreiser), 147

Slave narrative, 38, 201

Slave; or Memories of Archy Moore, The (Hildreth), 102

Small, Sam W., 63

Smith, Herbert F., 236 (n. 5), 244 (ch. 12, n. 6)

Smith, John David, 232 (n. 6), 233 (n. 9)

Social Darwinism, 28

Sollors, Werner, viii, 102, 103, 125

Souls of Black Folk, The (Du Bois), 6, 30

Spencer, Herbert, 12, 44, 232 (nn. 3, 4); *First Principles,* 91

Spirituals, 215

Sport of the Gods, The (Dunbar), 155

Stoddard, Lothrop, 219

Stowe, Harriet Beecher, 70, 81, 177; *Uncle Tom's Cabin,* 59, 117, 127, 155, 244 (ch. 11, n. 9)

Stowers, Walter H., 231 (n. 5)

Strangers to Ourselves (Kristeva), 122

Structuralism, 2, 3

Success story, 120, 152, 210

Sundquist, Eric J., viii, 82, 161, 230 (n. 6), 238 (n. 19)

"Talking Bones," 237 (n. 8)

Tannhauser (Wagner), 109

Tennyson, Alfred Lord, 116; "Morte d'Arthur," 110, 112

Thomas, William Hannibal, 233 (n. 9)

Thrasher, Max Bennett, 239 (n. 12)

"Tobe's Tribulations," 87, 92

Tourgee, Albion, 60; *A Fool's Errand,* 69, 180

Trickster, 77, 97, 103, 238 (n. 18)

Tuskeegee Institute, 218

Twain, Mark, 207; *Pudd'nhead Wilson,* 205, 206

"Uncle Remus at the Telephone" (Harris), 40

Uncle Remus tales (Harris), 78, 231 (n. 7)

Uncle Tom's Cabin (Stowe), 59, 117, 127, 155, 244 (ch. 11, n. 9)

"Up From Slavery" (Washington), 28, 30

Virgil, 31
Voltaire, 30

Wagner, Richard, 109
Waiting for the Verdict (Davis), 239 (n. 13)
Walworth, Jeannette, 63
Washington, Booker T., 52, 79, 181, 213, 231 (n. 5); political positions of, vs. Du Bois, 217–18; *Up from Slavery,* 28, 30
"Web of Circumstance, The," 53, 104, 119–21, 242 (n. 5)
Werner, Craig Hansen, 229 (n. 4)
"What Is a White Man?," 148

Wheatley, Phillis, 9, 31
White, Walter, 223
"White Weeds," 104, 106–11
"Wife of His Youth, The," 54, 104, 111–16, 118
Wife of His Youth and Other Stories of the Color Line, The, 103
Wilson, Harriet, 103
Wilson, Matthew, 181
Wonham, Henry B., 94, 98, 99, 229 (n. 3)
Woodcraft (Simms), 239 (n. 15)
World of Difference, A, (Johnson), 147

Youmans, Edward Livingston, 232 (n. 3)

Zizek, Slavoj, 120–21